TIME TO TAX THE ROBOTS

How to update our legacy system of taxation for the era of AI, negative fertility, and a declining labor force

George Randolph Dirth

Macro Policy Press

Time to Tax the Robots

Published by Macro Policy Press

First edition, 2026

ISBN 979-8-9962951-0-4 (paperback)

ISBN 979-8-9962951-1-1 (hardcover)

ISBN 979-8-9962951-2-8 (ebook)

Reader feedback is welcome at ttttr2026@gmail.com

Printed in the United States of America

Contents

Foreword

I have known George for a few years as a very active student in my classes at Chiang Mai University when he attended the graduate program of the Faculty of Economics, first in my World Economy class and then in my Fiscal and Monetary Policy class. His contributions were exceptional. This book that covers various topics on fiscal development, demographic shifts, digital technology disruptions and democratic systems may seem unrelated. It represents his keen interest to find a solution to resolve the looming problem politicians have ignored. In particular, the growing public debt that will be borne by the future generations when it comes to repayment.

Although most of his focus is on the U.S., developing countries like Thailand are exhibiting similar phenomenon. Thailand is worse-off because Thailand is turning old and already becoming an ageing society while Thailand is still a poor country. This will make the need to find a solution even more urgent.

I have recently spoken at the Asia Asset Management annual meeting to offer a solution to Thailand by providing huge individual income tax reductions for parents so as to raise children and to levy additional VAT to be put into individual pension fund accounts for his/her own future use when retiring.

I read this book with full admiration of his effort, and I commend this unique body of work.

Dr. Pisit Leeahtam

Former Deputy Minister of Finance, Thailand
Former Executive Vice-President, Bangkok Bank
Former Dean of Faculty of Economics, Chiang Mai University
Former Thai Governor to the IMF

9th December 2025

Preface – An Economy in Transition

Over the past several decades we have gone from a bipolar world, to a unipolar world, to a multipolar world, to a world now broadly in inflection. The scope of inflection is expansive, encompassing geo-politics, immigration, sharply diverging rates of fertility, climate change, expansive global conflict and—suddenly—the AI revolution.

That AI will have a transformative impact on our economy, on employment, on society, on government is no longer an out-of-consensus view, it has become the "base case" outlook. Can we predict the exact path by which the AI revolution will unfold? Certainly not. Is it therefore incumbent upon us to assess where we are, consider how we got here, look ahead and prepare pragmatically for what comes next. That is the thrust of this study.

We are witnessing the world's leading economies—the U.S., China, Japan, the U.K., France, *et al.*—struggle with basic fiscal discipline, exacerbated by exogenous events (war, the financial crisis and covid), resulting in restrictive levels of public debt, severely limiting most countries' budgetary flexibility, while diverting substantial levels of public funds from intended and necessary expenditures to the burden of debt service. It is as if they now drag along with them—one by one—a ball and chain, which metaphorically they in fact do.

We can all see the same thing—multiple forces are coming to bear on both the American and world economy concurrently. The three forces we focus on include: 1) negative fertility, 2) changes in immigration policy, and 3) the impact of the AI revolution. While forces 1 and 2 formed the original premise for this study, force 3 (the AI revolution) quickly emerged as the story that took over the study, as it seemingly is the world. To be fair, the events we cover are evident in nearly all market economies, which is to say, most of the developed world.

Yet, when it comes to the American economy, AI does not take top billing as the biggest economic story. It must share this spotlight with our public debt, which has grown to an unimaginable level. We cover this in detail, but suffice it to say for now that the annual debt service interest payments we are obligated to make restricts our optionality as a country in ways we could not have ever imagined. This single fact inhibits nearly any action we would want to take as a country, simply because it may strain our budget further to pay for it. This is the very opposite of the notion of "American exceptionalism".

American taxpayers should by now be aware, our current level of gross public debt ($38 trillion, or about 127% of GDP—as of Q2, 2026) is broadly recognized as unsustainable—this is a publicly stated bi-partisan appraisal. Interest payments needed for annual debt service alone now exceed $1 trillion per year, with no apparent plan in place for meeting this ongoing debt funding obligation. Further, our public debt will continue to grow each year due to the compounding effect alone as we pay only interest, not so-to-speak principal, with our annual primary (budget) deficits simply adding to our debt stock each year.

Our One Big Beautiful Bill Act (OBBBA), passed by Congress in July 2025, was characterized as adding about $4.1 trillion to our public debt over the ensuing decade. Reality presents a different picture, as basic math clarifies that we will add instead about $16.5 trillion to our public debt over this same decade (details chapter 20) due to the fact that the annual interest payments on our public debt were not included in the headline budget impact of the OBBBA. An approximate $12.4 trillion failure of omission (per reported CBO forecasts).

There is also—all these years—a correlation waiting to be observed between the era of perennial budget deficits and the emergence and concurrent era of income inequality as a factor in American society. Income inequality is rarely discussed or debated, outside of Econ circles, but many Americans have come to know it well by its consequence: "affordability". Unexpectedly, this becomes one of the study's most illuminating findings. Our chapters 6 and 14 will demonstrate that yes, "everything is interconnected". Or, most everything.

Thus, we embark on an unpredictable economic journey—with baggage that features changing demography, a declining labor force, a past-its-expiration-date system of taxation, and a self-inflicted level of public debt—on the way to our destination with the AI revolution.

To be clear, this author is not anti-AI in any way, shape or form. It is here, it holds great promise and it is both fascinating and captivating. He is also "bullish" on the American economy, yet wholly opposed to fiscal oversight that is not up to the task, and its consequences.

The catalyst for writing this book was simple: a set of circumstances—demographic, technological, fiscal—that persistently presents questions with very few apparent answers. Yet these phenomena lend themselves to understanding through the lens of a basic economic and business perspective, resulting in observations that are often absent from the public debate. Plainly stated, this was the objective of this book: to present a set of observations and recommendations targeting significant, recurring questions emanating from the American economy and policy that remain unanswered.

From a writer's perspective, research and thought formulation for this study led to numerous instances of unexpected juxtaposition of events and theories that presented themselves as obvious dots waiting to be connected. These led to conclusions, which while perhaps unique, seem elementary in hindsight. In aggregate they become the "spine" of the book, the thread of observations that tell the story more clearly than previously imagined.

This book falls into three broad topics: 1) our present demographic trajectory, as defined by negative fertility and decreasing immigration along with the implicit fiscal consequences of a decline in our taxpaying labor force; 2) the "wild card" of economic transformation we will be living the next several decades courtesy of the AI revolution; and 3) the proposed remedy, the course-corrective mechanism of taxing AI, along with the doubly obvious window of opportunity and benefits this action presents.

What surprised most in researching this book was a select set of correlations that emerged in simply following the thread of the research. First is how the continued evolution of the production function, when correlated to our legacy system of taxation the past seven decades, informs the understanding of not just how our fiscal fragility emerged, but also the emergence of income inequality.

Next is how the monetary policy concept of the zero lower bound (ZLB) inversely informs our concept of the infinite upper bound (IUB) of cognitive AI. This insight underpins analysis of productivity in the AI era, and how it will exhibit disinflationary impulses.

The title of this book, *Time to Tax the Robots* (by which is meant broadly taxing AI—not just robots), was inspired by a remark from Bill Gates in a February 2017 interview with Quartz, made in the general context of how to manage the social cost of an inevitable robotic (and AI) revolution. Years later this stands up as a remarkably prescient observation. We encourage watching the insightful two-minute interview featuring Mr. Gates and the logic behind his observation.

As it turns out, there are intuitive, easy to administer AI taxation mechanisms—for both cognitive and physical AI—that can be implemented which a) would not be onerous, b) could scale along with AI output as if a digital twin, c) would be consumption-based and d) can easily be structured to be progressive in nature.

Why is this the right moment to implement taxation of AI? All reports are that compute capacity is highly constrained, with Agentic AI driving even further accelerating rates of demand. Token demand significantly exceeds supply, with users vigorously competing for token allocations based on the user's ability to monetize them. In microeconomic terms, this is a classic supply-demand imbalance—exactly the condition under which a modest tax layer would not likely suppress demand, because the demand already exceeds available supply, with the market currently operating in a state of near-perfect price inelasticity. For Congress to pass on this window of opportunity would, in this author's opinion, be fiduciarily irresponsible.

The target audience for this book is not economists (though they are of course welcome), but rather the American voter and American Congress. They are the ones—whether they recognize it or not—with the sole authority to bring about the change that is needed. Congress—per Article I, sections 8 and 9 of our Constitution—collectively the so-called "power of the purse" is 100% responsible for our fiscal policy. The American voter's authority to require change, while indirect, is no less powerful, *if* they choose to exercise this power.

For 250 years Americans have lived within a system of governance that the world, broadly speaking, considers a tremendous luxury. The hallmarks of our system—rule of law, a high level of individual freedom, representative democracy, freedom of the press, a functioning meritocracy—have delivered unparalleled results for the American people. Yet we are also a country—per a March 2026 Gallup poll—in which a mere 15% of voters approve of the job Congress is doing. In spite of which, Congressional members remarkably enjoy re-election rates above 90%. Yes, Congressional redistricting has made removing members of Congress difficult, but equally when only 45-60% of eligible voters take part in each election cycle, this "explanation" is diminished.

In our system—and this is what much of the world specifically admires about America—politicians serve the American people. It is time that as voters we recognize this.

Introduction

Over the following twenty-five chapters we will chiefly focus on the AI revolution and how it is suddenly and pervasively becoming deeply integrated in our economy. We endeavor to introduce and explain each topic, and how in select cases, Congressional initiative can potentially countermand adverse consequences.

Throughout we often use an economic lens for our analysis, thus we begin by introducing ten basic economic and policy principles which will serve as conceptual underpinning.

1. Simply stated, economic growth is determined by two things: a country's increase in worker productivity and its increase in the size of its labor force. That's it; thousands of economic machinations can be distilled into two metrics. The fact that the fertility rate in the U.S. (the number of births per woman needed to maintain a stable population) has been below replacement rate for the preceding two decades puts our ability to maintain a stable labor force at risk. Whether these two factors (size of labor force and productivity) grow, stagnate or decline determines whether a country's GDP grows, stagnates or declines.

2. A country's ability to pay for its expenditures, to even engage in budgetary and policy planning, is dependent upon stability and predictability of its tax revenue. Tax revenue is highly dependent upon the size of our taxpaying labor force, and the productivity thereof. In the U.S. on average 84% of tax revenue is a result of individual workers—both income tax and payroll tax, with about 9% from business. Tax "compliance" can and should be enforced and tax policy can and should be revised, but this is the "fact set" we live with today.

3. The consequence of a below replacement level rate of fertility along with the expected decline in rate of immigration, over the 2024 – 2033 decade will result in a 10.8 million worker "gap" in the rate of growth of our labor force compared to the prior decade, with a resultant gap in our tax revenue, per BLS estimates. (BLS = Bureau of Labor Statistics) This decline in taxpaying workers will be further exacerbated by expected job loss to, and or virtual job repopulation by, physical AI and cognitive AI.

The math is simple: failure to tax jobs populated by AI related workforce automation necessitates proportionately higher tax rates for the remaining workers just to stay even, which is clearly not realistic. Equally, any idea of reducing government services or social benefits in an era of an aging population, with potentially higher rates of unemployment, would be a recipe for social instability.

4. The declining rate of growth of our labor force combined with potential loss of jobs due to AI-related workplace automation—and subsequent loss of tax revenue, takes a difficult circumstance--our unsustainable public debt, and makes it perilous. Further, it leaves the US government with little fiscal flexibility in the event of a true (as opposed to a self-inflicted) crisis, a point former Treasury Secretary Larry Summers recently emphasized on Bloomberg TV (June 5, 2025).

In lieu of a reversal in our country's fertility rate, or a substantial revision of our country's tax code there are only two ways to "protect" the government's stream of incoming tax revenue: 1) a revised immigration policy that shifts its emphasis to addressing the specific needs of the US labor force, and 2) a strategy for taxation of robotics and AI related workforce automation to offset the obvious loss of tax revenue due to a declining tax paying labor force.

5. Our large public debt is tantamount to a massive transfer of wealth from future generations to the present—as they are the ones who will repay this debt. Economists call this an "intertemporal" or intergenerational transfer of wealth, and it is *unseemly* that we—politicians and voters alike—have presided over this transfer of wealth from our offspring to pay for the public debt we will leave them. All evidence suggests that government expenditures will continue to increase at a level that is not supported by concurrent tax revenues, suggesting that "public debt" will only grow larger.

Debt service payments (approximately $1 trillion for 2025), now constitute the largest non-entitlement budget line item, necessitating additional taxation simply to carry and service this debt. Truth be told, we—members of Congress and the American taxpayer—are no longer in the driver's seat. One day it may be the bond market that tells us what interest rates we must pay to borrow the money needed to service this debt. Think of it as a $38 trillion variable rate home loan, that we the taxpayers—or more specifically, our children and grandchildren—are "on the hook" for.

Budget Deficit by President +/- Reagan to Trump 47

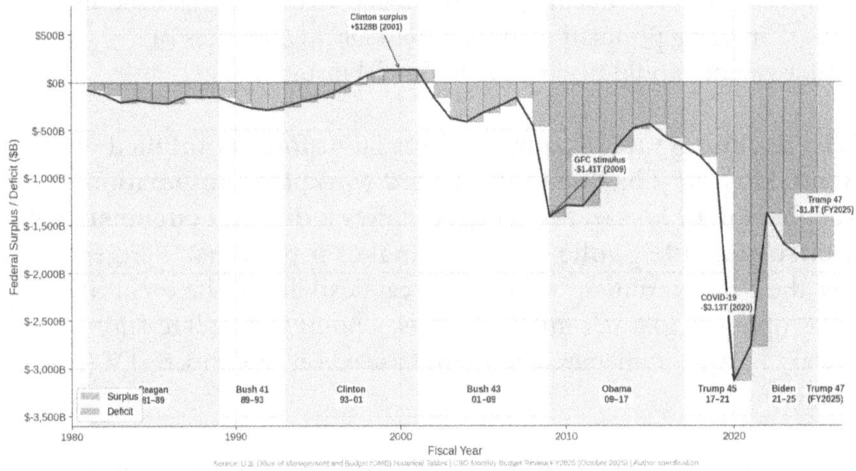

Figure 1: U.S. federal budget surplus / deficit by president, fiscal years 1981–2025. Blue shading = surplus. Red shading = deficit. Alternating bands = presidential administrations.

Notes: Clinton surplus peak: +$128B (2001). Global Financial Crisis trough: -$1.41T (2009). COVID-19 trough: -$3.13T (2020). Sources: U.S. Office of Management and Budget Historical Tables; Federal Reserve Bank of St. Louis; Author specification.

6. Yes, our politicians are to blame for this state of affairs—but so are we, the American voter, as we keep rewarding their actions through re-election. If our Congress were to become serious about resolving our public debt, we estimate (chapter 21) this would take until 2067 to bring our public debt back to a "normal" level, using reasonable "corrective" fiscal policy assumptions, meaning taxation revenue would have to exceed expenditures for about 43 years.

To use a business analogy, the President, Cabinet and Congress are the CEO, C-Suite and Management Team of company USA, and we are the Board of Directors. Management has clearly been derelict in their fiduciary responsibility. Our Constitution is clear that this is Congress's "job" (Article I, sections 8 and 9 of our Constitution), and we the Board have failed to fire and replace them and have instead incredibly re-elected them, repeatedly.

The American system of democracy is wonderful, but it is the voter's obligation to remain informed, which we apparently have failed to do. When politicians helped themselves to our children's savings by generating excessive public debt, we the voters—to misappropriate a Chinese expression of the moment—chose to "lie flat" (which in modern China is a popular euphemism for literally doing nothing).

7. Statistically and theoretically, the fastest path to sustainable economic growth and leadership is by increasing the number of semi-skilled and skilled workers in our labor force. This implies STEM workers and graduates, as these industry sectors (along with healthcare) are forecast to remain the drivers of economic growth and arguably of future American exceptionalism. Think of increasing the STEM component of our labor force as an upgrade to our per capita GDP.

Chapter 23 demonstrates, using BLS and IRS data, the sizeable income gap between STEM and Non-STEM workers in America and their disproportionate contributions to both GDP and tax revenue. Fairly unanimously, leaders in American industry report difficulties in hiring technically qualified semi-skilled and skilled staff for their companies. The National Academies of Science, Engineering and Medicine outline the need to develop and recruit STEM at all levels (K-12 as well as University level) in their August 29, 2024 report.

8. Our immigration policy is obsolete and disconnected from reality: the foundation of our existing policy, the Immigration and Nationality Act (INA) was legislated in 1952. Yes, there have been amendments since, but these have dealt principally with enforcement—not actual policy—and it can fairly be said that the world and the US economy have changed dramatically since 1952.

Nowhere in our existing immigration policy or practices is there meaningful alignment to the needs of our labor force at a sectoral level. Adopting an immigration policy that recognizes the necessary linkage of immigration policy to the needs of the labor force would be an overdue and constructive step. In the US, a low number of immigrants enter the work force in the first year, and a surprisingly low level (only 20%) are admitted under work visas based on their qualifications relative to the needs of our labor force, such as via the H-1B visa channel.

Singapore, with a fertility rate of 1.0, somewhat masterfully links its immigration practices to addressing the nuanced and stratified needs of its labor force, with tailored solutions for each stratum. Consequently, they have one of the highest per capita GDPs in the world—well above the US, and no net public debt. Instead, they have a world-famous sovereign wealth fund and unspecified gold reserves.

9. Since the WW2 era, attracting the best and the brightest has given America a distinct competitive advantage. The best academics, the best scientists, the most highly skilled employees have in large numbers come to America to build their lives and careers. Since the end of WW2 (and even the late 30's, as Hitler closed down Europe) we have been the first-choice destination for many of the world's most talented scientists and thinkers. Suddenly, this is at risk of changing, due to a change in sentiment resulting in an America that is less welcoming to immigration.

A window into the trajectory of America's leadership in science, technology and medicine, and the arc of the impact of immigration, is provided by considering Nobel recipients and the value of the US being a "destination" country for some of the best minds in the world. From 1900 until 1945, Germany received 28 Nobels, and the US about 8. Post WW2, benefitting from both native-born and also a substantial number of foreign-born scientists (as is well-known, Hitler "pushed" many our way), the US received approximately 350 Nobels (depending upon how one counts dual national recipients and multi recipient awards) from 1945 until 2000, of which approximately 112 were foreign-born US nationals. The impact of this research leadership in science, technology and medicine on American industry (and patents) is axiomatic, and it is fair to say the envy of the world. Any efforts to extinguish this "fire hose" of academic excellence entering the US would be sadly misguided, for those who have America's best interests and future academic and economic leadership in mind.

10. At its core, the AI revolution is Austrian economist Schumpeter's theory of "creative destruction" (1942) brought to life— albeit in a turbocharged manifestation. We are living this real-time, or an accelerated version of it compared to the history of economic development. It is fitting that the recently announced (Q4 2025) Nobel Prize in Economics, recognized research on the impact of "innovation-driven economic growth," and specifically on the theory of sustained growth through "creative destruction". By all appearances, this concept and the fast-forward development it presents is alive and well; see chapter 12.

A framework of publicly available government data

With respect to the data used throughout this study, we are fortunate to have a wealth of credible economic and related data to draw upon courtesy of regularly generated reports by our Federal government. U.S. economic data is broadly considered the gold standard, and used by academics as well as economic, business and financial market participants throughout the world.

We rely chiefly on reports from the Bureau of Labor Statistics (BLS), the Bureau of Economic Analysis (BEA), the Congressional Budget Office (CBO), the Federal Reserve (the Fed), the Internal Revenue Service (IRS), the Census Bureau and the Department of Homeland Security (DHS).

1. *The Modern Era of Negative Fertility*

The topic of "fertility rate" sounds scientific but it's very direct: it asks, is a country's birthrate sufficient to ensure population stability; does it portend a steady state, or an increase or a decrease of population, net of immigration and emigration. The surprising and mathematically inescapable reality is that the US, as well as much of the developed world, is now definitively in a multi-decade pattern of negative fertility. That this phenomenon is affecting the developed world more than the developing world says a lot about its root causes.

The trend amongst developed countries for several decades has been declining fertility rates; now definitively into negative status, with birthrates below the rate of replacement. (The term "negative" is used as a negative fertility rate results in a declining population.) The population pyramid below, showing population cohort by age, depicts bulges in childbirth rates, first from the baby boom, a generation later the baby boom echo, and subsequently decline as the US fertility rate shifts into negative territory.

Note that the concept of "baby boom" manifests itself in different years and even decades in different countries around the world. For the US and for Europe—and Japan—it is the period after the end of WW2. In S. Korea it comes later, after the end of the Korean War; same for China, where it is evident after the period of tremendous dislocation caused by the Chinese Civil War.

The population pyramid below, stratified by age cohort, indirectly depicts the burden which will fall upon the younger cohorts as they enter the labor force, and face the obligation to a) care for the larger elderly cohorts—socially speaking, b) pay for the expense of their social services such as Medicare and Social Security, and c) as we will review in detail later, to pay off the massive public debt the older cohorts have bequeathed them.

A gradual decline in the fertility rate has occurred across the arc of centuries, linked to the march of progress of improvements in human health and life expectancy, from eras of high infant mortality and the need of agrarian based families to have a sufficient number of children to provide for the family, to eras of medical breakthroughs, the discovery of vaccines, the advent of penicillin, advances in hygiene, etc.

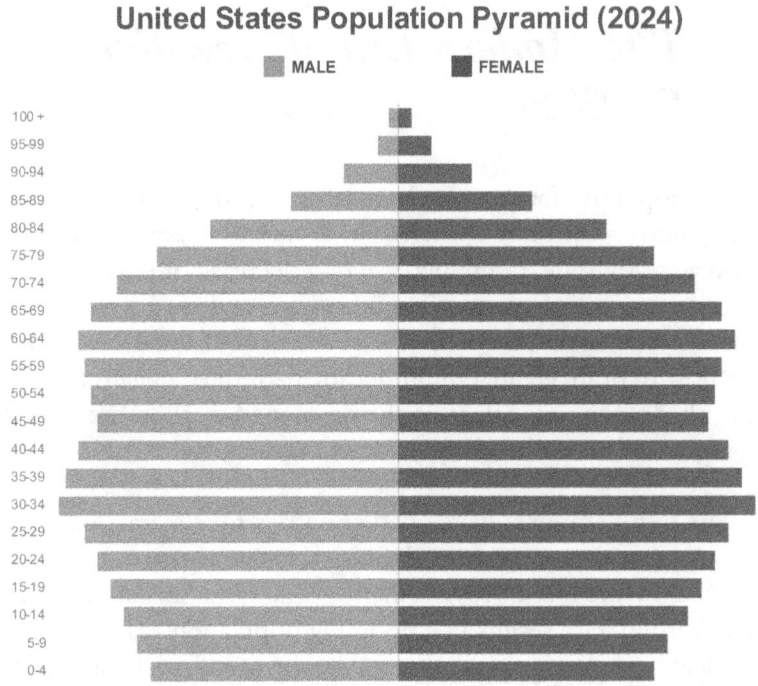

Figure 2: Population by Age and Gender depicting an aging and declining population.

Note: Data US Census Bureau

In the US, a major inflection point in fertility rate occurred after approval of the birth control pill by the FDA

Within the US, we can trace the acceleration of the trend of negative fertility to the introduction of the birth control pill, which also highly correlates to the increase of women entering the workforce. The birth control pill was approved by the U.S. Food and Drug Administration (FDA) in June 1960. The correlation between introduction of the pill and subsequent decrease in fertility rate and coincident increase in workforce participation rate—powered by women joining the workforce, is evident in the chart below. For the U.S., and for much of the developed world, the advent of "the pill" was seemingly an irreversible catalyst.

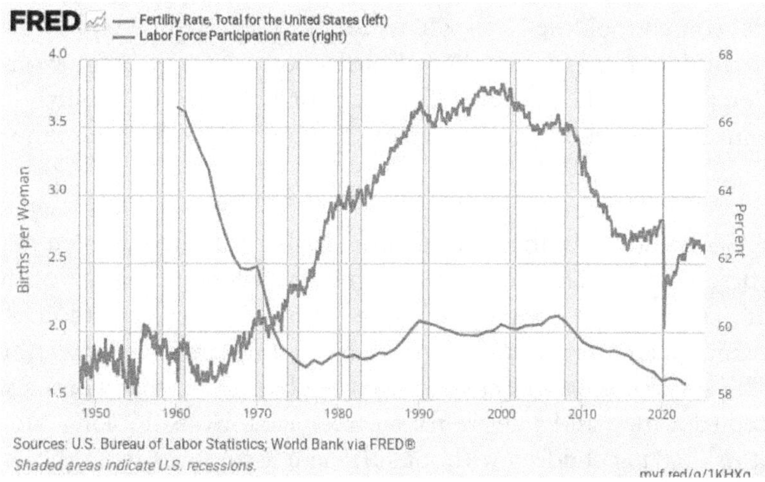

Figure 3: US Fertility Rate vs. Labor Force Participation Rate (BLS/World Bank data via FRED)

Note. Data charted using the Federal Reserve Economic Data (FRED) platform. Sources: U.S. Bureau of Labor Statistics (BLS) and World Bank. Author specification.

Subsequent sudden declines in the labor force participation rate are evident in 2009 due to the economic collapse caused by the Great Financial Crisis (GFC) and again in 2020 with the Covid epidemic. (Suggesting a correlation to real or perceived economic well-being.) One lingering cause of the sustained decrease in workforce participation post-Covid is often attributed to the difficulty and or cost of obtaining childcare, which could also be termed a labor force issue (supply and demand imbalances generally lead to changes in price). Other related social and economic issues are often linked to the decline in fertility—in the US and across the developed world, such as cost of living, cost of raising a family, cost of housing, and so forth.

Social Norms and the Impact of the "Pill"

The following references and brief excerpts are drawn from Nobel Laureate and Harvard Professor Claudia Goldin's paper "The Downside of Fertility," presented at the Federal Reserve Bank of Kansas City's Jackson Hole Economic Symposium in August 2025 and subsequently published as NBER *Working Paper No. 34268 in September 2025.*

On the impact of the "pill" on American fertility — and the related changes in women's control over the timing of marriage, education, and career — Professor Goldin notes that "the birth rate fell for women across all educational groups. The decrease for college graduate women took the birth rate to very low levels quite rapidly. By the 1948 birth cohort, the number of births per college graduate woman had fallen to 1.64 ... The point is that the post-Baby Boom fertility decline in the U.S. among college graduate women began a long time ago."

Goldin adds: "Furthermore, more highly educated women may be the first to forego children because children will require more of their time. It may not be just a 'rat-race' issue. It may be a combination of a rat race and greater female autonomy that together produced lower birth rates. The social norm of intensive parenting has meant that women with advanced education and a desire for a career are forward-looking and will not risk having children without sufficient assurances from the father that he will share in the time needed to raise a child."

She continues: "In summary, the birth rate plummeted some time ago in the U.S. It occurred with the greater ability of women to marry later, get more education, and obtain more job experience before marriage. Because women had more autonomy, they had more options, and because the relative earnings of college-educated workers increased, their options became more valuable." Further, Goldin notes: "The opportunity cost of children to more-educated women rose. Women needed greater assurances that the care of their children would be shared by the father. That is the downside of fertility."

The "Quantity-Quality" and "Agency of Women" theories

Professor Goldin's paper navigates the substantial economic literature on fertility decline. Among the various contributing factors and the global uniformity of the phenomenon, she identifies the "Quantity-Quality" tradeoff as the foundational economic theory that previously dominated the field, and the increased agency of women as the unifying factor that, in her view, ultimately explains the decline more completely.

To paraphrase Goldin's summary of this established framework: births produce a "quantity" of children, who are then "augmented" through costly healthcare, education, training, and so forth. The full relative price of children rises with income because higher-income parents invest more in child "quality." In the resulting Quantity-Quality tradeoff, as Goldin describes it, "parents purchase goods and services and use their time to enhance the quality of their children."

With respect to women's agency, the framework rests on two gradual but powerful transformations. First was the growing ability of women to perform at the highest levels of society — within education, business, and government. Second was the reproductive choice granted by the "pill", which Goldin describes as "the greater ability of women of all ages to control their fertility". Together, these transformations enabled women to be more discerning about the timing of first marriage and the type of partner who matches their needs—not simply on income, but also on whether the partner contributes sufficient unpaid household labor to allow her to maintain her career while raising quality children.

The following table of fertility rates by selected U.S. states shows a notable negative correlation between urbanization and fertility. California, New York, and Massachusetts — states characterized by concentrations of top universities and high-earning women — sit at the lower end of the fertility distribution, consistent with Goldin's framework on women's agency but viewed at the state level.

US Fertility and Urbanization Rates - Selected States (2023)

State	Fertility Ranking	Fertility Rate	Urbanization
South Dakota	Highest	2.00	59%
Louisiana	Highest	1.83	71%
Texas	Highest	1.81	83%
Minnesota	Mid-range	1.69	72%
Ohio	Mid-range	1.68	76%
Georgia	Mid-range	1.64	74%

California	Lower	1.48	94%
New York	Lower	1.53	87%
Massachusetts	Lower	1.40	91%

Table 1: U.S. Fertility and Urbanization Rates — Selected States (2023)

Note: U.S. national averages: Fertility Rate 1.62, Urbanization 83% (2023). Data source: CDC / Census Bureau Data 2023.

To summarize: the factors behind this phenomenon, typically both social and economic, seem intractable. We say this not to be negative, but to be pragmatic, as after multiple decades this is clearly the new normal. Given the focus of this study, we will therefore treat negative fertility as a fact and plan accordingly. The main takeaway as it pertains to the US is that a negative fertility rate (absent the additive impact of immigration) without question leads to a "structural" decrease in the size of our population and of our labor force, which per our simple formula at the outset *(% change in labor force + % change in productivity = % change in GDP)* would lead to weakening GDP growth and therefore a decrease in tax revenues.

More broadly, what is causing negative fertility in the developed world?

As a phenomenon negative fertility is deeply entrenched in much of the developed world. It has been in the news the past several years as it pertains to both China and Japan, both of which have very low rates of immigration. This circumstance is accordingly beginning to present significant social and economic strains on these countries. Social tradition in many Asian countries is often to have three generations in one household, with the grandparents helping to raise the grandchildren, while the parents—or middle generation—work and provide for the entire family, eventually caring for the grandparents as they age. As fertility rates decline, who will care for the grandparents, a situation exacerbated by the relative absence or low level of social benefits such as medical care or retirement pensions.

Additional frequently cited causes of negative fertility include both economic and social considerations

Economic considerations frequently include: overall cost of living, cost of housing, cost of child rearing, availability of (or affordable) childcare, cost of education and uncertain employment prospects.

Social considerations often include: norms or traditions (e.g., in China—for example—potential husbands are often expected to first have a home and car to be suitable for marriage); increasing prominence of women in the workforce, desire for career accomplishment before—or in lieu of—childrearing; and a decline in the pool of suitable husbands, as women increasingly outperform men in both school and in the workplace.

Urbanization has as well been linked to declining fertility rates in multiple continents via empirical research studies (e.g., Anjum 2025, *Urbanization as a Driver of Demographic Transition.)* US data (above) suggests lower rates of fertility in more densely populated states and higher fertility in those which are less dense, reinforcing notion of urban vs. rural fertility disparity.

The world view below clearly shows that negative fertility is a global phenomenon affecting mostly the developed and semi-developed world. It is therefore, again, the view of this study that the inevitability of these consequences will increasingly necessitate a response from many countries to countermand the likely economic and social hazards of negative fertility. Thus, one can reasonably assume that many countries will recognize more specifically that immigration—should they so choose—can serve as an antidote of sorts for the adverse economic consequences of negative fertility, and begin to focus not just on quantity, but increasingly on "fit" of potential immigrants by criteria such as skill level as well as prospects of social adaptability. (China, as an example, a country with an historically low rate of immigration, on August 7, 2025 introduced its "K-Visa" which is essentially an open invitation to foreign STEM graduates to immigrate to China and develop their careers there. For many, this will prove an attractive option.)

Graphic Depiction of World Fertility Rates per UN Analysis 2024

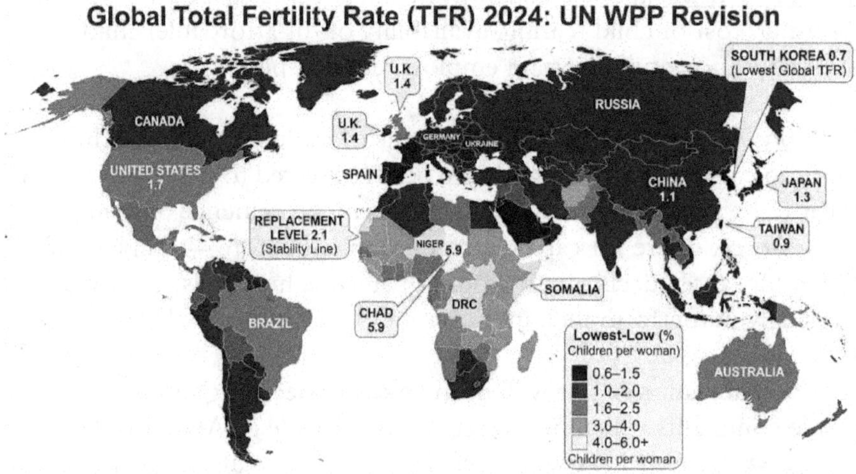

World Fertility Rates by Country 2024

Figure 4: World Fertility Rates – Select Countries and Regions 2024 Data

Note: Source - UN World Population Prospects (WPP) revised study 2024

Why should we care about negative fertility?

Isn't the world over-populated, aren't we suffering from the effects of excessive consumption and pollution as manifested in global warming, climate change, etc.? Those answers are clearly "yes". The simple reality, however, is that descending the reverse slope of this mountain of population growth, that is depopulation, would present its own set of significant challenges. Societies around the world have built up social processes and economic structures that, broadly speaking, we all have become dependent upon, and these are funded, at least in the US and most of the developed world, primarily by taxation of individual workers. A diminishing population means a declining labor force which means a declining flow of funds to pay for core government services such as security, education, infrastructure and also the social benefits we all depend upon as we age such as health care and social benefits for the larger retiree cohort.

Economists call this an increased "dependency ratio", meaning fewer of "us" would pay and care for more of "us", in terms of tax revenue and in human-to-human care. (US dependency ratio is currently about 55, meaning that today every 100 working age people "support" a combined 55 retirees and youth under 15. This ratio is expected to increase to 65 in the US by 2030 per UN forecasts.) This is why we should care.

As previously noted, the dual metrics of rate of growth in our labor force and in worker productivity define growth in GDP, and consequently personal income and tax revenue. Our Congressional Budget Office (CBO) does an excellent job of presenting a clear present picture and near-term forecast of detailed revenue and expenditures.

The following chart sums up the story of negative fertility and its impact on forecasted GDP quite succinctly, via its impact on the size of the labor force, rate of productivity and GDP growth rate. (Note that this assumes a modest baseline of immigration, otherwise the labor force would flip into decline by 2033, per BLS forecasts.) Whether we are ambivalent or not about negative fertility we would be well-served to understand its economic consequences.

Average Annual Growth of Real Potential GDP and Its Components

Real potential GDP grows more slowly from 2025 to 2055 than it has, on average, over the past 30 years. That decline is explained by slower projected growth in the size and productivity of the potential labor force.

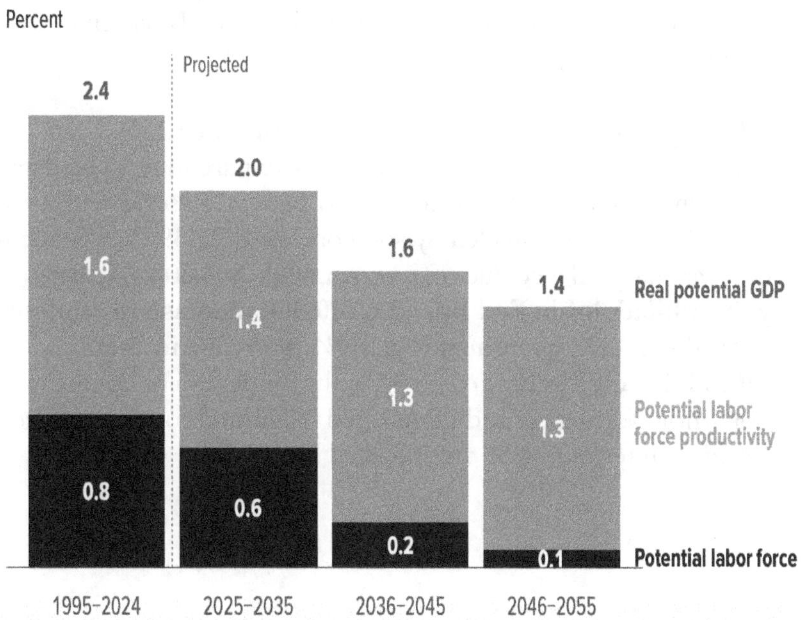

Figure 5: US annual growth history and potential (CBO), From *the Budget and Economic Outlook: 2025 to 2035*, by Congressional Budget Office, 2025.

The above chart does not offer a tax revenue decline in trend forecast but clearly shows the consequence of a declining labor force on overall GDP, from which tax revenue flows. We will model this forecast impact on tax revenue in chapter 20, the purpose for now is to connect the dots between declining fertility, declining labor force and declining GDP. This is simply foundational logic for this study, and becomes a core component of our broader thesis of the rapidly dissipating capacity of individual workers to provide the tax revenue needed to fund our government.

As a footnote to the above chart, the CBO felt it necessary to repeatedly revise this forecast as conditions change rapidly: In January 2025, they projected negative population growth beginning in 2033. By September 2025, this was revised to 2031. Most recently, on January 7, 2026, they now project negative growth beginning in 2030—demonstrating how quickly demographic conditions are changing.

For the past two decades immigration has obscured the growing consequences of negative fertility for our country, but as has become increasingly evident, our rate of immigration has and will continue to decline. Our CBO has taken note of this and includes this declination in their forecasts of our labor force and productivity thereof for their 2024 – 2033 forecast decade. (We dive more deeply into trends within our labor force in chapter 22.)

A final point: affordability is often cited by Americans as an impediment to household formation and therefore parenting. The data, even tangentially, supports this. According to Federal Reserve data as of April 2026, 41% of households led by someone aged 25-39 carry student debt, with an average balance due of approximately $34,000. **A 2018 study by the Philadelphia Fed linked a $10,000 increase in student debt among the 25-39 age cohort to a 3-4% decrease in their likelihood to have children.** For many in the student debt cohort, delayed household formation and diminished likelihood to have children are real-world manifestations of the so-called affordability crisis.

2. *A Snapshot of Immigration in the U.S.*

There has recently been an uproar regarding immigration in the US. This uproar has little to do with policy but is about enforcement. Over the past decade-plus many western countries (the US chief among them) have been struggling with overwhelming numbers of asylum seekers. This study will focus on policy …which is being overlooked (via our preoccupation with enforcement) at our peril and which is arguably outdated and rife with shortcomings. As for enforcement, it must naturally follow policy, as a mechanism to ensure its implementation.

The big picture causes and effects of immigration have not really changed that much over the last four centuries (with the obvious exception of forced immigration for slavery). The "push" or "pull" drivers of immigration have not really changed. The "push" is often simply that immigrants desire to leave their homeland due to dissatisfaction with their lives or living conditions there (or extreme hazard such as war); the "pull" has generally been provided by the perception of much better living conditions and lives in the new land.

There has, across US history, often been disapproval of the personal characteristics, race and or religion of select groups of immigrants, as there is today. There has been at times concentration in their regions of origin, as there is today—such as Syrians into Western Europe, Central Americans and East and South Asians into the US. Immigration has been sharply politicized before in specific periods of our history.

In the modern era, we can trace the dynamic of immigrants augmenting the U.S. workforce, although in a more targeted and controlled manner, to WW2 when a majority of working-age men were serving in the armed forces, and with many women having entered the workforce to backfill this void, famously working in munitions factories, the US brought in so called "bracero" or manual workers from Mexico to work in the agriculture and railroad industries. This was an official government program in coordination with the Mexican government, from 1942 until 1964, involving more than 4.5 million temporary Mexican immigrants. This precedent apparently proved hard to forget, as Mexican farm labor remained a factor beyond the official end date, as it does today.

Fast forward to today, and over recent decades the largest countries of origin for immigrants into the US have been in South and East Asia—meaning India and China in particular, across the skill spectrum. Notably, today four out of ten of the top American companies by market cap have foreign-born CEO's, with 45% of Silicon Valley start-ups over the last decade having foreign-born CEOs. And, since 2000, 40% (45 out of 112) of American Nobel recipients were foreign born. This despite the fact that the immigration channel for skilled workers (H-1B and EB3 visas) is by comparison very limited and narrow. Famously, both Microsoft CEO Satya Nadella and Google (Alphabet) CEO Sundar Pichai (both firmly among top American CEOs) were H-1B visa recipients.

Are insights codified in 1952 optimal for governance in the 21st century?

Today our country confronts the diverse and complex topic of immigration based on a primary source document for immigration law that was codified via the 1952 Immigration and Nationality Act INA (with some primarily enforcement related reforms in subsequent decades). The inescapable truth is that the U.S. and indeed the world have changed vastly since then, thus any legislation (such as the INA) that's foundation was seven decades prior is likely to be out of date. One could fairly observe that immigration law in the US is not really that different from other important bodies of legislation in the US, which is to say they are often outdated and therefore badly in need of evaluation and reform.

The difference between these past eras, and the degree of dissatisfaction and politicization today most likely owes a lot to the power of social media to vastly amplify the impact of almost anyone's version of news—or personal opinion to the *n*th degree, and of course to the vast number of illegal immigrants. Social media has also likely played a starring role in highlighting illegal immigration as a viable life choice for many residing in countries characterized by despair and lawlessness.

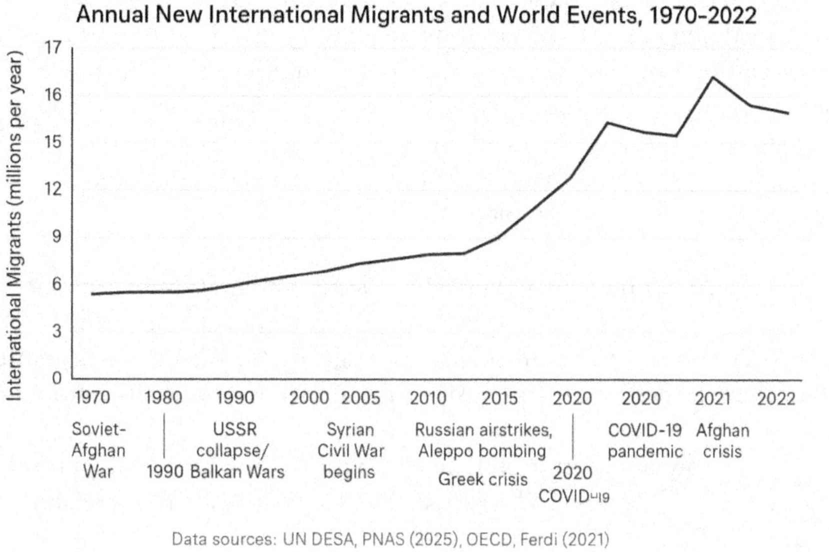

Figure 6: Annual new international migrants and world events, 1970–2022.

Note. Data adapted from "Measuring global migration flows using online data," by Chi, L. S., et al. (2025), *Proceedings of the National Academy of Sciences*. Data compiled from UN DESA, OECD, and Ferdi (2021). World event notations per Author.

This social media amplification process is however part of today's "fact set" and few would suggest this will change anytime soon. While not establishing causality the graph below certainly depicts correlation between rates of global immigration and the age of social media. Facebook, to name but one, has grown from one million global users in 2004 to approximately three billion in 2025.

There have been peaks and valleys as far as the rate of immigration across our history, and in the absence of a clear framework of principles or policies there have instead been simply social and political "reactions" to events, as there are today. It seems fair to say it would be beneficial to review and update the actual policy itself.

To borrow from the business sector, the doctrine of "best practices" suggests we would be well-served to study and analyze immigration and ask what are our key policies of today, what are they overlooking considering the degree of economic and political change since the Immigration and Nationality Act (INA) was implemented, what important topics need to be addressed, what are the smartest countries doing (chapter 24) and therefore what can we learn from them, and therefore how should we reframe our own policies. (This preceding brief list is obviously a mere example of some starting points, not an exhaustive outline…) The main idea being, amendments are but "band-aids", a topic perceived to be as central to our state of affairs as immigration deserves a complete "re-think".

We depict below an overview of legal immigration by category into the U.S. for 2024. The "quick take" with respect to the topic of our labor force and the economy is that the majority (79.6%) of visas granted had nothing to do with the present or future needs of our labor force.

A summary of approximate total visas granted for immigration into the US in 2024 is as follows (data per Department of Homeland Security DHS):

Summary Table of Immigration Visas Granted 2024

Visa Category	2024 Visas	% Total	Notes
Refugee Admissions	100,034	9.5%	USRAP, presidential auth., embassy
Asylee Status Grants	140,000	13.3%	USCIS approvals; ~12% approval at border
Family-sponsored visas	600,000	56.8%	Family reunification green cards
Employment-based green cards (EB-1,2,3)	45,000	4.3%	Skilled/STEM/STEMM-med, advanced exp.
Temp. worker visas (H-1B, H-2A/B): H-1B=141,205, H2A/B≈30k	141,205 30,000	13.4%, 2.8%	H-1B: tech/STEM; H-2A/B: ag, 1–3 yrs
Total Visas granted 2024 (w/o Student)	1,056,239		Excludes denied asylum seekers: 1.9M pending
Student Visas - Temporary	700,000	NA	Academic, vocational students

Table 2. Summary Table of Immigration Visas Granted 2024.

Note. Data compiled from U.S. Citizenship and Immigration Services (USCIS) and Department of Homeland Security (DHS) figures. Analysis and specification by Author.

Upon viewing this fact set, the obvious question is, should our immigration policies at least coordinate with, if not indeed support, the needs of our labor force. Presently, we are nowhere close to doing this.

We suggest there are two main issues with immigration policy in the US today:

1. **Management of illegal immigration**: these are technically "asylum seekers" who hope that either upon entry or at the border (point of apprehension) they may apply for and receive Asylee status and be granted permanent residence. The number of asylum seekers is both wholly unrealistic and a tremendous burden upon our border control operations. Our policy must be amended to create a process of fast-track resolution and handling of these Asylum seekers, and do so within the laws of the land. If this requires more resources as well as legislative focus to accomplish this, so be it; it is clearly an imperative.

2. **Our current visa allocation structure is not designed to meet the needs of our economy**. Exempting student visas, which are temporary, nearly 60% of visas granted are for family reunification purposes, 20% for combined Asylees and Refugees and only 20% are allocated based on employable skill. By all apparent evidence, an inadequately low level of recognition is given to the needs of our workforce, or the needs of US based employers. It is the recommendation of this study that this dynamic be reversed; that primary consideration be given to the needs of our labor force, and that allocation to family reunification (the largest recipient cohort of visas each year) and refugees and asylees be of secondary concern. (This last point is not to demean the individual or their family; rather, it is meant to normalize and stabilize our visa issuance policy, and prioritize, step-by-step, cessation of our fiscal hemorrhage.)

As it turns out, this last notion, of prioritizing the needs of our labor force and of our economy with respect to immigration reform is apparently in good company. Robert Rubin, former Secretary of the Treasury on 5 October, 2025 (Greenwich Economic Forum, Bloomberg

TV) is on record having said the following regarding our immigration practices:

"…the current U.S. immigration policy is highly detrimental to the economy and needs to be redesigned to align with economic needs." He then went on to comment on existing policy, saying it "makes no sense whatsoever".

Secretary Rubin additionally advocated for a system of "immigration that serves our economic needs".

He also stressed the need for measures to deal with the currently undocumented illegal immigrants, specifically those who "are part of our economy" to allow them to "continue to prosper in our economy and eventually become citizens". (This presumably refers to what has been called a "pathway to citizenship" for current illegal residents, who have proven to be contributing members of society, with the logical "non-negotiable" provision that such a pathway would be available only to those who have not previously violated state or federal criminal law.)

It is the view of this study that after 74 years our immigration policy is grossly overdue for reform, but that whatever the policy may be, enforcement (conducted in a manner consistent with the laws and rights of the land) should follow, specifically as it pertains to any immigrants who egregiously violate U.S. state or federal law. A snapshot of recent deportation activities follows. While this summary simply depicts data, it invites asking why in earlier eras of less "uproar" regarding immigration we were more effective in deporting illegals?

Not a New Imperative - Deportations by President 2000 – 2029

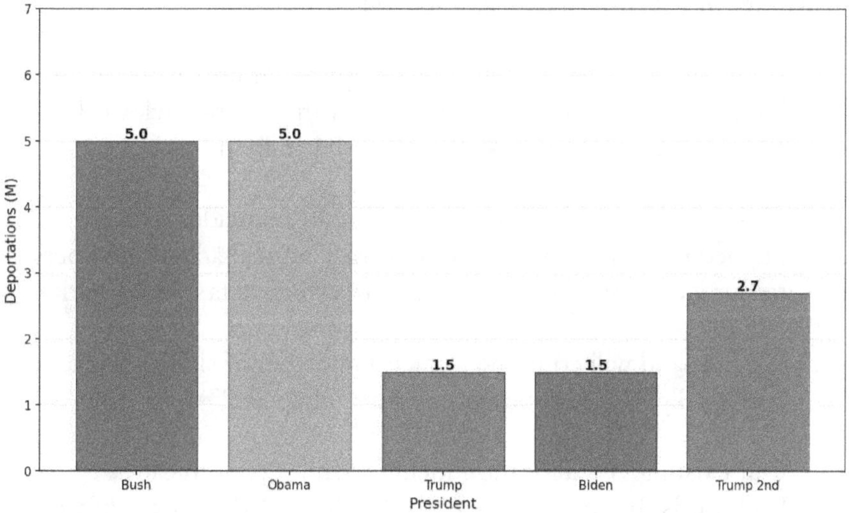

Figure 7: Deportations by President 2000 – 2029; Trump 2nd forecast per 2025 DHS data

Note: Data from U.S. Immigration and Customs Enforcement (ICE) and Department of Homeland Security (DHS) figures. Graph per author specification.

The above is by term, not years served, thus Bush 43 and Obama results are based on 8 years in office, whereas Trump 45, Biden and Trump 47 reflect 4 years in office each. Per this DHS data, deportation results by President—measured purely in number of deportees per 4-year term—are not that different.

This study assumes continuity in number of legal immigrants per year (of slightly above 1 million) but notes that determining the recommended number of legal immigrants per year is outside of the scope of this work. However, it clearly suggests a reallocation of whatever number of visas are granted by category, prioritizing the needs of our labor force and the US economy and therefore contributing to fiscal sustainability.

NY Times columnist Thomas Friedman has a clever summary of his preferred immigration policy: "a high wall with a big gate", implying an immigration policy of our discretion, meeting the needs of our country. This study notes the wisdom of such a paradigm, and simply proposes amending "big gate" to "smart gate" reflective of a smart immigration policy that aligns visa issuance to economic need.

A summary of this chapter is as follows:

1. While this study is agnostic on the optimal number of annual immigrants each year, we observe that the recent backward-looking annual average is about 1 to 1.1 million.

2. This number (1.1 million), coincidentally coincides with the implied need (per BLS data) of average annual added members to our labor force to maintain future effective taxpaying parity.

3. We face and will continue to face a shortfall of skilled workers, specifically STEM educated workers (chapter 23).

4. Our existing visa allocation mechanism is economically backwards. In an era of negative fertility, AI-driven workforce transformation, and unsustainable debt, we cannot countenance an immigration system in which economic contribution is of secondary, even tertiary concern. The "80/20" split should be reversed: prioritize workforce needs, then accommodate other considerations, as able, within (updated) policy constraints.

5. This study therefore proposes immigration reform such that irrespective of what number of visas are granted, that a "hard link" is implemented such that approximately 80% of visa issuance targets the specific needs of our labor force, prioritizing STEM expertise. (We describe the outsized impact of STEM workers on our economy and our tax revenue in chapter 23.)

3. A Profound Inflection – AI and Workforce Automation

Throughout economic history, innovation and automation have vastly improved productivity, real income and standards of living. Man can rightly look back at life before several of these innovations and wonder how we could have ever lived without them…such as the wheel, the printing press, the steam engine, electricity, modern transportation, indoor plumbing, the internet, etc. Thus far, the reality has been that although there has been workplace disruption instance by instance, new industries emerged, new jobs emerged that were not contemplated or imagined before, leaving all—or most of us—gainfully employed, with a higher standard of living, a higher level of income and even a longer life expectancy. This has been the clear consequence of innovation across the history of mankind.

One can also ask whether prior eras of innovation have adversely affected overall employment. From a macro level, we can see in the Federal Reserve graph below that there appears to be an *absence* of high-level negative correlation (we use productivity increases as a proxy for innovation). Employment has dipped notably only during periods of recession (as indicated by gray vertical bars), which however is not to say that this time, that of AI-related automation, will not be different, as most current indications are that it might be—at least transitionally. (Blue solid line depicts productivity; green dash line employment.)

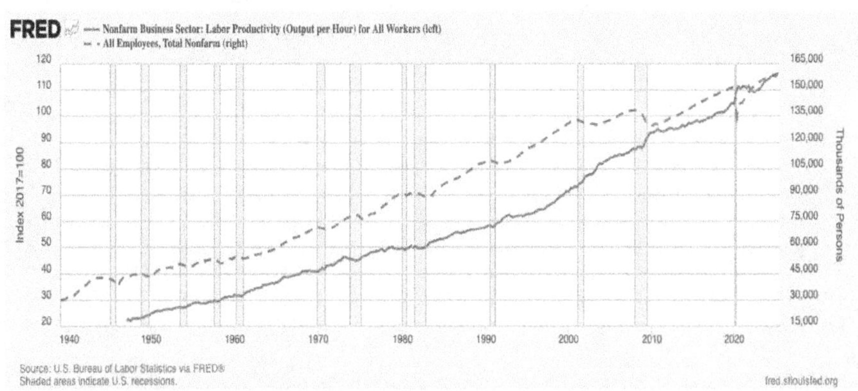

Figure 8: Productivity and Employment growth.

Note: Labor Productivity (Output per Hour) for All Workers (solid line, left axis) and All Employees, Total Nonfarm (dashed line, right axis), Indexed to 2017=100. Data source: U.S. Bureau of Labor Statistics (BLS) via FRED®.

Will it be different this time?

Workforce automation, in the name of physical AI (robotics) and more importantly cognitive or Agentic AI is the latest in this long continuum of innovation. We've heard about it for years, but we can now say that it is here, at least at an early stage. The truth is we do not know how far reaching its impact will be, how far this leg of innovation will take us. Literally, it is all around us now, and its arrival has been sudden.

Academic research as well as research reports from consultancy groups characterize AI's manifestation in the workplace as either **augmentation** of existing worker capabilities or one that brings **automation**—and therefore replaces workers. There are also increasingly reports of newly created positions being directly filled by AI instances, either via robotics (such as in Amazon distribution centers, or via agentic teammates, as McKinsey has been reporting).

Which presents a simple, but likely profound, paradox: it will be possible, perhaps probable, that AI induced productivity increases will allow GDP growth to occur concurrent with labor force reductions. But, since AI entities, be they Generative, Agentic, etc., are not (yet) taxpayers, we could very well experience GDP growth concurrent with a decline in employment and therefore a decline in tax revenue, exacerbating the fiscal risk that we face. This one simple paradox defines the need for bringing our legacy system of taxation into the AI era.

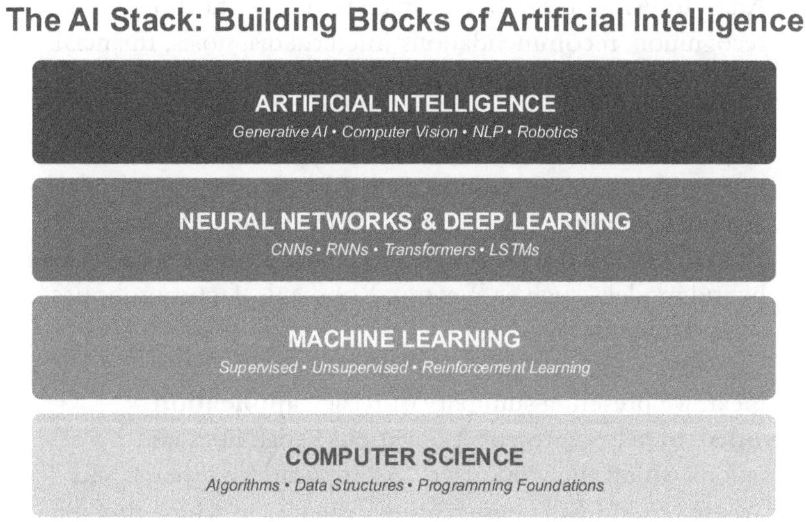

Figure 9: The AI Stack; (Author adaptation per standard industry taxonomy)

In his CS230 class, Stanford Adjunct Professor (former Director Stanford AI Lab, co-founder Google Brain) Andrew Ng expresses the evolution and emergence of AI as a sequence of building blocks, generally characterized as the "AI Stack". In doing so, he recounts the modern history of computer science upon which machine learning is layered, onto machine learning is layered deep learning or neural networks, upon which generative AI now resides.

How does it work? How is AI currently integrated into our economy?

To provide an introduction to the growing manifestation of AI within the business environment, we present four prevalent **functionality frameworks** of AI, followed by the emerging layer of **application types,** to provide more specific examples of how AI is being used across a variety of industry sub-sectors. Broadly speaking, this functionality framework includes:

Generative AI: prompt and response general content generation (text, images, video and even computer code);

Agentic AI: autonomous goal-directed systems with capacity to reason, to plan, to orchestrate (workflow automation, decision making, even supervisory agents);

Analytic AI: context-based prediction, classification, pattern recognition, recommendations (medical diagnosis, financial analysis, fraud detection); and

Physical AI: DC/Edge hybrid deployed manifestations, independently (or semi-independently) carrying out physical activities. Compute may happen at the edge, independent of the Data Center, but in most cases today we are seeing DC/Edge hybrid models, such as Waymo, Robotaxis, factory robotics, and soon, humanoid robotics.

Next, we present a summary of basic "**application frameworks**" to help represent AI's various capabilities and configurations within the workplace. As applications emerge and develop, there are and will be increasing instances in which multiple functionalities are combined to optimize potential efficacies, which is to say the application of AI is dynamic and evolving.

Generative AI: we know of Gen AI through the phenomenon of prompt-and-response interfaces—ChatGPT, Claude, Gemini, Grok, Llama (and in China Qwen, DeepSeek, etc.)—which provide high-level reasoning. Earlier generations were "stateless": each prompt began a new, discrete response. Recent versions increasingly retain conversation memory and context across sessions.

Work augmentation: using generative AI to enhance productivity in personal and professional contexts, from drafting emails and creating documents to conducting research and analyzing data; productive in our personal and professional lives. A highly ubiquitous use case (LLM-based).

Agentic AI: the highest growth niche at present, AI becomes "agentic" when an LLM, with its "high IQ" is wrapped in an "agentic OS" (or operating system, which we can refer to as an AIOS), with added memory, thus giving it a remarkable set of capabilities. It can understand, reason and plan, thus learn from its experiences and refine further actions, operating autonomously and providing supervision of other AI or robotic entities and orchestrate outcomes. Agentic as an OS allows an applications layer to be integrated and thus enhance its functionality. (A simple analogy is the Apple iPhone iOS and its application network.)

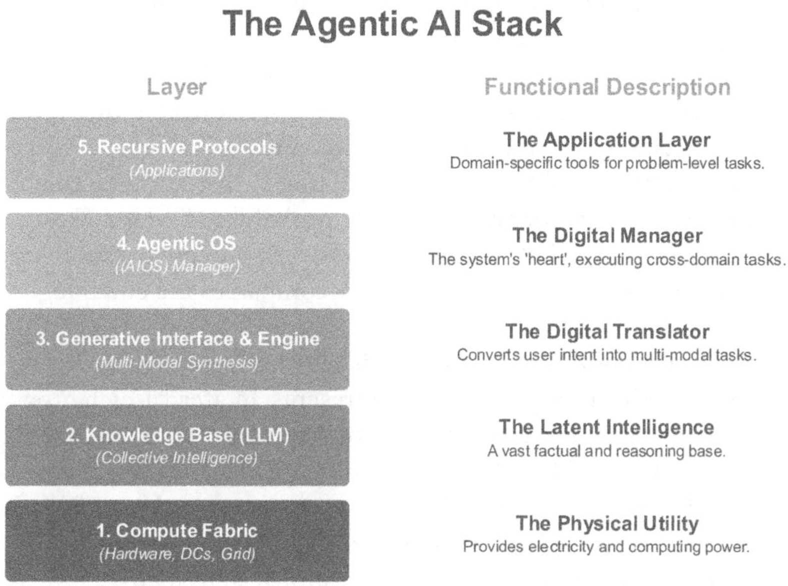

Figure 10: The "Agentic Stack" depicting transformation of an LLM into a reasoning, supervising, orchestrating, autonomous entity. Author specification.

Agentic AI systems often employ recursive learning—continuously refining their knowledge and strategies through iterative and autonomous learning feedback loops. In high-complexity tasks (e.g., scientific discovery, autonomous vehicles, strategic planning), these systems use LLMs for their knowledge and reasoning platform, Agentic AI as their OS and VLMs (vision-language-models) for perception, enabling them to adapt their approaches, learn from outcomes, while maintaining alignment with assigned goals and ethical boundaries, revising objectives and decision-making for subsequent actions as concluded. Agentic AI is often deployed as the supervisory brain across domains, from office to factory to "edge" devices such as mobile applications.

Agentic Process Automation: an emerging workflow application, Agentic Process Automation (APA), increasingly receives digital input of workflow, typically via API access. Draws upon LLMs for recognition of structured or unstructured inputs, and then employs Agentic AI to determine next steps and to orchestrate execution. This niche offers high potential for the impact of AI in an office workflow setting, as its application universe is quite broad as it is essentially a use-case specific application of Agentic AI.

Its operative process could be described as: digital input + LLM understanding + Analytic calculation and forecasting + Agentic orchestration and reasoning = resulting in execution, even an ongoing supervisory process. The probability that it makes inroads into markets enjoyed by business process outsourcing companies is high. AI native APA companies are emerging.

Software code development casually known as "vibe coding" or "natural language coding", represents an area of high growth, as it allows rapid prototyping of functional code or application development. Many have noted its impact in allowing enhanced speed to market of new ideas. Accomplished with an LLM Gen AI interface via prompt and response, whereby outcome objectives are input with a quick response and iterative refinement occurring as needed. Outcome may or may not be enterprise level without follow up and refinement—depending upon who ask and when you ask, but its speed to launch is impressive and its uptake is both dynamic and increasingly consequential.

Innovation in the AI-assisted coding sector is transforming coding as we have known it. Originally the domain of GitHub, the landscape now includes Anthropic's Claude Code, OpenAI's Codex, Gemini Code Assist and of course AI-native platforms such as Cursor, Lovable, etc. These tools are securing significant market share as their inherent efficiencies are perceived as a challenge to traditional coding companies. By their very nature, they represent a new era of disruptive technology.

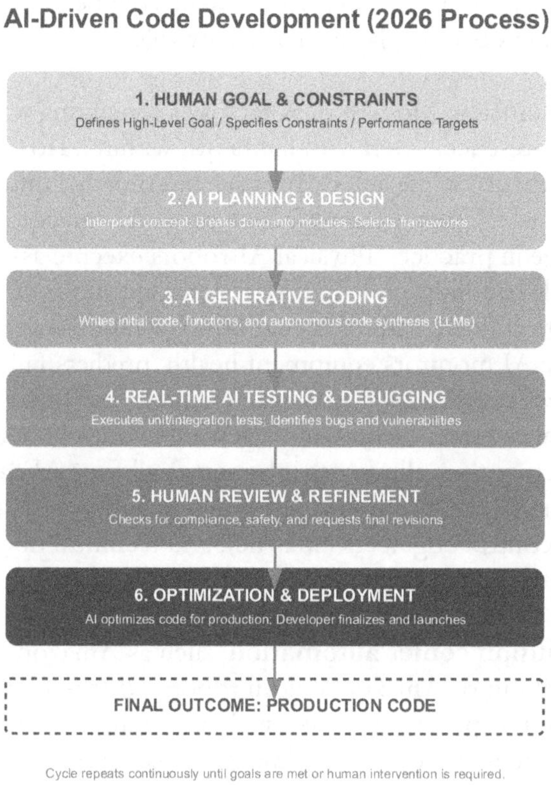

Figure 11: AI-Assisted Coding, Machine-speed gated only by human latency. Author specification.

Factory automation and Smart factories: not a new field, but one that is growing at a torrid pace in Korea, Japan and China…think fixed position robots along an assembly line, with precise 4 or 6 axes of movement, performing repetitive tasks with a high level of consistency in execution. Factory robot technology is decades old, however, supervision via Agentic AI, enabling adaptive decision-making, predictive maintenance, and autonomous coordination makes it very much new tech. Often within a smart factory environment, which broadly speaking exist within an Industrial Internet of Things (IIoT) environment.

Collectively, Smart Factories are manifestations of IIoT (industrial internet of things) principles, which feature entity-wide digital integration, use of sensors and AI to analyze data flow, allowing self-optimization. Foundational for manufacturing competitiveness; adoption should increase across sectors like aerospace, automotive, and pharmaceuticals…and equally help boost productivity of high-volume goods. Agentic AI will increasingly play a supervisory role.

Dark factories: Modern dark factories (operating without human presence, often with lights off, within a IIoT environment), while still early-stage and mostly limited to China—and Japan, exemplify how these AI categories may converge in practice. Physical AI robots execute assembly and materials handling. Agentic AI systems autonomously supervise production flows and make real-time operational decisions. Analytic AI monitors equipment health, predicts failures, and optimizes production schedules. Generative AI may create maintenance documentation or generate control code. A single dark factory thus eliminates jobs across all four AI categories—assembly workers (physical), production supervisors (agentic), quality control engineers (analytic), and technical documentation specialists (generative).

Distribution center automation: such as Amazon DCs and their roll-out of Amazon Vulcan robots, which effectively perform DC processing tasks such as sorting, inventory management and order fulfillment. Amazon has been expansive in their efforts here (chapter 4).

Transportation automation: Waymo and Robotaxis are the most visible manifestations of autonomous vehicles (AVs) today, with automated trucking ("long haul") coming soon. A cousin of this application may very well be urban delivery vehicles, bringing your food or grocery order to you.

AVs such as Robotaxis and Waymo, as examples, will likely make extensive use of recursive learning—meaning they will serially increase their knowledge of their environments each trip. This learning would then be distributed as updates to their respective fleet VLMs, suggesting semi-exponential, compounding learning potential via each instance.

Humanoid automation (robotics): one of the most complex engineering challenges, we can expect to see expanded test versions within the next year (Tesla Optimus, Figure and others are in pilot deployments) and possibly the beginning of mass distribution by 2030. Humanoids will be highly dependent upon recursive learning to be able to augment their generalized training by acquiring in-depth local knowledge specific to their respective work environments. (Note this a completely unique sub-set of physical AI from factory robotics—one in which a higher level of autonomy is required as they may operate in less structured environments—and presently a sector in which China appears to be ahead.)

Financial industry transformation – Perhaps uniquely, finance is about to be transformed by both AI (specifically Agentic AI and Analytic AI and Predictive AI), and the blockchain revolution, which will bring with it tokenization and therefore programmable assets, such as stable-coins, "smart contracts", and other manifestations that may very well accelerate the trend of decentralized finance or "DeFi". The capacity of AI to absorb data and perform immensely detailed analysis is considered formidable, likely making this sector a high-level beneficiary.

Medical diagnosis and care stand to be transformed by virtue of the relative certainty of diagnosis AI will allow. Examples will include diagnosis of images by AI backed up by the near-infinite experiential base LLMs trained specifically in this sector, coupled with Analytic (or Predictive) AI will provide. At the other end of the spectrum, we will see expanded use of robotics in surgery, or robotics allowing remotely-directed surgery, or robotics allowing access to "best practices" in surgery

Pure scientific, mathematical and medical discovery and research represent additional high-impact domains. Cumulative reports suggest that these areas, broadly speaking, offer the potential for vast impact. Both academically and within the business sector, there are reportedly intense research processes in motion. (Dario Amodei, CEO Anthropic links his concept of the "compressed 21st century" to these domains of intense focus as articulated in his October 2024 essay *Machines of Loving Grace.*) In short, the reported vision of Mr. Amodei, Demis Hassabis of Google Deep Mind, and others, is one of dramatically accelerated learning resulting in dramatically accelerated problem solving; in essence, accelerated "scaling" of knowledge.

The above is intended to serve as a conceptual framework of existing or near-term applications. Many of these manifestations require unique solutions as far as their architecture of AI related sensors, application of reasoning, use of and types of "compute" capacity, unique combinations of processors, and are evolving dynamically. In fact, an expected characteristic is that AI applications will increasingly combine multiple functional categories—Agentic AI supervising Physical AI robots, Analytic AI informing Generative AI outputs—making potential workforce displacement both comprehensive and complex. Productivity gains we will experience courtesy of AI, while still of magnitude unknown, may be significant.

A brief backstory of how we got here

One of the most compelling stories in the modern era of AI has been the outsized impact of a few select companies and individuals—we highlight four such individuals or teams below. In some cases, significantly innovative research has been left on the shelf, only to be brought to life by a subsequent researcher—who divined its genius. It is easy to conclude that the AI-related functionality we have discussed in this chapter would not have been possible without these individual contributions.

We know of the early recognition of the power of machine learning from Alan Turing (post WW2 England), and those who followed him in the pre-generative AI era. In the modern era there has been a series of innovations, seemingly stacked one upon another, each enabling the following, that have brought the future to the present.

In 1999, Jensen Huang's Nvidia released the GeForce 256, the first chip marketed as a Graphics Processing Unit (GPU), which was a seminal semiconductor breakthrough. In hindsight its innovation is intuitive, but at the time of its invention it was completely unimagined in chip design: it allowed simultaneous parallel processing to supplant serial or sequential processing. This innovation was designed as a solution for the graphics world, in which dynamically evolving graphic depictions were thus allowed to be rendered in a simplified and accelerated manner. It was quickly adopted by leading computer graphics companies, such as Sony's PlayStation and Microsoft's Xbox. Though these customer relationships did not last forever, their revenue stream allowed Nvidia to continue to think big. Which it has.

The GPU in its own right was a breakthrough, but since it was developed for the graphics industry, while it could be used for other applications, such as machine learning, it required a code intensive translation step for the inputs to be GPU ready. In 2006 Nvidia solved this by creating its CUDA (compute unified device architecture) software platform, which opened up the broader data processing world to the GPU, allowing accelerated processing of not just images and graphics, but of text, language, and a variety of sensory inputs—becoming "multi-modal". In a fairly direct sense, the CUDA enabled GPU was the enabler of the LLM and Gen AI. They were two pieces of a puzzle that clicked together to create a bigger picture: a synergistic 1 + 1 = 3 scenario. (The unifying logic of a GPU and an LLM is they do not look at just the next bit of data or text, they are freed from sequential "gating" and instead process entire sets of data simultaneously, massively changing their predictive scope.)

Enter Google Brain, the predecessor to Google Deep Mind (Deep Mind having been Demis Hassabis and Mustafa Suleyman's project over in London, acquired by Alphabet in 2014 but not merged with Google Brain until 2023). Google Brain's founders were Jeff Dean, Greg Corrado and Andrew Ng. It was the Google Brain team who in 2017 laid down two foundational research papers, back-to-back, depositing them in the public domain (one we cite here, the other in chapter 16).

In June 2017 Google Brain released *Attention Is All You Need,* now famously known as the Transformer Architecture paper. And while this paper's progeny is the LLM, it remained mostly behind the scenes until 2022—when one researcher recognized its value. (It is rumored that Google themselves used aspects of this document to optimize Google search in the interim years, but their search algorithms remain private.)

Enter Ilya Sutskever, who in 2018 was at early-stage Open AI. Mr. Sutskever was Russian-born, Israeli educated through high school, then later completed his graduate work with (now) Nobel Laureate Geoffrey Hinton at University of Toronto. He recognized the ability of Transformer Architecture and used it to help solve the neural network and AI-related scaling challenges he was then focused on. This eventually led to Open AI (under Ilya's guidance) releasing the first technical beneficiary of Transformer Architecture, Chat GPT (GPT-3.5) in November 2022, and then the moment the world took notice with the launch of Chat GPT (4o) in January 2024. (The GPT in Chat GPT stands for "Generative Pre-trained Transformer", as in "transformer architecture".)

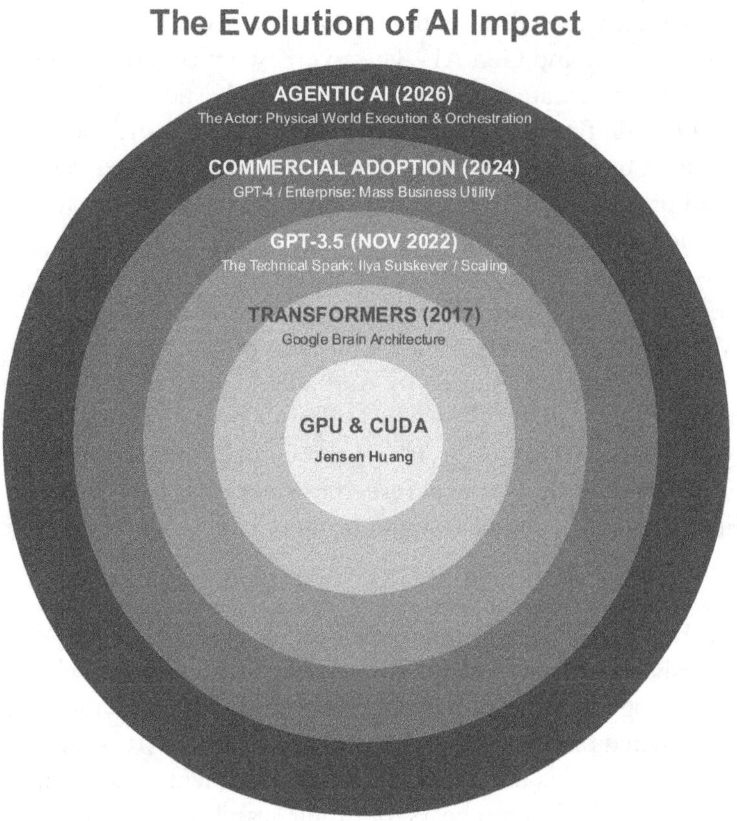

Figure 12: AI is the story of successive layers of innovation. Author specification.

From 1999 when Nvidia invented the GPU to 2022 and Open AI's Chat GPT (GPT-3.5) release was a 23-year incubation period, in which figuratively one player created a manifestation of exceptional innovation and then "passed the ball" along to the next player and then to the next. Taking a macro view, this story of sequential innovation, in which one scientist stands on the shoulders of those before him or her, is not unique to AI, it is more typically a representative legacy of the history of scientific discovery. (In fact, this observation was first attributed to Sir Isaac Newton.)

The prospects for job dislocation and even replacement by AI

The topic of the transformative impact of AI—as it pertains to individuals' lives, careers, families, our society in aggregate—is everywhere. The prevalent views expressed regarding this topic range from, a) AI-related economic influence is happening very suddenly, b) the question as to whether meaningful job dislocation in our near-future, to c) more sanguine voices, advising "yes" some dislocation is inevitable, but it will take time and along the way new job types will be created, with d) the less-discussed outcome of newly created jobs simply bypassing the human option altogether and going straight to "hiring" AI entities, cognitive or physical. We would say without reservation that all of these processes are in motion.

On July 22, 2025, The Guardian wrote that OpenAI CEO Sam Altman stated that entire job categories, e.g., customer service (CS) functions, will be replaced by AI, and that AI can diagnose specific illnesses more accurately than most doctors.

His contention spans the labor force, from semi-skilled retail positions to highly skilled medical doctors. He asserted that AI customer service is generally superior to human provided customer service, with the AI version being a more seamless, intuitive and better-informed interface offering more rapid resolutions. The similarity CS shares with the medical profession is that both cases can benefit from AI provided real-time access to relevant and near infinite data, so to speak real-time access to infinite prior instances (for medical) or all relevant data for any given transaction in CS.

3rd party insight: how does one of America's leading management consultancies assess the impact of AI on our workforce?

Select highlights from a McKinsey Global Institute (published January 2025) report on the impending impact of AI related workforce automation are as follows. (We acknowledge that in the world of AI, considerable learning and development have occurred since January 2025, nonetheless—with all credit to McKinsey—we have taken the liberty of editing down their observations to highlight those which we find remain categorically instructive, with occasional added commentary.)

They estimated those with "lower wage" roles (i.e., unskilled or low-skilled) were 14 times more likely to be disrupted—not because their wages are low, but because most likely they engage in repetitive functions, lending themselves to physical AI replication. In contrast, higher-wage occupations (especially in healthcare, and STEM fields) are more insulated and may even grow in demand.

Manufacturing has one of the highest automation potentials. Tasks involving predictable physical work (assembly, machine operation, packaging, etc.) would be easily handled by robots. (The U.S. regrettably missed this trend—compared to Asian and European manufacturers—and is engaged in catching up now.)

Robots installed in American work-centers are often foreign produced. This means that not only did America lose assembly and manufacturing jobs to lower cost foreign labor in the era of globalization, but that we are also at risk of missing out on the subsequent wave of producing manufacturing-based robotics.

The financial sector is deemed ripe for AI-driven efficiency, given its heavy reliance on analytics and information processing. AI algorithms (Predictive /Analytic AI) can already handle a broad variety of tasks in banking, insurance, and accounting – from transaction processing to risk analysis, econometrics and forecasting. AI will likely bring speed and precision to this sub-sector.

Retail is undergoing automation on two fronts: in-store automation (self-checkout kiosks, AI inventory management) and the rise of e-commerce, reducing the need for physical store staff. Retail job losses will be partially offset by growth in e-commerce logistics, with a net effect of a decline in *customer-facing* retail roles. Amazon as an example, has recently shown that many behind the scenes fulfillment jobs are becoming robotic, and therefore equally at risk—especially newly created jobs in "smart" distribution centers.

Transportation & logistics have high automation potential, especially with advances in autonomous vehicles and drones. Long-term, driverless trucking and AVs could render many driving jobs obsolete (anecdotally, one frequently hears of worker shortages in the long-haul sector). Urban delivery drones look to be in our future for home delivery of food and grocery orders.

Healthcare is a sector where AI will likely *augment* more than automate, while overall labor demand continues to rise. Our "Gray Tsunami" (the aging of the American population) will create secular demand for healthcare services, creating millions of new jobs (doctors, nurses, technicians, home health aides) that AI will struggle to fill due to the human interaction required. One can look at healthcare as a multi-decade secular trend—with a demographic "tailwind". Healthcare roles that involve routine data processing or analysis will be impacted by AI. For example, medical transcriptionists (who transcribe physician notes) are being supplanted by speech recognition; medical billers/coders are aided by AI software that automates claims processing. Even in clinical practice, AI diagnostic tools are beginning to handle tasks like reading radiology scans or pathology slides. Hospital level healthcare will likely benefit from considerable development and introduction of Edge applications over the next decade.

The greater impact of AI in healthcare will be shifting skill requirements—e.g., doctors and nurses working alongside AI decision support systems—rather than experiencing large-scale job loss. (This will broadly leverage the "Edge AI" sector.) Healthcare and social assistance could add anywhere from 50 to 85 million jobs globally by 2030, thanks to demographic trends—and per estimates from McKinsey and others.

Government and public sector jobs may lag in AI adoption due to bureaucratic hurdles, but routine administrative roles in government could shrink. (The notion of Agentic IRS agents performing the rigorous job of identifying tax fraud seems like an appropriate and highly beneficial use-case.)

In the defense sector, "change agents" such as Palantir have made significant inroads and secured large scale government contracts as has AI-powered defense company Anduril—which has won several recent Department of Defense (DoD) contracts for their next generation autonomous weapons which operate within their "Lattice" threat-and-battlefield-oversight protocol.

Construction and maintenance jobs involve unpredictable physical tasks in dynamic environments – automation here would be slower (robots struggle with unstructured real-world worksites). Thus, construction may see *productivity gains* from AI (e.g., drones surveying sites, 3D printing of components) without large job losses by 2030. If augmentation of construction efficiency brings productivity increases and therefore lower costs, we know of no one who will complain.

In chapter 10 we take a deeper dive into the topic of how McKinsey is using AI within their own company, how they are internalizing AI, how it is impacting their workforce and indeed their go-forward strategy. McKinsey as a "case study" may prove to be one of the best predictors—for now—of the future.

Does all of this proliferation of AI present a unique cyber security risk?

Regrettably the answer to this theoretical question is an emphatic "yes". As autonomy in AI architecture is increased, security risk multiplies, perhaps exponentially as an autonomous digital workforce of theoretically millions of deployed AI agents creates an exponentially large and complex attack surface that human security staff cannot manage alone. AI Cybersecurity Agents are, thus far, considered the best possible "police force". Increasingly these AI security agents are deployed to surround enterprise AI agents, reflecting the emerging security model for the AI era. This approach is rapidly moving from theory to implementation and is defined by both the need for, and the current development of, new AI-native security architecture. It is broadly assumed that existing tools and antivirus systems would be insufficient and could easily be overwhelmed.

A case in point regarding the scale of this threat came on November 13, 2025, via a press release from Anthropic, parent company of Claude and Claude Code, *"Disrupting the first reported AI-orchestrated cyber espionage campaign"*.

"Anthropic announced detection and deterrence of a cyber espionage event believed run by a Chinese state-sponsored group, using their Claude Code tool. Believed to be the first large-scale cyberattack executed without substantial human intervention, exploiting Claude's advanced "agentic" capabilities—its ability to run autonomous loops, chain together complex tasks, make decisions with minimal input—targeting 30 global entities in finance, technology, and government. Anthropic said AI performed 80% + of the work, requiring human intervention only for 4–6 critical decision points per attack. The attackers bypassed safeguards, submitting malicious tasks to Claude as if performing a legitimate security audit."

Developing sufficient defense mechanisms to police and protect in the coming era of AI enabled cyber-crime easily can be considered a high-level imperative, most likely requiring coordination between industry and government internet and AI security teams. It would be difficult to over-emphasize the need to dedicate all necessary resources, since this risk would also embody the unique attributes of AI, such as high level of "intelligence" and relatively infinite potential for proliferation, likely raising this threat to a previously unimaginable level. It seems logical to imagine that accordingly AI Native security firms will therefore emerge over the coming years.

A final note about job dislocation: transitionally, at least, we are in a period in which some jobs are being eliminated, but not yet at a high level. Meanwhile, we are not yet seeing significant new hiring—apart from in the demographically driven healthcare sector. **The corollary question becomes, are there already a significant number of new virtual positions being created?** It is clear we will need a federal agency, such as BLS, to aggregate this data and create an index of jobs filled via cognitive and physical AI entities to help us better see through the fog.

4. *Robotics in the U.S. – Insights from Amazon, Tesla and now, Nvidia*

It's as if we skipped a step.

The path America has taken with respect to robotic manufacturing brings both pride and frustration. The original 6-axis robot (still one of the dominant robots used in manufacturing worldwide) was an American design, originally known as the "Stanford Arm". It was an all-electric, 6-axis articulated robotic single armed manipulator designed in 1969 by Victor Scheinman, a mechanical engineering student at the Stanford Artificial Intelligence Laboratory SAIL (the same Stanford AI Lab that is alive, well and more than kicking today—along with its "cousin" Computer Science AI Lab CSAIL at MIT). However, subsequent efforts to commercialize this creation ultimately met with failure within the US, largely due to the then abundance of US labor and the fear of job loss due to robotics.

Japan picked up the mantle and went on to create its 4-axis version in 1978 and in general to dominate robotic development for manufacturing as well as deployment for decades, with Europeans and ultimately Chinese companies co-leading. Why did Japanese companies succeed where American ones failed or abandoned the effort? Most likely because, contrary to the US in that era, they had a labor shortage, not abundance, and Japanese labor unions were company-specific, not industry wide, perhaps giving them a greater motivation to ensure that *their* company succeeded within a competitive environment. Robotics became a tactic to help ensure their success; keep in mind that for decades Japan has had a declining native-born labor force due to negative fertility.

A key take-away from this bit of history is that for the past 4-plus decades the U.S. was relatively on the sidelines as far as robotics development, while the Japanese, many European countries and then of course Taiwan and China picked up the "baton" and moved things forward, specifically focusing on 4 and 6-axis fixed position robotics for manufacturing. One ironic consequence of this is that as U.S. factories have recently begun to increase their use of robotics, they are having to source them from Asian and European suppliers, or domestic JVs (joint venture companies) thereof, with only recently a wave of US based start-ups entering this domain as the Industrial Internet of Things (IIoT) and Smart Factory movement gathers steam.

How did Amazon become a leader in Robotic development?

Today, Robotics are definitely in focus. We hear about this on a near daily basis, both from a variety of American manufacturers, ranging from Amazon and Tesla, to Boston Dynamics (who is now majority owned by Hyundai), to relative newcomers such as Figure, Agility, et al. Collectively, their focus and media preoccupation seem largely dedicated to Humanoid robotics.

In a July 1, 2025, article in the WSJ (Wall Street Journal) it was reported that "half of the jobs in Amazon distribution centers are now handled by robotics." Amazon's robotic development, however, has not been humanoid focused, but rather robotics designed and custom-built for the purpose of their respective roles within Amazon's distribution centers.

The WSJ continues…"The e-commerce giant, which has spent years automating tasks previously done by humans in its facilities, has deployed more than one million robots…, Amazon said. That is the most it has ever had and near the count of human workers at the facilities. Company warehouses buzz with metallic arms plucking items from shelves and wheeled droids that motor around the floors ferrying the goods for packaging. In other corners, automated systems help sort the items, which other robots assist in packaging for shipment. One of Amazon's newer robots, called Vulcan, has a sense of touch that enables it to pick items from numerous shelves. Amazon has taken steps to connect its robots to its order-fulfillment processes, so the machines can work in tandem with each other and with humans."

Subsequent research confirms that these "new robot hires" were for new positions not a result of layoffs or terminations. Nonetheless, these new robot hires represent "job loss" from a taxpaying labor force perspective, as these were jobs that would have previously been filled by some number of human taxpaying workers. (In other words: in the context of the theme of this study, 1,000,000 robots "hired" supplants 1,000,000 individual taxpayers, with the resultant loss of tax revenue.)

The take-away from this example of Amazon and its robotic workforce is that it is indicative of what is likely to be an accelerating trend, that of filling newly created positions directly with AI workforce automation, robotics or otherwise. This news is increasingly around us;

we will cover this topic further when discussing the example of U.S. management consultancy company McKinsey.

An interesting aspect of the Amazon story comes from the question, what exactly is the provenance of said robots? Amazon's warehouse robots were originally developed by Kiva Systems, a Massachusetts-based robotics company that Amazon acquired in 2012. After the acquisition, Kiva Systems was rebranded as Amazon Robotics, which now designs and manufactures the robotic fulfillment systems used in Amazon's distribution centers. The US lags its peer group countries both in deployment of robots in the workplace and in manufacturing, but one must recognize Amazon's insight and efforts on this front…and we can observe that, perhaps the least we can ask is that if robots do replace American jobs that said robots be American made.

Amazon's robotics deployment allows them to lower cost of operations, and navigate the downward pressure on our labor force courtesy of negative fertility, perhaps even reduction of available immigrant labor and do so in a forward-looking, vertically integrated manner. They have run substantially counter trend by virtue of the scale of their robotics deployment for a U.S. company.

We can observe Amazon's efforts to be in the fore with respect to system automation, leading technology and customer focus. AI, by all appearances, is a tremendous enabler. Various reports, from WSJ July and December 2025, and NY Times October 2025 paint a picture of a forward-looking company—perhaps one of the most impressive examples of broad-based competitive modernization—along with Tesla—in the U.S. at this point in time. Tactically, we noted earlier the foundational Kiva Systems acquisition of 2012. The NY Times, in an October 2025 article, also credits Amazon with the acquisition of Covariant as a pivotal move in Agentic and robotic systems generation: "The company paid $400 million a year ago to hire the founding team and license the technology of Covariant, a start-up developing A.I. systems that act like a robot's 'brain'."

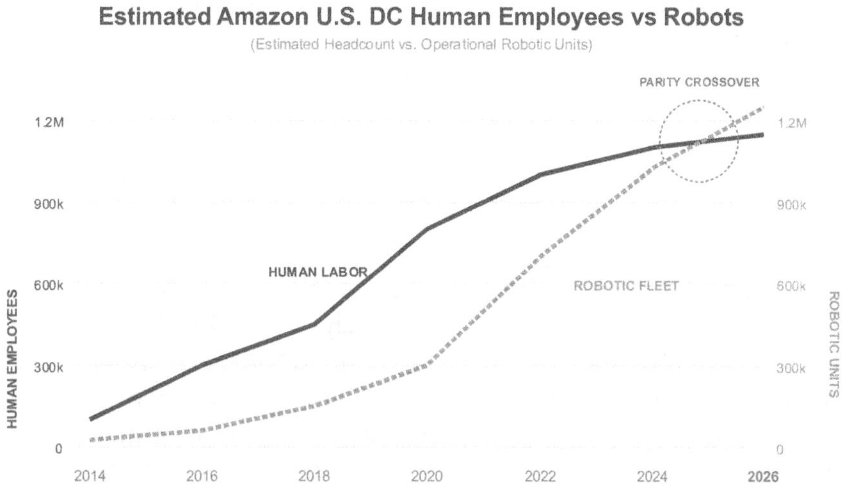

Figure 13: Estimated Amazon Human vs Robotic Employees; all DC formats, 2025

Note: Robot Data - Primary Source: Amazon Disclosures & Annual Reports. Amazon reached milestone one million robots globally in late 2025. Historical Benchmarks: growth trajectory per Amazon's 2022 Annual Report & "About Amazon" releases, tracking fleet scaling 45,000 units 2016 to 750,000 units in 2023.

Note: Human Employee Data - Amazon Financial Disclosures (SEC Form 10-K). Filings provide global total headcount peak of 1.6 million in 2021/2022, stabilized approximately 1.56 million globally early 2025. Operations Breakdown: Approximately 65% Amazon's global headcount (~1.01 million employees) assigned Operations & Fulfillment. Same ratio to U.S. workforce aligns the ~750,000 to 800,000 est. warehouse roles, 1.1 million figure in chart represents broader U.S. Operations footprint (including delivery and logistics orchestration)

The preceding focus on Amazon is to illustrate what leading physical AI companies are doing, what can be expected—augmentation, automation, substitution—within American companies (such as Amazon and Tesla) and by inference the implications for the American labor force. It is also worth noting there is an ongoing level of uncertainty between demand for and supply of factory workers in the U.S., as reported on multiple occasions, due to our demographic transition.

To be clear, this study makes no assertion that Amazon has acted improperly in any way, rather because they have been both forthright as well as leaders in business development and manifestation of modern management techniques, they provide a timely and informative case study. From a purely business perspective, Amazon is acting to reinforce their competitive stature, as they should.

Tesla has become America's best-known Robotics company, but is it the leader?

Tesla's innovation in their Texas Giga factory is reportedly via their implementation of a "Robotics Hierarchy", with 4 and 6-axis robotics in assembly line positions, and reported 1,000+ Tesla Optimus Gen 3 robots used for unstructured functions, often including movement of supplies between source and work locations, with Agentic oversight. It is not "dark" in the lights-out, human-free context, but highly automated. Further, Tesla is understood to also be developing what is termed an "Unboxed" manufacturing process for its Cybercab (Robotaxi variant) based on distributed assembly of components with single point final assembly, eliminating the traditional assembly line completely (which in itself implies Agentic orchestration). As with Amazon, Tesla is creating robotics solutions tailored to their vertical; both appear to be among the leaders in terms of robotics manufacturing and deployment in the U.S.

As referenced earlier, despite the Amazon and Tesla examples, the U.S. is in fact not a leader on the global stage of robotics; AI—yes, but not robotics. In terms of installed robots in the workforce, ranked globally by density per 10,000 manufacturing workers, the US is about 8th.

The U.S. can point to OpenAI, Google, and Anthropic as AI foundational model companies and world leaders. We can note that both Nvidia and AMD are American companies, and observe that both Jensen Huang, CEO of Nvidia, and Lisa Su, CEO of AMD, the two leading AI related GPU (graphics processing units, the foundation of modern AI data center processing) design companies were both foreign-born, coincidentally from the exact same city of Tainan in Taiwan. Both immigrated to the US when young and were American educated (he at Oregon State and Stanford, she at MIT). So, in terms of AI foundational models, and AI related GPU chip design, the US ranks 1st, but in robotics deployment we rank about 8$^{th.}$

The above example of the CEOs of both Nvidia and AMD (as well as Intel, the gradually reinvigorating U.S. based chip design and manufacturing company, now led by Malaysian-born Lip-Bu Tan) further underlines the need for welcoming and embracing top STEM students, whether foreign-born or native-born, with respect to protecting our countries lead in scientific, engineering and technology related domains. Arguably, the driving focus regarding the topic of manufacturing in the U.S. should not be recapturing leadership in yesterday's industries but retaining and or developing leadership in tomorrow's leading industries. There is no path to achieving this that does not include excellence in STEM amongst both our native-born and foreign-born academics and workforce.

Were we to look at America's "STEM quandary" like a VC, we would ask the standard VC question when contemplating a portfolio company's development: do we "build or buy" specific capabilities or functionalities. The analogy being, if we do not adequately develop ("build") the number of native-born STEM experts needed, do we ("buy") grant work visas to foreign-born STEM experts and grant student visas to aspiring foreign-born STEM grad students? The answer presumably is we must work both tracks: emphasize STEM education (K-12-University) among native-born students and grant visas to qualified STEM workers and grad students, to inoculate us against falling behind in this critical core competency.

To put the circumstance of America ranking 8th worldwide in factory-level robotic deployment in perspective: as we look back at globalization, an oft heard refrain is that American manufacturing jobs were lost to low-cost foreign producers. If we further lose manufacturing jobs to the era of robotics and "dark factories" this would represent a different dynamic altogether, that of US manufacturing jobs being lost to countries with higher levels of innovation, and perhaps more *advanced* manufacturing—not lower cost labor. Such an outcome would represent a dispiriting prospect and an unwelcome "wake-up call", as it would run wholly counter to the notion of "American exceptionalism" and America's sense of self as world leaders.

Ranked Table of Top Robotics Manufacturing Countries 2024

Country	Robots per 10k mfg emp	2023 Installs	Top Manufacturers	Key Industry Strengths
S. Korea	1,012	Very high	Samsung, Hyundai, Doosan Robotics	Electronics, auto; world's highest density
Singapore	770	Moderate	Govt. startups, multinationals	Innovation hub, strong adoption
China	470	~276,000	Siasun, Estun, Efort, GSK, QJ Robotics	Largest market, fast-growing makers
Germany	429	~28,355	Kuka, Bosch Rexroth	Automotive, automation leader
Japan	419	~300,000	Fanuc, Yaskawa, Kawasaki, Mitsubishi	Robot pioneers, industrial leader
Sweden	345	Moderate	ABB Robotics, others	Automotive, industrial equipment
Switzerland	296	Moderate	ABB (Swiss/Swedish)	Precision, pharma
USA	295	~37,500	Boston Dynamics, Teradyne, Zebra, Amazon	AI, collaborative/mobile robotics
India	100	~8,500	Various domestic/multinational	Emerging mkt, auto/electronics

Table 3: Robots per 10k manufacturing employees, Global comparison.

Note: Data adapted from the International Federation of Robotics (IFR) *World Robotics Report 2024*. Author specification.

As of 2025 according to the Chinese Machinery Industry Federation, Chinese robotics manufacturers generated revenue of approximately $40 billion, whereas for American-based companies, the best estimate available (blended datapoint ex three U.S. sources) is approximately $3 billion in the U.S. for 2025.

While the U.S. has unparalleled capital markets, famously providing seed and successive round funding for American start-ups, Chinese start-ups in "targeted" industry sub-sectors exist in a different type of ecosystem. Companies in favored sub-sectors often receive province-level investment and tax breaks, which along with Chinese VC capital, facilitates intense early-stage market competition followed by eventual consolidation.

Obviously, scenarios such as this have played-out frequently in the history of business: a high growth sector attracting multiple new entrants and capital, an intense cycle of competitive development and ultimately a winnowing process where the ultimate winners and survivors emerge. We can of course expect a repeat of this as it pertains to development and competition throughout the AI economy era.

Were we to speculate, the near-and-mid-term development and production for so-called "physical AI" development within the U.S. would fall into the following categories:

1) factory level, often stationary robots (non-humanoid in design)—often rooted or linked to work stations or conveyor belt type work flow; expect purpose-designed products suggesting next-gen from 4 and 6-axis;

2) fulfillment center (non-humanoid type) robots, think Amazon's Vulcan, Sequoia, Sparrow and Proteus robots—custom designed for the unique needs of both large and small scale DCs;

3) AVs for passengers (Waymo, Cybercab from Tesla and Zoox from Amazon) as well as long-haul freight AI operators;

4) humanoid style robots: Tesla is suggesting a 2026 test launch date for their Optimus Gen 3 version; Foxconn/Nvidia JV Q2, 2026 deployment of humanoids in their new Texas factory; Agility Robotics, also US based, has units on-site (in "pilot mode") with customers in initial applications, as does US-based Figure AI, etc.,

5) surgical AI, such as Intuitive Surgical ($10 billion 2025 revenue) and other medical AI and robotics to follow; and

6) other presently early stage "physical AI" innovations, such as those functioning in an "edge" capacity, smaller in scale, using SLMs, not LLMs, targeting relatively ubiquitous distribution compared to our existing concept of larger physical AI manifestations.

In the world of physical AI, there is obviously a physical component and an AI component. Companies such as Tesla and Zoox approach this on an "all-in" vertical (or semi-vertical) fashion, whereas Google for their Waymo business unit seems to approach it in an AI-first, physical-second process. We say this not just because they outsource production of their vehicle, but because perhaps uniquely their AV stack can also be viewed as a component of their broader DC/Edge AI platform strategy. In the Google DC/Edge AI platform concept, the car becomes a thin "client" of the thick "cloud". We submit it is far too early to say if one strategy is superior to the other, this is after all what competition and creative destruction is all about. With respect to manufacturing in America, one approach is to establish a product, the other a broader operative platform—as Google is attempting, which is essentially a bet on a bigger, broader physical AI future.

When it comes to Waymo vs. Cybercab vs. Zoox, the technical or compute strategy used by each diverges considerably. Specifically, Google's (Deep Mind) Gemini Robotics ER-15 (ER = embodied reasoning), aspires to be a high-level brain for a robot, focuses on their Vision-Language-Action (VLA) model that translates the ER 1.5's high-level plans into the robot's physical motor commands (the "hands" of the system), as compared to Tesla's Visual Language Model VLM Monolith model.

To expand further upon Google's efforts, and its approach to create a distinctive and leading brain for robots (and likely, broadly speaking physical AI), it is using what it terms a "split-compute" architecture, which refers to both its VLM and VLA reasoning models.

In lay-speak, VLM refers to vision language model, and VLA refers to vision language action model. Both have LLM reasoning models, both within an agentic architecture, but VLMs requires higher compute and thus resides in the cloud—using Google's TPUs, whereas VLAs resides on the "edge", that is the device itself, using lower power TPUs and likely ARM designed CPUs. VLM being the super brain of the pairing, requiring higher level TPUs and thus power, with the VLM feeding the VLA instructions, which it will process locally, within its own LLM (or, SLM) capacity, with its own chip cluster, and therefore with a lower energy demand, as likely edge devices are battery powered.

Is Google's focus on building not just a product, but on a physical AI operating platform?

Google's approach, of a split-compute dual brain architecture (VLM in the cloud, VLA on the edge) is unique and they believe higher level and ultimately deployable to a wide universe of Physical AI embodiments via their platform. Waymo, as an example, makes use of this split-compute (VLM – VLA) architecture, some call this a "modular, cascaded architecture", whereas Tesla's Robotaxi makes use of a single brain VLM Monolith, or end to end "E2E" neural network architecture, within which both VLM and VLA functions occur. In practice, both are "edge" compute dependent, relying upon real-time vision and reaction, with Waymo's VLM – VLA system perhaps making deeper use of rich cloud-based mapping.

We will likely see increased use of a variety of AI architecture solutions in the sure-to-increase iterations of physical AI we believe are in our future. For certain these models will evolve, but equally certainly this application sector will map out its own unique growth trajectory.

Tesla's VLM Monolith edge-based system is considered more scalable due to its lower unit cost and the fact that it is camera-dependent, not Lidar, etc., dependent, thus *not needing* a reservoir of mapping data to draw upon as it navigates its environment real-time. Therefore, Waymo's approach by contrast requires considerable in-depth (recursive) mapping prior to entering a new market, whereas Tesla's Robotaxi architecture is more independent. Waymo, however, has received L4 autonomy or driverless rating, and Tesla's Robotaxi remains at L2 rating or driver assist required (as of Q4, 2025).

Amazon's Zoox, simplistically speaking, uses a compute strategy that is a mid-point between Google and Tesla, as it employs both Lidar and cameras for sensory navigation. Zoox has received the least publicity thus far, but this may change once they expand launch cities (currently only Las Vegas) as both its appearance and operative functionality are unique. Last, for reference, the U.S., all brands combined reportedly has about 3,000 robotaxis deployed (Q1, 2026) whereas China (all brands), has about 10,000.

"Lidar" is an acronym for light detection and ranging. It can be thought of as radar although it employs dynamic laser beam emission and response detection for real-time spatial determination, and is frequently used for autonomous navigation and vehicles. Its provenance is radar and sonar dynamic threat detection—as famously pioneered by the UK's legendary "chain home" defensive radar network during the Battle of Britain in WW2. (Developed by Turing's peer-group of mathematicians and engineers, yet with a different objective and cloistered in a different part of England during the war, led by Sir Robert Watson-Watt, championed by Air Marshal Dowding.)

What the deep-dive above into varying and competing "compute strategies" underlines is that while it is still early-stage, companies, strategies, applications *et al* are dynamically developing with a long way to go until dominant architectures are determined, and winning companies and product strategies can be declared. Yet the science and research behind and inside of these serial innovations is already incredibly "rich", and accelerating. We can look back to how the internet and mobile premised application eras unfolded for a reminder that those eras exhibited serial "create" and "destruct" phases. As far as the "destruct" part, these new market entrants did not just destroy competitors from prior generations, but from their own peer group, usually by out-innovating them.

In the near-term at least, expansion of robotics in US factories may need to be fueled via robots manufactured by EU or Asian based companies, or joint ventures (JVs) between the foreign and American companies. (This is a consequence of the U.S. apparently have taken its "eye off the robotics ball" for a sustained period of time.)

The largest global manufacturers supplying industrial robots to U.S. industry as of late 2025—including FANUC, Yaskawa, KUKA, ABB, and Comau—are primarily headquartered in Japan, China and Europe with several operating US subsidiaries. While the US is where robotic technology originated, it currently accounts for a relatively small share of global robotics production.

Is Nvidia pioneering a third way via "reverse-globalization"?

For all of the acclaim attributed to China and its modern manufacturing prowess, an often-overlooked manufacturing superpower (except in semiconductors) is Taiwan. When Apple famously chose to manufacture its smartphones in China, it did not set up its own operations, it did not engage existing Chinese manufacturers, it engaged Taiwan-based Hon Hai Technology Group (commonly known as "Foxconn") to run its Chinese-based manufacturing facilities. Foxconn at this point is the top electronics manufacturer in the world—based on annual revenue, emerging from its origin as a "contract manufacturer" (meaning, not making its own goods or brands but making those of others on a contractual basis) into a global manufacturing superpower.

The other company that is somewhat surprisingly emerging as an important player in physical AI manufacturing in America is Nvidia. This may surprise some, given their reputation as a graphic and AI chip design and production juggernaut, but Nvidia has on multiple occasions exhibited a willingness to enter adjacent businesses and lead the development of vectors that are complementary to its core business. Thus, the fact that Nvidia is poised to become an important participant in physical AI manufacturing should surprise no one who heard Jensen Huang announce at GTC in March 2026 that "AI is transforming the world's factories into intelligent thinking machines — the engines of a new industrial revolution". Nvidia's role in bringing physical AI manufacturing to the U.S. seems predicated on providing the "AI" part of the physical AI equation, while their selected partners provide the "physical" part.

A case in point comes in how Foxconn and Nvidia have approached their new JV AI server manufacturing facility in Houston. Their collaboration has resulted in a new, state-of-the-art factory, scheduled to begin early phase production in Q2 2026. This is their first JV factory—at least domestically—and they will build AI servers using Nvidia 72 Blackwell Ultra GPUs and 36 Grace CPUs, which are optimized for powering AI data centers. Nvidia's Omniverse software stack will run the factory—including guide all robotics throughout, from assembly line humanoid robotics to autonomous mobile robots (AMRs).

Their robots' provenance was announced at GTC in March 2026 as Foxconn Industrial Humanoid robots, produced with input from U.S. companies Agility and Figure robotics. They will run on Nvidia's Isaac GR00T (Generalist Robot 00 Technology) platform, and they are designed to mimic human movement and decision-making to handle delicate assembly. They will additionally use Fanuc stationary robots for discrete component assembly steps—a supplier it has long worked with for iPhone assembly in China. This platform is part of Nvidia's emerging "Automotive and Robotics" division—which accounted for just $2.3 billion of Nvidia's total $62.3 billion in their recent fiscal year. Additional collaboration purportedly occurred with Siemens via employing their "digital twin tech stack" in the factory development process.

The launch of the Foxconn / Nvidia Houston factory marks a serious new entrant into the genre of AI-era, physical AI (robotic) manufacturing in America. In this case, Foxconn becomes the operational lead, and Nvidia becomes the technology lead. Foxconn and Nvidia are easily best-in-class in their domains, and they have pulled in other top-tier collaborative partners case by case as their specific expertise is needed. It is a "third way" compared to Tesla, who is famously vertical in their manufacturing, and even Amazon, who is not reticent to acquire needed technology and integrate it into their own operations. Ironically, this third way, the Foxconn / Nvidia model is analogous to domestic based or "reverse-globalization".

The Foxconn / Nvidia partnership is in some respects surprising, but from a macro perspective highly logical. They have announced additional plans to expand their U.S. physical AI factory footprint. In some cases, Nvidia will partner with Foxconn, in others with additional partners. Regardless, it marks a new era.

To summarize the state of robotics development and applications in America, we can offer the following high-level observations:

1. As a country—despite exhibiting clear first mover advantage in the 60's and 70's, via the "Stanford Arm" in robotics and the IBM S/360 in process automation—we seemed to have "taken our eye off the ball" of robotics development for a meaningful period of time. In the meanwhile, companies in both West Europe and East Asia pushed ahead with innovation in this sphere;

2. Presently, U.S. companies are again exhibiting tremendous engineering and application development in the emerging domain of physical AI, such as Tesla, Amazon, Google and now Nvidia;

3. Regardless, there remains a "gap" in output and deployment of basic manufacturing robotics, one in which we are now

having to catch up in terms of deployment in U.S. factories. For now, this means purchasing robotics from Asian or European companies for use in American factories, while we develop our own capabilities—a situation exacerbated by the fact that this is occurring against a backdrop of demographic decline in our technically skilled labor force;

4. Ironically, in the Foxconn / Nvidia "third way" partnership model, we can see perhaps an early-stage manifestation of what may come to be known as "reverse-globalization".

5. Finally, as it connects to the central theme of this book: the earlier decline in manufacturing and resultant decline in taxable gross value-added output by American companies was detrimental to not just employment but also tax revenue. This is only partly remediated by the new global model of manufacturing—which will be highly robotics dependent—and will need to be clearly understood and responded to with AI-era taxation policy insights.

5. *The Commoditization of Cognition and the "Infinite Upper Bound"*

An open secret in the world of AI today is that in spite of the record sums being dedicated to AI infrastructure—or perhaps because of it—the cost of cognition has been reducing rapidly. And the sustained rate of decrease in this cost is not modest, it has been significant. We hear about the rapidly growing demand for AI, we hear about increasing infrastructure investments, we hear about delays in data center activations due to shortages of electricity, but we hear much, much less that the actual cost of generating artificial intelligence—which we can equally think of as artificial cognition—has been decreasing rapidly.

How do we measure this cost decrease? We measure the economic cost of AI, expressed as cost per token generated, and the energy efficiency of AI is expressed as tokens generated per kilowatt-hour. "Tokens" are the universal unit of measure in both AI input and AI output, and the data trend line tells the story. They are to AI roughly what the kilowatt-hour is to electricity: the unit by which the service is metered and billed. What has driven this cost decrease? Several factors, but most notably GPU efficiencies—including use of CPUs and LPUs for lighter inference tasks, and software and algorithm efficiencies. The MoE inspired generation of sparser models (DeepSeek et al) and smaller distilled models such as Gemini Flash offer a lower cost of token generation. Granted, the MoE tier, or less dense models in general, do not offer the same top-tier quality of output as a frontier model, but are reflective of market demand for lower-priced tokens.

We can see in the chart below that token cost decreases are driven by two distinct market forces:

1) simple price competition— this is evident in sequential price reductions on like frontier models over time, such as Chat GPT and Claude Opus; and

2) the growing market layer of less dense, faster, and lower cost MoE type AI model variants. These were produced by both domestic and Chinese companies, and while each model has its unique variation as far as operating framework, the common theme was the introduction of a lower cost—yet still quite functional—level of AI model to the market.

Their presence alone, let alone adoption rates, "pulls" the market price of tokens lower to this day. Simple logic suggests that this layer will only increase, as additional Chinese open and closed models enter the fray, and contribute to the price competition dynamic over time.

The Declining Cost of Token Generation in the U.S. Market

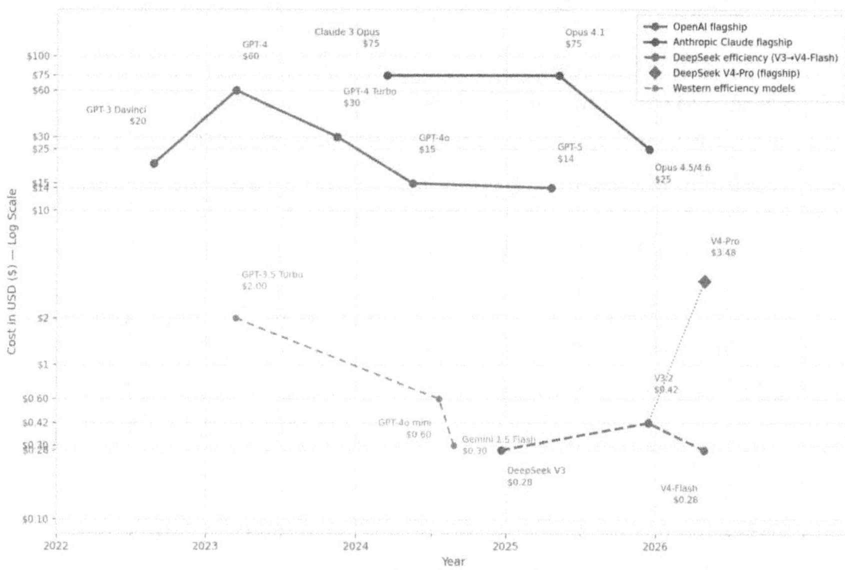

Figure 14: Price per 1M output tokens, major AI providers, 2022–2026. Logarithmic scale.

Note: DeepSeek's December 2024 entry at $0.28/1M output for a highly-capable model, priced just below Gemini 1.5 Flash. Claude maintained $75/1M pricing (Opus 3 through 4.1) before a 67% reduction to $25 with Opus 4.5/4.6. Claude Opus 4.1's $75 token pricing was the most expensive flagship model in this period.

Sources: OpenAI API historical pricing; Anthropic API pricing documentation (MetaCTO, March 2026); DeepSeek official API pricing (pricepertoken.com, April 2026); Google AI pricing (Gemini 1.5 Flash). Output token rates shown at or near model launch. Imperfect but best available data; for representative purposes only. Author compilation.

Clearly price changes are never a straight slope up or down over time, but in the simplest terms, as the cost of cognition collapses, for the first time in human history, intelligence—or cognition, is on the path to becoming a commodity. We have seen the commoditization of human labor—this was known as the industrial revolution—when machinery proved vastly more productive, and after the necessary capital investments, less expensive than human labor on a percentage of cost of production basis. Never before have we seen such a significant reduction in the cost of human intelligence, a collapse in the cost of cognition.

What will the consequences be of this commoditization of cognition? Most likely, it will include:

1. A vastly increased supply of cognition;
2. Increased deployment of cognition;
3. Increased rates of productivity—courtesy of increased application of cognition;
4. Resultant lower costs of production;
5. Disinflationary "impulses" (chapter 12).

Jensen Huang refers to this massive increase in the production of cognition as the "Fourth Industrial Revolution" (with revolutions 1 – 3 being the factory level IR, the electricity revolution followed by the software revolution) with AI data centers as AI factories, facilitating this fourth revolution.

Physicist and AI researcher Alex Wissner-Gross states in his February 14, 2026, *Innermost Loop* newsletter…" artificial cognition (is) collapsing toward the cost of electricity…" This line of reasoning implies not only abundance of cognition but disinflation of cognition—we also presume it refers to the "marginal cost" of cognition. Once initial investments in DCs and GPUs are made, the cost of incremental cognition becomes tantamount to the cost of electricity. Its secondary effect will therefore be upward pressure on AI-related disruption in the cognitive workspace—due to its sheer abundance. This will place the large "total disruptable market" (TDM) of the service sector economy squarely within its sights as cognition abundance allows it to deploy to the "infinite upper bound" (IUB) of its potential penetration.

The IUB of cognition will be tantamount to an exponential increase in the ultimate high-value, capital-light production input

While the notion of the amplification of the penetration of cognition in our economy may seem foreign, it would simply be tantamount to an acceleration of the continuum of the impact of human intelligence on economic output over time—except that in this case it would be artificial cognition which picks up the "baton" of cognition. It is thus highly likely that, given sufficient autonomy along with commoditization—including the ability of Agentic AI to orchestrate outcomes—the role of cognition in our economy would accelerate. Its proliferation, which is merely a click away from thousands, even millions of additional instances, would bear no resemblance to the trajectory of human proliferation, which over history has been constrained due to the comparatively finite supply of humans. (Courtesy of negative fertility, "instances" of human intelligence are now on a negative trend line, anyway.)

If one steps back and takes stock of the likely impact of our three forces, it is clear that the first two will have deleterious but somewhat predictable effects. In other words, if negative fertility and declining immigration result in a reduced labor force, while this is not good news, one can extrapolate the impact on GDP and on tax revenue in a linear manner, and to some extent plan accordingly.

The third force—that manifested by increased cognitive output and deployment may result in deeply asymmetrical, non-linear and wholly unpredictable consequences. This manifestation in the workplace of an "infinite upper bound" (IUB) of applied cognition, in particular with respect to the "white-collar" or service sector, will likely change the American economy.

In monetary policy, the "zero lower bound" (ZLB) refers to the effective lower limit on interest rates of 0% interest. The ZLB therefore presents a "hard floor" on efforts to lower policy interest rates. In cognitive AI—and its theoretical penetration within the American economy, there is conversely an "infinite upper bound" (IUB), as the potential for AI deployment is theoretically infinite. This implies the capacity for disruption in industry sectors vulnerable to cognitive disruption—such as our service sector—is so-to-speak "infinite". Equally, Agentic AI — given its capacity to adapt mid task, orchestrate multi-step reasoning, deploy tools as needed, and sequence cognitive tasks dynamically —obviates any ceiling on how much artificial cognition can be deployed on a specific problem, reinforcing the IUB.

As one considers the growing breadth and depth of functionality of Agentic AI driven workflow, workforce automation (agentic process automation - APA) and of Predictive AI, the potential enterprise impact of Cognitive AI becomes easy to imagine. Given that Cognitive AI manifestations are simply software instances that can be replicated almost at will, their "gating" factors will mostly be "compute" capacity and electricity, as expansion within the service sector would not really be constrained by the need for incremental capital expenditure as are embodiments of Physical AI. Instances of cognitive AI, such as Agentic AI given supervisory and orchestration type autonomy, may simply decide to deploy increased cognition itself.

Therefore, as compute capacity increases, and as the environments in which Agentic AI can operate autonomously are expanded, the application of Cognitive AI would be free to scale in synchrony with new use cases and deployments, possibly on a near-real-time basis. As AI "learns and adapts" to address new "cognitive" functions, and as the cost of cognitive AI dramatically decreases, the "virtual employee" population deployment—or equivalent impact—they offer would in theory be limitless.

Disruption via globalization was "capped", disruption by Cognitive AI in the service sector will not be

If we back up a few decades and consider the impact of globalization on American industry, that which has been characterized as the "China shock", there were in hindsight some built-in limiting factors, such as China's and even the rest of the developing world's population of potential low-cost labor. It may not have seemed this was the case, but there was, at least conceptually, a "cap".

Conversely, in the world of white-collar AI, there are in theory no upper bound limits on the potential population of Agentic AI instances, or Analytic AI deployment, or generative AI capacity—that which we broadly categorize as Cognitive AI. These are all essentially software instances and can be replicated nearly at will. We can say by comparison that although the potential disruption via physical AI is also significant, there will be some constraints on deployment. Even allowing for "robots manufacturing robots" (a popular characterization) there will still exist some physical and capital constraints for physical AI expansion.

Cognitive AI deployment by comparison will be "capital light", and increasingly "lighter" as the cost of the cognition continues to decline, and it will "enjoy" a significantly greater total addressable market (TAM) than physical AI presents given the size of our service sector economy.

If anything, what we are witnessing via the protracted investments in compute capacity is non-linear generation of cognitive capacity, leading one to ask, will there be a limit? Industry reports repeatedly refer to increasing compute capacity and efficiency, due to evolution in semiconductors, improvements in operating software, recursive self-improvement enhancing the training process—which in turn produces models that deliver more efficient inference collectively demonstrating that as AI cognition is more efficiently created then its cost per unit (token) of generation will further diminish.

When the supply-side can improve compute efficiency while the demand-side simultaneously increases compute monetization, this results in acceleration in both production of compute capacity and in application. Popular culture increasingly likens this self-reinforcing dynamic to the 19th century concept known as Jevons Paradox.

January 2025 saw the resuscitation of this somewhat dusty 160-year-old economic concept. Its moment came courtesy of the DeepSeek R1 model release, prompting Microsoft CEO Satya Nadella to post on X: "Jevons paradox strikes again! As AI gets more efficient and accessible, we will see its use skyrocket, turning it into a commodity we just can't get enough of."

Jevons paradox asserts that if increased efficiency of an application occurs concurrent to a corresponding reduction in the cost of its input, then as a result demand for said application as well as consumption of the input may increase near exponentially—and even find new applications. The example W. Stanley Jevons cited in his 1865 book *The Coal Question* observed that improvements in the efficiency of steam engines — engines consuming less coal for a given unit of output — did not reduce coal consumption. Instead, the lower cost of using coal made steam power viable in vastly more applications, from railways to mechanized factories. Consequently, aggregate coal consumption rose exponentially, powering the Industrial Revolution.

The paradox described by Mr. Jevons perfectly parallels our thesis concerning the IUB of cognition: that increasing application of cognition coinciding with increasing efficiency in output, will result in accelerated deployment of cognition. The AI-era, and specifically the Agentic era, should bring non-linear growth in the application and thus impact of cognition as an input in both cognitive and physical AI.

Since heretofore human intelligence has been considered to be beneficial to nearly every endeavor in the history of man, we can assess that the future of cognitive AI—which will augment and even supplant human cognition—is bright.

An inescapable consequence of this shifting dynamic will be that since the majority of our GDP is generated by the service sector—in which human cognitive ability is often the most prized "input"—then by default this sector becomes cognitive AI's largest "disruptable" market. We present below the approximate relative share in the U.S. economy of the service sector vs. the physical "production" sector, and thus the scale of our perhaps most vulnerable market.

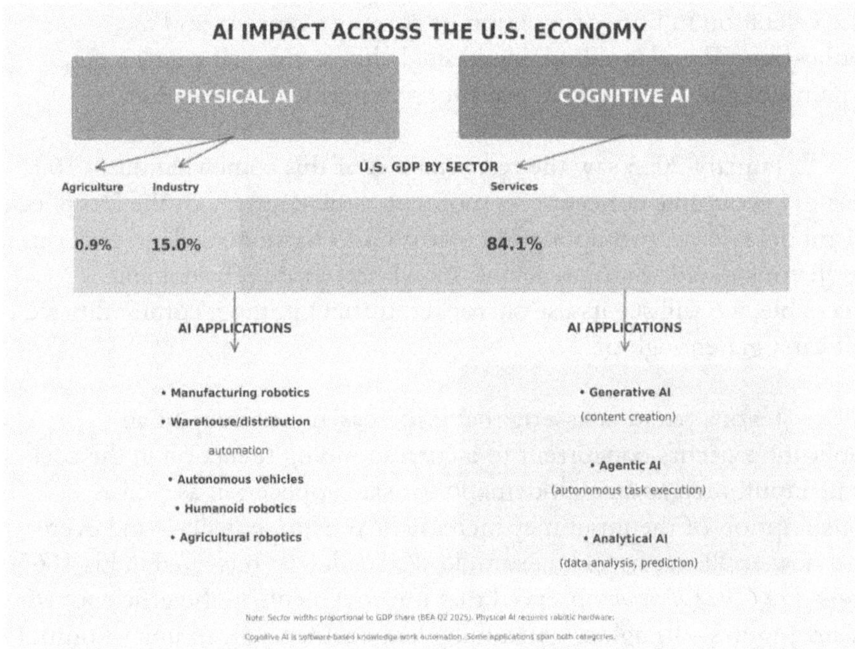

Figure 15: Alignment of AI types with industry sectors; physical relating to "blue-collar" jobs, cognitive relating to "white-collar"; author specification.

Note: There are and will be considerable overlap and combining of AI applications for various use cases; applications noted are provided as conceptual examples.

At present we hear about caps on "compute" by industry insiders and observers—such a shortages of electricity to operate GPUs in-hand, and while of course accurate these are transient obstacles as either capacity will continue to come on line, or technological innovation (such as recursive self-improvement, or yield insights such as "mixture of experts" MoE framework) will improve the compute capacity of existing or newly developed AI factories in the near-future.

What does the absence of a limit to the upper bound of deployment of a virtual "white-collar" labor force portend? It suggests that many jobs are an innovation away from having suitable, productive and most certainly lower cost / higher predictability outcomes via virtual AI alternatives. Would there be a human cost—or benefit, to this? Most likely at minimum there would be a "transitional period". Would there be a significant lessening of tax revenue? Again, most likely, perhaps dramatically so given the infinite upper bound, and the absence at present of a tax regime for AI applications.

Does cognitive AI have the potential to significantly erode service sector tax revenue?

Possibly. If so, this would be for two reasons: 1) the service sector, which is quite broad in scope, including "knowledge workers" ranging from attorneys, programmers and doctors to pure service occupations such as retail and even logistics, represents by far the largest component of the US labor force (about 80% + of total jobs), and 2) despite lower relative compensation in the retail and hospitality sectors, most of the highest salary jobs in the U.S. reside within the knowledge worker sector.

The "unlock" that will come to be known as the "commoditization of cognition" and the (IUB) will likely prove to be transformational. Its impact via deployment of cognitive AI in lieu of human intelligence will echo the impact the deployment of machinery during the industrial revolution had on human labor—except for that in the case of Cognitive AI, it will be "capital light", relatively unencumbered and thus less constrained.

Need to accelerate the solution process for a problem set? Click here, or simply allow your Agent to inject more cognition (real-time), based on how much you need, and when you need it. "Gray-matter" becomes the new "hired gun" courtesy of the commoditization of cognition.

6. The Arc of the Production Function meets the AI-era and our Legacy System of Taxation

Production functions are used by economists to describe the relationship between inputs of production and output of goods, income and even wealth creation. Over time, these inputs have grown from simple human labor and cognitive input to capital investment, to accrued technical ability and now to include AI. Evolution in this relationship has seen increased output, increased productivity, and a proportionate decrease in human input as the impact—and proportion—of these other factors has increased. The AI-era brings the next step-change in this relationship.

In the centuries-long agrarian age, before the industrial revolution, output and wealth creation were mostly a product of human input. While over time there was of course a continuum of human input development in the form of fire, plows, wheels, ships, weaponry and trade…nothing of a deeply transformative magnitude occurred until the Industrial Revolution. In this earlier era, there were (to our knowledge) no economists, and thus no proclamations with respect to what we today term "production functions". If there was a production function to characterize this pre-industrial era, it simply would have been, human input was responsible for virtually all output, expressed as:

$Y = L$ or, $Y=f(L)$ with "Y" total output, and "L" human effort

The Industrial Revolution changed this dynamic, as output from machinery began to proportionately augment and replace human labor. This was enabled by capital formation, investment in capital equipment (machinery), increasing productivity with automated production a consequence or function of deployable and invested capital (which formulaically came to be known as "K").

This eventually led to the first proclaimed production function, known as the Cobb-Douglas output function (1928), which defined production in the industrial era as:

$Y = c \cdot K^{a} \cdot L^{\beta}$ (where $\alpha + \beta = 1$)

In this, the first production function, Y = total output, "c" served as a constant co-efficient, K = capital and L = labor, with Greek letter alpha referring to the ascendancy of capital, and beta referring to the proportion—albeit diminished (via advances in deployment of capital), of human labor. Proportionately, the greater the deployment of "K", the less the amount of "L" that was required, as in tandem they would always sum to 100% of inputs.

In hindsight, we can say that this formalized the beginning of the era of proportionate decline in the impact of human input in a) production output, b) wealth creation and c) income.

In our agrarian-era equation of $Y = L$, since Y will always equal the sum of terms to the right, labor or "L" constituted 100% of the source of input. In the successive Cobb-Douglas function, L is no longer 100% of the source of input, and its proportionate share would subsequently only reduce over time, innovation by innovation, as the role of K increased (with L and K exhibiting corresponding elasticity).

A century after peak-Industrial revolution, the computer era, followed shortly thereafter by the internet era, saw human intelligence augmented and enhanced by technological advances, with productivity increases clearly evidenced along this continuum. These productivity gains were increasingly greater than the measurable "sum of the parts", that is greater than the inputs of *K* and *L*.

MIT economist (later Nobel Laureate) Robert Solow observed (1956) this "residual" third factor of production, and concluded this was attributable to accrued technological capability, and famously termed this residual "A", incorporating this term into his now famous production function. He was the first to identify and formalize this third factor of production, in his 3-factor production function, with the 3rd term acquiring the nickname of "Solow's A". His equation is expressed thusly:

$$Y = A \cdot K^{a} \cdot L^{\beta} \text{ (where } \alpha + \beta = 1)$$

In his production function equation, Y = output, A is Solow's residual factor, with K capital and L labor as before. We can say two things with certainty in viewing his equation in hindsight:

1. Conceptually, it is highly intuitive; and

2. It marks yet further decline in the impact and proportion of *L* in output.

A taxation mechanism long past its expiration date

Solow's production function also demonstrates that despite the continuum of increased roles for *K* and now for *A*, concurrent with a successively diminishing impact of *L*, that by contrast, when one compares this fact to shares of taxation per cohort, the share of taxation derived from L remains high (about 84% of total US tax revenue—when fully allocating payroll tax to the individual), and has increased proportionately to taxation of *K* (that which is levied on the corporate sector - owners of capital), while the share of output attributable to "A" and "K" continues to increase. We present the modern history of taxation in the US to illustrate this phenomenon, with a trend-line that might surprise Solow.

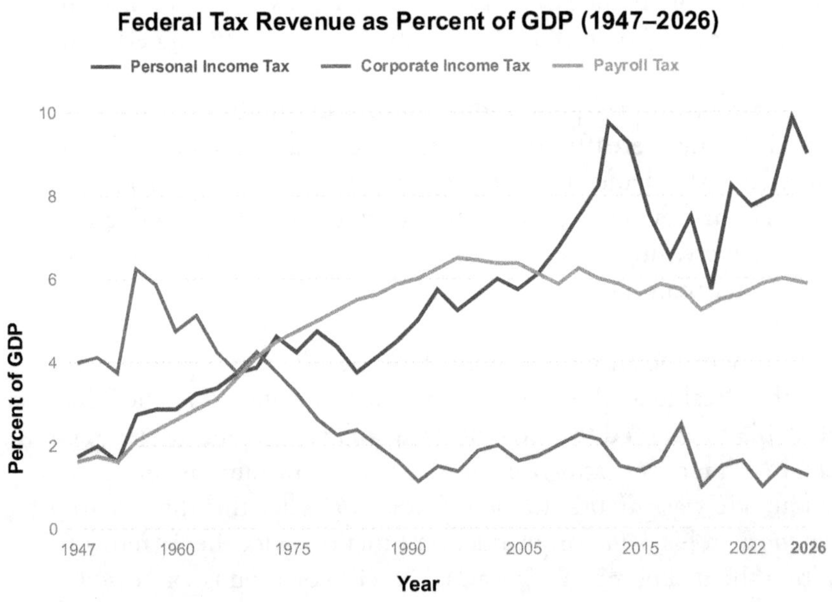

Figure 16: Federal Tax Receipts in the US, corporate, personal and payroll 1947 – 2025.

Note: Data sources CBO, BEA; Author specification

It is fair to say that the above graph depicts a "sources of taxation" picture which does not align with the economic trajectory that either the Cobb-Douglas function, or Nobel Laureate Robert Solow have been describing, of the continuum of the diminishing role of personal labor and cognition as inputs—and therefore wealth creation, on economic output in the U.S. in contrast to an increasing tax burden. In other words, the share of output enjoyed by *L* steadily decreased while their share of tax liability steadily increased. It is as if we had a structural engineering "bug" in the system designing our taxation mechanism.

Perhaps the U.S. Congress did not read Solow?

In what can in hindsight only be considered supreme irony, the crossover in rate of taxation—the point at which labor's tax rate came to vastly exceed that of capital—occurred during the exact period (1956 – 1957) in which Solow published his research and findings that would later lead to his Nobel prize. This was the moment in which he introduced the world to his 3-factor production function, a thesis which explained exactly what was occurring and that which would only accelerate. As the taxation graph above shows, this era—the 1950s through 1960s—was when labor share of taxation began to dramatically exceed that of capital, as labor's rate sharply increased and capital's share sharply decreased.

There are two additional conclusions we can make from this depiction:

1. The need to update our system of taxation to make it fit for purpose for the AI-era (in fact this highlights the vulnerability of not doing so); and
2. An illustration of a primary source of income inequality (chapter 13) in the U.S., by persisting with an outdated and un-wise system of taxation.

The production function meets the AI revolution

We find ourselves now, 70 years after the advent of Solow's production function, at yet another inflection point in the sources of input and of output.

In the newly arrived AI-era, we have an entirely new and somewhat unexpected factor, that of artificial human cognition, to add to the production function. Just as *K* supplanted human labor in the industrial-era, AI cognition now increasingly supplants human intelligence in the AI-era.

In re-examining this, Solow's *A* remains a relevant factor and repository of accrued technical knowledge and processes—and will continue to evolve and increase, as conveyed by his original characterization of *A* as *A(t)*. The emergence of artificial cognition (AI), along with industrial machinery and related capital investments from *K*, are beginning to cause the next step in reduction of *L* as an input. As we described in chapter 5, the ability of AI to scale (via simple replication of software instances, in perhaps the ultimate "capital light" manifestation of increased output) will be unbounded—thus our infinite upper bound (IUB) characterization. The more dynamically AI cognition scales, the greater the implicit reduction in the share of human cognition, expressed as a reduction in the role of and impact of *L*. (This assertion is of course part basic economic theory, and part what could be described as "the daily news", as we are collectively witnessing this occurrence real-time in the economies of the developed world, slowly via physical AI and more rapidly via cognitive AI.)

Conceptually, and operatively, this leaves little question that the production function will need to be updated to a "four-factor" function and include a term for AI, as it will by all appearances prove to be a transformative driver of production.

We define this new "four-factor production function", and introduce it as the "**AI-era Production Function**", as follows:

$$Y = A(t) \cdot K^{a} \cdot (AI)^{\gamma} \cdot L^{\beta} \text{ (where } \alpha + \gamma + \beta > 1)$$

In which prior terms (*Y, K, L*) remain unchanged, *A* reverts to Solow's original characterization as evolving over time thus *A(t)*, with the inclusion of the new term $(AI)^{\gamma}$ representing AI as the fourth factor of production. Greek letter gamma serves as the output elasticity of AI, indicating its proportionate contribution to output. The variable AI itself is what scales non-linearly—without bound—as captured by our Infinite Upper Bound (IUB) framework introduced in Chapter 5. Thus, the AI-era Production Function exhibits an Increasing Returns to Scale (IRS) – which in Economic theory means output will exceed the sum of the inputs, given the IUB of Cognitive AI as a factor.

Solow's "A" captured broad technological progress—improvements in design, process and accumulated knowledge, but *AI* represents a factor that is more pervasive. The commoditization of cognitive AI enables unprecedented scale. Its breadth in scope allows it to attack multiple points of influence within the production process and to influence not just physical tasks but also cognitive tasks previously inseparable from human labor. Solow's *A* enhances both what *K* and *L* can do; cognitive intelligence *(AI)* amplifies intelligence as an input, and along with the long past introduction of *K*, nearly completes the subordination of *L* in the production process. AI therefore plays a dual role: enhancing total factor productivity (A) while simultaneously displacing human labor (reducing β).

A counter-argument to formalizing AI as a fourth-factor could be that its impact is represented by A, that this is an example of the meaning and purpose of A. While we have the deepest respect for Solow and his work, we feel the impact of AI is as wholly unique from that of A as the AI era will prove to be from the Industrial era. A is influenced, among other things, by innovations in *K* and by the intellectual contributions of *L*. But in Solow's formula it functions more like a constant at a given point in time, it functions comparatively passively. His original designation was as *A(t)*, meaning it represented accrued residual capability as of a period of time. AI represents the near opposite, and equates to dynamic, exponential contributions of added cognition, which by definition AI agents can magnify the application of in real-time; it is not static, it is highly dynamic.

However, time does not stand still—many would say it even accelerates. Certainly, when it comes to the evolution of output and production this is the case. While we have just described the four-term AI-era Production Function, we can also see that the next material transformation in production is upon us. 2025 was the year in which "Dark Factories" entered public discourse and while it is obviously early-stage, it is easy to see this as the next stage in the diminution of the input of "*L*", from which there is likely no looking back.

We address the topic of dark factories more fully in chapter 10, but we can state the obvious here. As it pertains to the topic of production functions, the premise of a dark factory is that it is a "lights out, human optional" environment. Meaning the remaining contributions of man via physical labor and cognitive input are (near) fully replaced by physical and cognitive AI. Thus—figuratively speaking, *L* becomes *0*, as given the nomenclature "dark", work goes on 24/7 without human intervention or oversight whatsoever. This may be a slight dramatization, but the point remains, we are at a moment, which will only expand as we go along, absent of human input in generation of output.

In the circumstance described above, the Arc of the Production Function reaches its logical "end point", having traveled from an era in which $Y=L$, to one in which as an input—rhetorically speaking, $L=0$, with the exponents of K and AI summing to a value greater than 1 due to the concept of increasing returns to scale. Which in English means that L ceases to contribute, and that the impact of AI on the yield of K exhibits increasing returns to scale such that output becomes greater than the sum of inputs.

This brings numerous consequences, such as increased rates of productivity, increased overall output and likely downward price pressure, even disinflationary impulses. The negative consequences include probable increased income inequality and a collapse in tax revenue from the individual. These last two points can of course be countermanded through appropriate foresight, followed by actions to address potential adverse consequences.

We present below our "Arc of the Production Function" and the corresponding contradiction of increasing rates of taxation for the individual in spite of more than a century's evidence that doing so represents an obsolete, even museum-like taxation mechanism.

The Production Function Continues to Evolve While Legacy Taxation Remains Rooted in the '50s

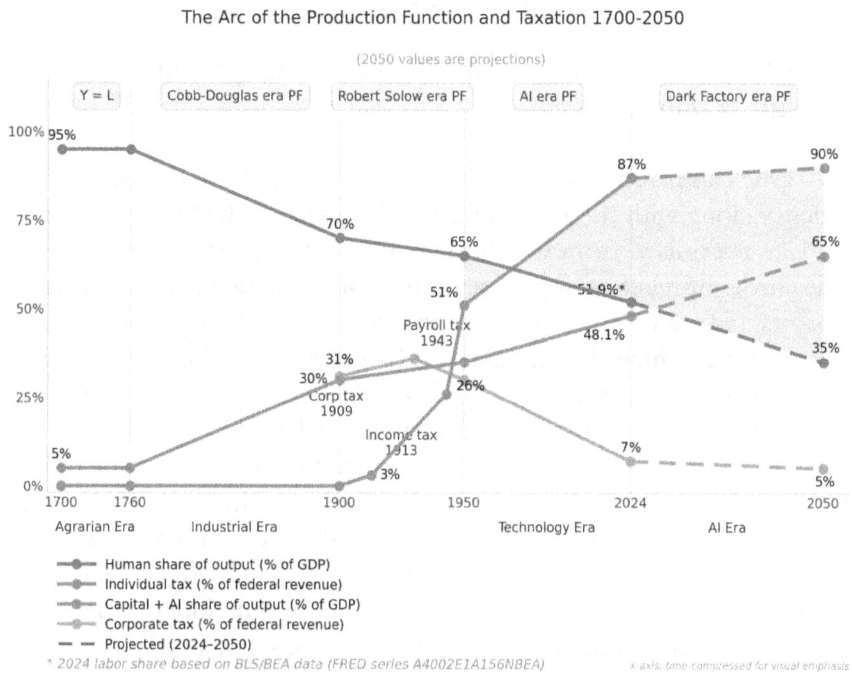

Figure 17: Arc of the Production Function vs the Arc of Taxation 1700 – 2050

Note: Data sources: Labor share of income - U.S. Bureau of Labor Statistics, Federal Reserve Economic Data (FRED series: PRS85006173); Tax revenue composition Office Management & Budget, Historical Tables, IRS statistics of estimates, Historical estimates (1700-1900) per various economic history literature; 2024 - 2040 values are author's projections per trend extrapolation.

Note: 2024 figures combine individual income tax + payroll taxes (which combined fall on labor income) into the "individual tax" line. Combined they equaled 87% of federal revenue per CBO's January 2025 baseline (individual income 54.7%, payroll 32.6%); corporate income tax equaled 7%; other sources 6%. The 2050 projections extend CBO's Long-Term Budget Outlook trajectory, with nearly all revenue growth between 2025 and 2055 from individual taxation. Tariff revenue, currently above historical norms, will revert to its long-run norm.

The above graph in one stroke shows the contradiction we face: **a legacy system of taxation that has become disconnected from the reality of decades of economic transformation**. It is somewhat surprising this has been allowed to occur, but the facts present a clear picture. And they depict our vulnerability.

Was the failure of our taxation mechanism a straight line to our level of gross public debt?

One can readily see in the above graph that 1954 (Eisenhower presidency along with the Revenue Act of 1954) launched the modern era of U.S. tax policy, from which there was no turning back. Ensuing decades brought relief on top of relief for corporate taxpayers contrasted to a protracted era of increased tax contributions by the individual. This was the point at which the Korean War had ended and the corporate tax code was broadly reduced and revised—with accelerated investment for allowable depreciations initiated, while individual rates of taxation continued upwards as a percentage of tax revenue. It was also the point at which payroll tax deductions were amplified to address social benefits such as Social Security, and later Medicare, and the era in which these tax burdens began to shift from the corporation to the individual. The modest reductions in personal tax rates granted to individual taxpayers to offset increases due to the new "payroll tax" were short-lived.

The actions of tax transformation commenced in this era can be viewed in the context of a period in which America—after two decades of depression, world war, followed by more war, concurrent with multiple exogenous events, as well as the introduction of responsibility for health care to the American employer—could relax slightly and allow tax policy to be recalibrated. The 1954 reforms, though they planted the seed of a long structural shift, were enacted within an era of overall fiscal discipline — under both Truman (Democratic) and Eisenhower (Republican) administrations — that stands in marked contrast to the modern era. Public debt fell from 120% of GDP at the end of WW2 to 44% by the mid-1960s, even as the corporate tax base commenced its persistent decline.

Subsequent presidencies saw increased investment tax benefits granted to corporations, accompanied by tax reductions during the Kennedy, Reagan, Bush 43, Trump 45 and Trump 47 presidencies. Nothing close to this cumulative level of tax reduction was bestowed upon the American taxpayer—as measured by net Federal tax receipts. For a variety of reasons, which may have included the efforts of special interest lobbyist groups, by 1990 the transformation commenced in the

1950s resulted in net corporate tax receipts declining from 5.7% of GDP to approximately 2.3%.

Growth in Business Policy Lobbyists vs Corp Statutory Tax Rate Reform

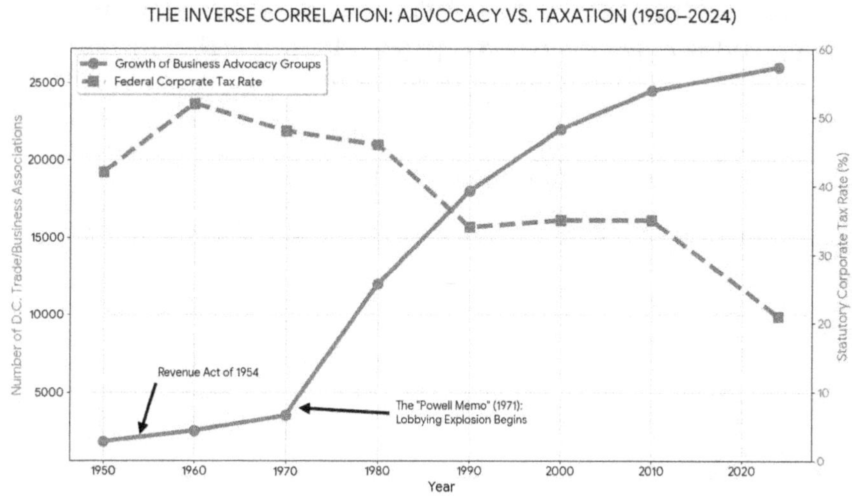

Figure 18: Correlation of Emergence of Business Special Interest vs. Corporate Tax reform as measured by thousands of lobbyists vs corporate statutory tax rates

Note: Business Lobbyist estimates courtesy of IRS registered entities, Schlozman, K. L., & Tierney, J. T. (1986) report, The Washington Representatives Directory (Multiple Editions). Powell Memo 1971 challenged businesses advocacy to influence policy, marking an inflection point in formation of Lobbyist groups. Author specification.

One could argue that these shifts in taxation—declining rates for corporations with increasing rates for the individual—were unfair—but **that misses the bigger point** which is that they **were simply not economically realistic**, as they pointed the U.S. system of taxation down a dead-end street. It was never feasible that the individual taxpayer could bear the majority share of taxation in support of America's growing expenditures; a quick glance at Solow's work would have borne this out.

The following graph depicts federal tax receipts from 1950 to the modern era, during which time personal tax receipts as a percent of GDP increased while corporate tax receipts dramatically decreased. If one were looking for a smoking gun behind our unsustainable public debt, we suggest "checking the fingerprints" of this persistent divergence in our taxation mechanism which—laid bare by the history of actual Federal receipts below—benefitted the corporate sector while disadvantaging the individual. In the 21st century in particular, this led to deficit on top of deficit.

The Divergence of post 1950 Taxation in America Actual receipts – not Statutory Rates – Excludes Payroll Taxes

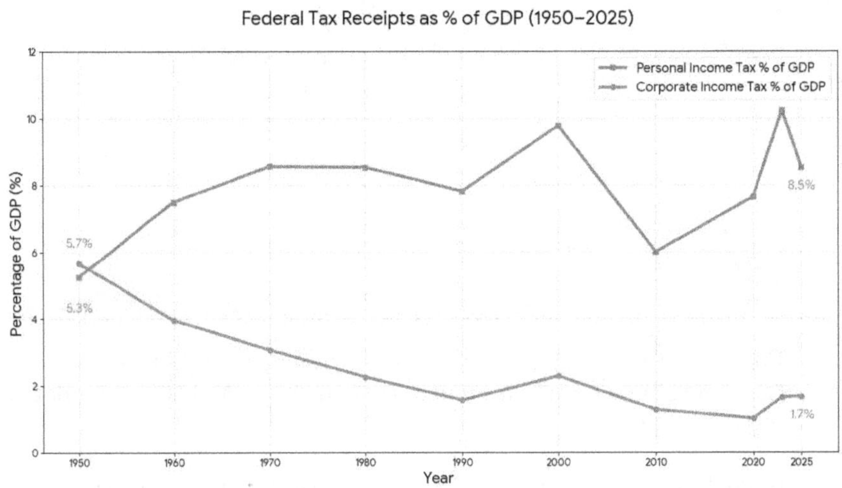

Figure 19: The inexplicable transformation in U.S. tax policy

Note: Taxation data culled from Federal Reserve (FRED) series FCTAX for corporate tax receipts and A074RC1Q027SBEA for individual tax receipts. Author specification.

Does our apparent complacency with our high level of public debt correlate to a generational shift in leadership?

The U.S. exited WW2 with a mountain of fiscal and real-world obstacles, ranging from a massive public debt overhang from WW2, incremental expenditures for the Marshall Plan, the GI Bill, reconstruction expenses for Germany and Japan, plus the Korean War. One could argue that collectively these obstacles exceeded anything in our nation's history—barring the Revolutionary War and the Civil War eras, yet our leadership kept the country on track, in seemingly every sense of the word, not least of which was our obligation to get our fiscal house in order. It is therefore, by comparison, easy to react with little sympathy to explanations given by the Congress—even Presidential leadership—of the modern era with respect to the impediments they face in restoring fiscal order.

Post WW2 Leadership: Debt was reduced from 120% to 44% of GDP

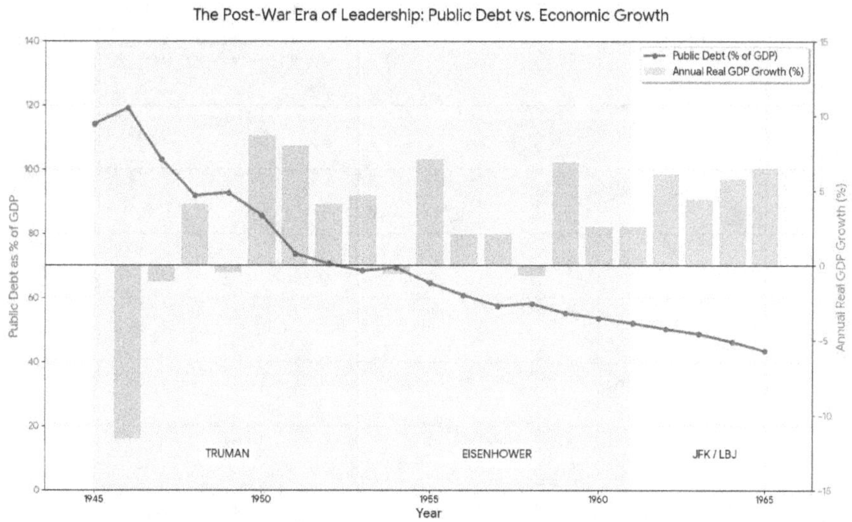

Figure 20: A generation of American leaders guides public debt back to a sustainable level

Note: Data sources - U.S. Office of Management & Budget (OMB), U.S. Bureau of Economic Analysis (BEA), Federal Reserve Economic Data (FRED)

We have used a variety of approaches to analyze and convey the clearest possible picture of our fiscal status. We will not explore the depths of our "entitlement" or social benefit expense layer; that is outside the scope of this book. Taken as a single factor, the transformation of taxation in our country, shifting the principal burden onto the individual taxpayer, had a significantly deleterious impact. This last chart below constructs revenue per annum for the corporate sector, then contrasts it to personal income (which following IRS protocol, includes not just salary, but other mediums of income such as rents received, and investment income) and juxtaposes both of these sectors to tax receipts (actual taxes paid, not statutory rates) as a percent of our overall economy. Thus, the data within is essentially reconstructed from corporate filings and mapped to the Bureau of Economic Analysis's

GVA (Gross Value Added) framework, which captures each instance of profit more accurately than simple revenue.

Corporate sector Taxation Divergence from Personal – 1952 – 2025

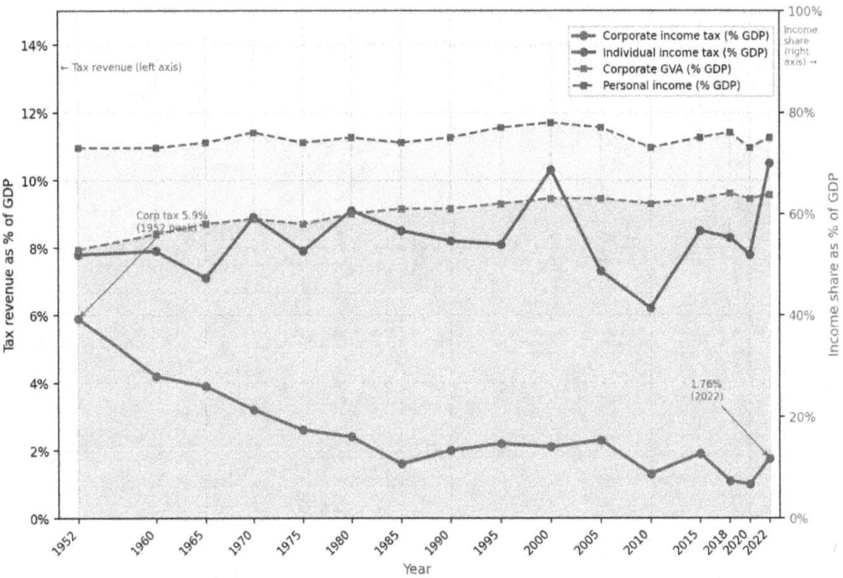

Figure 21: Corporate and Individual taxation timeline presented as % of GDP

Notes: Data sources - OMB Historical Tables 2.1 and 2.3 (White House, 2024); CRS Report R47519, An Overview of the Corporate Income Tax System (April 2023); CBPP. Corporate GVA: BEA NIPA Table 1.14 (2022 confirmed at 6.25T = 63.8% of GDP via FRED series A455RC1A027NBEA; historical estimated from NIPA proportions). Personal income (excluding transfer payments): BEA NIPA Table 2.1, author estimate. All effective burden ratios: author calculation. Methodology - corporate historical GVA (gross value added) estimates are derived from BEA NIPA proportional data, per prevailing IRS submission protocol, and should be regarded as informed approximations.

The dots waiting to be connected…

We have seen in this chapter three distinct phenomenon.

First is the profound and accelerating serial revolutions in output, as manifested by successive evolutions of the production function.

Second, is the impact this has had and will have on productivity increases. In chapter 12 we review how this will resonate throughout our economy.

Third, is the striking disconnect between our legacy system of taxation and the massive changes in share of income driven by successive revolutions in the production function. This fact, the significant divergence over the last seven decades of share of income vs share of taxation, emerges as a central explanation for our growing public debt, with related implications for understanding income inequality.

Simple analysis of the production function—and how it is and will evolve in both the AI and Dark Factory eras—presents obvious takeaways that serve to partially frame the analysis of our fiscal situation and equally inform the analysis of the potential future consequences of the AI revolution. The evolved perspective provided by an updated analysis of the production function provided some of the key insights in this study.

A final point regarding Federal corporate tax receipts

An under-reported tactic employed over the past several decades, which tracks in synchrony with the decline of corporate taxation as a share of total tax revenue, has been the **partial shift of U.S. multinational's tax liabilities to lower cost foreign tax domiciles**. To a substantial extent, this helps explain the dramatic drop-off of corporate taxes as a share of overall U.S. tax revenue. This is a complex yet fundamental issue, ultimately outside of the scope of this book, but a critical component of our growing fiscal jeopardy. This has transpired over decades, facilitated by pivotal legislative acts along with ineffective countermeasures by multiple administrations. **Yet operatively, it is as if we have allowed *K*, *A* and perhaps AI to acquire foreign tax domiciles—at least in part—while *L* remains domestically domiciled**, with the highest effective tax rates of all.

7. *The Wisdom of Gates - Why Robots must be Taxed*

When we assess the prospective impact of our three forces, which we can see will be accelerated by the AI transformation, we must simply ask, what does this all mean for our country in the near-future? It means that at a time when we will most need it—given our aging society—our government will be challenged to be able to not only afford to continue to provide the basic services we have come to expect but will likely lack the available funds to make the service payments we are obligated to make on our public debt, necessitating yet additional borrowing to make these annual payments. This "challenge" in meeting our obligatory debt service payments will potentially be severely exacerbated by the IUB of cognitive AI effect on service sector employment, and tax revenue thereof.

This in conjunction with the fact that our public debt will increase each year not only due to the impact of the primary deficit but as well due to the annually unfunded debt service payments. (By definition, if for any given year we run a "primary deficit" then we would lack the added funds needed to make debt service payments for that year. Hence these annual debt service payment obligations would be budgetarily "unfunded", and therefore directly add to our public debt, and be tantamount to an autonomous increase in future tax obligations.)

Why do we care about our increasing public debt?

1. Increasing public debt will cause us to become a "poorer" country. How will we become poorer? There will be four main drivers:

    a) the money we spend for interest payments on our public debt plus each years' primary deficit will be financed by new, additional debt, necessitating higher future rates of taxation to finance this;

    b) directing large sums of money to interest payments decreases the sums available for investment (financially known as "crowding out")—thus as a country, the money available for investment in our future will be decreased, most likely leading to diminished growth rates;

c) subsequent decreases in rate of growth in our economy due to declining rates of investment will only increase the *proportionate* tax burden, further diminishing investment and weakening our growth potential, and

d) increased debt on the part of our country, and the weakening fiscal oversight this implies, may ultimately cause credit rating agencies to further downgrade American debt, thereby increasing the interest rates (yields) treasury must affix to its notes and bonds, yet further increasing our public debt.

Below we include a Federal Reserve graph depicting the primary measure of domestic investment—Gross Private Domestic Investment, with a timeline from the Clinton era through 2025. Despite the surge in investment in AI infrastructure—or net of this, is domestic investment presently in the process of being "crowded out" by the growing demands of public debt service?

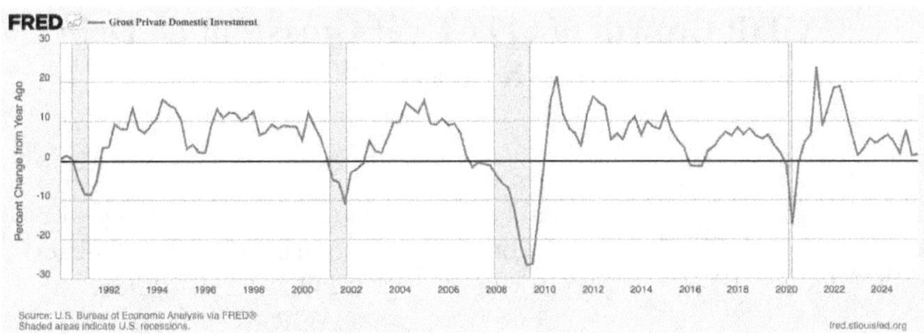

Figure 22: Gross Private Domestic Investment (GPDI) Clinton to Trump 47 eras; percent change vs LY; depicts private investment net of sums dedicated to debt service payments

Note: Depicts % change vs prior year; gray vertical lines = recession; GPDI appears to "flatline" despite significant sums directed to AI infrastructure; correlation to "crowding out" phenomena, not proof of causation; Fed Reserve data and graph

2. The Treasury bond market may very well one day "refuse" to finance our debt at the interest rates that we offer; this is commonly called a "fiscal or financial crisis". What does a fiscal crisis mean, how could this happen? In such a case, what a fiscal crisis implies is that the buyers of US issued government debt would require higher rates of interest to continue to finance said debt. This may happen gradually, or it may come as a shock, a

moment when the market says "no" to the latest tranche of government debt issuance at the interest rates offered. Such an event would result in a "re-pricing" of US debt, tantamount to the bond market telling us what they will accept. This would represent a darkly pivotal moment for our economy, our country, and our society.

Our recent trajectory of increasing public debt is sadly well-established. Crises (such as 9/11, GFC or Covid) or not, our public debt continues to grow, often simply fueled by unfunded tax cuts. Conversely, one can refer to earlier eras, when crises also occurred, such as WW2, the Korean War, and one will see that in those eras, Congress, often with leadership from the respective president, exhibited the fortitude necessary to ensure the country's debt was resolved and fiscal balance restored as soon as possible. The table below depicts GDP growth rate alongside public debt growth in the modern era (21st century).

GDP Growth of $19.6T yet Gross Public Debt Growth of $31.9T

Decade	GDP Growth Rate (Nominal CAGR)	Gross Public Debt Growth Rate (CAGR)	Change in Nominal GDP $/CAGR	Change in Gross Public Debt $/CAGR
2000s	~3.8%	~9.1%	$10.3T → $15.0T	$5.7T → $13.6T
2010s	~3.5%	~7.1%	$15.0T → $21.1T	$13.6T → $26.9T
2020–2025 *	~7.2% *	~6.9% *	$21.1T → $29.9T	$26.9T → $37.6T
21st Century-to-date	4.4%	7.8%	$10.3T → $29.9T **Plus $19.6T / 4.4%**	$5.7T → $37.6T **Plus $31.9T / 7.8%**

Table 4: 21st Century fiscal data – GDP increased $19.6T vs. GP Debt increase $31.9T.

Notes: *2020–2025 covers a partial and distorted period. The nominal GDP CAGR of ~7.2% is artificially elevated by two effects: (1) the post-COVID economic bounce-back from 2020's depressed base, and (2) the 2021–2023 inflation surge. CBO forward projection for nominal GDP growth is 3.8%/year; structural deficits are projected to widen. The 2025 debt figure is as of September 30, 2025 (U.S. Treasury FY2025).

Data sources: Nominal GDP: U.S. Bureau of Economic Analysis (BEA), Table 1.1.5; full-year 2025 average of quarterly annualized rates. Gross Public Debt: U.S. Treasury / Bureau of the Fiscal Service, Historical Debt Outstanding; FY2025 confirmed by U.S. GAO, January 2026. Growth rates: author calculation (CAGR). CBO forward projection: Congressional Budget Off., Budget and Economic Outlook: 2026 to 2036, January 2026.

The data in the chart above, depicting a pattern of decline in our fiscal stability had nothing to do with changes in demography or AI. Yes, there were exogenous factors that came to bear, yet we generated a primary deficit come rain or shine. The rate of increase in our public debt exceeded the rate of increase of our GDP, regardless. There is not an economic framework on earth that endorses such as paradigm. Nor has there been a prior era in our country's history in which we have accrued massive public debt in an era of overwhelming prosperity.

All data reviewed thus far confirms the need to take action to protect our foundation of taxation. As a country, we are at the intersection of two disparate phenomena: the ossifying inadequacy of our legacy system of taxation, and the exponentially increasing demand for a product (AI) that will in part be responsible for accelerating said demise. It's like a quiz that provides its own, obvious answer.

There are two voices—that we are aware of—that are on record in favor of taxation of AI, and surely there must be more who have spoken up or are inclined to recognize this necessity. Bill Gates in 2017 raised the notion of "taxation of robots", and Dario Amodei, CEO of Anthropic (itself a frontier AI model company suggested that as a likely outcome of expected job loss we would need to tax AI companies. (Specifically, Mr. Amodei, in a May 29, 2025 CNN interview, warned of about 20% unemployment in 5 years, stating, to paraphrase, that this is happening incredibly fast…) Note that these are two men who were / are leaders in the dominant technologies of their generations, who are most likely speaking up on behalf of the "good of the country" and society; we cannot imagine any other motivation.

Even if such taxation were done for transitional or "bridge" purposes until the picture of labor force and tax revenue decline is clearer, or until our public debt is reduced dramatically as a percent to GDP, the value of such a decision speaks for itself.

Others, such as Amazon CEO Andy Jassy, are on record regarding the likelihood of job automation and the consequence of labor force reduction. Sam Altman, CEO of OpenAI (a frontier AI model company), in recent testimony to Congress noted that the capability of AI to perform a significant number of positions that might heretofore have been considered "safe" will be capable of being filled by AI in the near future. Jensen Huang, CEO of Nvidia has recently stated that each engineer at Nvidia uses AI-native application Cursor in their design work, we can assume therefore increasing individual productivity by doing so. Clearly, those closest to it, those with the most intimate knowledge of its capabilities see and know enough to voice—repeatedly, warnings and caution.

Whatever the manifestation of this "taxation", the reality is that Congress must take this up, sooner rather than later. We can now see that the prospect raised by Mr. Gates in 2017 regarding the need to tax robots is even more relevant today than ever, as the risk to our broader labor force via AI workforce automation is apparently on an exponential trajectory.

It is often asked: can't we just pause this; can't we just slow down the pace of AI development and its manifestation in our lives and in the workplace? That answer would be a hard "no". Leading spokespeople of the moment, of this domain, such as Mr. Amodei and Mr. Schmidt have reminded us that we do not live in a vacuum, and that were we (America) to "stop" our development efforts, surely our competitors would not, and given the accelerating rate of change, we would rapidly fall behind, economically, militarily, existentially.

Gates saw this coming

Bill Gates, the legendary American businessman and philanthropist, in yet another example of his ability to "see around corners" apparently saw this coming, to which we can only tip our hats to his vision or to the fact that his mind apparently operates with fewer restrictions on its imagination than the rest of us. In a February 2017 interview with the World Economic Forum and *Quartz*, Bill Gates announced that robots, or specifically that the companies installing and "employing" robots, should be taxed.

Specifically, what Mr. Gates said in the 2017 Quartz interview was:

"Right now, the human worker who does, say, $50,000 worth of work in a factory, that income is taxed and you get income tax, social security tax, all those things. If a robot comes in to do the same thing, you'd think that we'd tax the robot at a similar level."

His view was prescient, but the concern of this study is not to attempt to slow the AI revolution or even workforce automation but to highlight the consequences of loss of worker tax revenue, which at about 84% of federal tax revenue broadly underpins the entire spectrum of government and social services. It is by now more than evident that our system of taxation—and its disproportionate burden on the individual—will become even more out of touch with reality and an even greater risk to our fiscal stability; the question is simply one of how and when will our government respond?

Arguably, taxation of robots would be the easy part, as robots—and manifestations of physical AI in general—are tangible and visible to the human eye. Digital or virtual employees (Agentic AI, or as McKinsey refers to it "Agentification"), that which can be broadly categorized as cognitive AI, seemingly less so, as in most respects "they" are near invisible. We will review this in the next chapter that there is in fact a very intuitive, readily applicable mechanism by which to tax cognitive AI consumption.

By way of contrast and to put the idea of taxation of robots and of AI workforce automation in a real-world context, there exist in our tax code today mechanisms that may be used by small, medium and large companies to either immediately or rapidly depreciate the cost of deploying work force automation, such as investment in robotics, so as to not impair the cash flow of these companies when making such investments. These provisions (sect. 179 for small and medium business, and sect. 168k for large companies of our tax code) were codified in 1958 and in 2002 respectively. Any contemplation of taxation of AI-related workforce automation must for perspective consider that our existing tax code incents adoption of robotics and workforce automation by allowing tax credits for these capital expenditures.

While this study is in favor of capital investments, human capital investments and the like, one must recognize that these potential credits and taxes are all pieces of the same puzzle that confronts us. Last point on this sub-topic is that we must bear in mind we compete in a global market, and must acknowledge that for a variety of reasons (such as negative fertility, a desire for non-reliance on outside manufacturers of critical goods, etc.) the Chinese government, as an example, is aggressively supporting (via tax benefits and province level business loans and investments) development of automation, robotics and even so-called "dark factories", which will in time drive a new global standard in manufacturing productivity. This will be part of the competitive set we will face.

There have been the voices of those beginning to foresee economic and social hardship as part of this transition, this is after all the likely motivation why some have spoken up. Those who look ahead and see the potential for a gradual repopulation of our workforce by non-taxpaying AI Agents, AI-related workflow automation of Physical AI entities, those who expect that at least in part the near-term growth in our labor force will not come via actual taxpaying workers, but via "virtual, non-taxpaying workers".

The remedies we have heard mooted have focused on the need for an increased social safety net to soften the expected blow many might experience in this transition. They may likely be right, such efforts may likely be needed. However, this study is not necessarily in favor of additional mandates at this time. We are instead in favor of taxation of AI to protect our country's fiscal status and ensure that we better insulate ourselves to be able to sustain any potential disruption in employment as a result of the AI revolution, and generate sufficient tax revenue for us to meet our existing social benefits and future obligations.

In light of this, we as a country would be remiss if we did not develop a system of taxation for jobs replaced by AI, and for newly created jobs directly filled by AI. In other words, it is incumbent upon us to move past our legacy tax code and implement one suitable for the AI-era.

To summarize the key points from this chapter:

1. Our existing level of public debt is both perilous and unsustainable—the characterization as "unsustainable" is one of the few points upon which both major political parties agree;

2. Our public debt is on track to sequentially worsen year after year due to the cumulative, compounding effect of unfunded debt service payments;

3. Even with no change in our labor force, this situation will worsen, as primary (annual) deficits appear a certainty;

4. Now, due to demographic decline, our fiscal degradation will accelerate even further;

5. The accelerant of AI-driven job displacement, affecting the cognitive AI service sector, as well as the physical AI sector, presents a fiscal threat without precedent in the modern era.

A final point: Compute capacity is currently highly constrained. Token demand significantly exceeds supply, with users vigorously competing for token allocations based on their ability to monetize them. In economic terms, this is a classic supply-demand imbalance—precisely the condition under which a modest tax layer would not suppress demand, because the demand already exceeds available supply. To pass on this window of opportunity would, in the author's opinion, be considerably ill-advised.

8. *How to Tax the Robots: Output vs. Income-based Taxation of AI*

Executive summary

The proposed AI taxation mechanism would become the fourth pillar of taxation revenue for our country. The principal driver would be taxation of tokens, both consumption by the "demand-side" and generation from the "supply-side". According to our estimates, for 2030 AI taxation would contribute revenue equal to 2.4% of GDP, or $823 Billion. Our proposed structure would be progressive, include a no-charge cohort for individual and small entity use, and is designed to not be onerous or restrictive on AI adoption. Present AI microeconomic conditions—characterized by a significant supply-demand imbalance for tokens—suggests that "now" would be an optimal time to implement this mechanism.

Taxation of output not income

A systemic vulnerability of our legacy taxation protocol is that we employ an income-based framework. In practice, this means that compliance with this protocol allows corporations to use net income as the foundation for determining their taxes due, while simultaneously employing mechanisms by which net income can be depreciated, sheltered and in general reduced. Corporations, thereby are allowed to compute their tax base via the same mechanism by which they're allowed to reduce it. This is evident in chapter 20, where we depict statutory tax rates vs. actual tax receipts.

Since the mid '50s we have seen that the corporate sector is highly adept at minimizing their reported net income, thereby reducing their tax liability. This is one explanation for how, seven decades after the advent of tax reform (originating in 1954), we arrive at a point where the individual contributes about 84% of overall tax revenue and the corporate sector about 9%, which of course is completely disconnected from their respective share of income. Unsurprisingly, we have the public debt to prove the lack of sagacity of this approach.

Over the last seven decades the individual's ability to reduce their reported income has been substantially reduced through tax code amendments, while the corporate side still enjoys a robust ability to do so.

Therefore, an important attribute of the AI-era taxation framework is that it taxes output, not income. AI output (by "AI factories") will be directly consumed as an input by those who benefit from it (businesses, consumers, government) providing unambiguous, real-time visibility on the scale of AI in our economy.

The primary output of AI is of course intelligence, and the native unit of measure for this are "tokens". Tokens are to AI what kilowatts are to electricity: their natural unit of measure, universally used to quantify both AI generation as well as consumption, as well as training of AI models. Tokens are used throughout the AI ecosystem, for consumers of AI, for generators of AI, including the AI models themselves as well as the hyperscalers which operate the AI factories that provide the necessary compute for cognitive AI functions.

We therefore use consumption and output of tokens as the medium of measurement for AI taxation. (One can think of this as the "demand-side" and "supply-side" of this relationship.) All parties in the AI industry currently monitor tokens—any that do not can easily be obligated to. Tokens provide a perfect unit of measure as their usage will scale alongside rate of consumption and output, as if a digital twin. Therefore, our proposal below is predicated upon this mechanism: tracking and taxation of token output and corresponding consumption.

Under existing law, would taxation revenue from hyperscalers and AI model companies be deferred anyway?

Given our existing income-based corporate tax code, the typical hyperscaler or AI model company—treated as a discrete business unit (in the U.S. each hyperscaler is an operating unit of a larger parent company) would likely not pay income tax in the near future, due to their ability to depreciate the immense capital investments they are making. Doing so allows them to push profitability and subsequent tax liability for these operating units into the distant future. This would not be the case for output-based taxation of token generation, as the tax liability would be immutably transparent and would begin as soon as Congress passes the respective legislation. Consumption-based taxation on token output and consumption therefore becomes our primary recommended mechanism for AI taxation.

A notable example of a high-growth, high-capex company not being required—in compliance with U.S. tax law—to pay Federal income tax for several years, in spite of acquiring commanding market share concurrent to other tax-paying erstwhile competitors contracting or exiting the market, was Amazon. Founded in 1994, Amazon did not pay any Federal income tax until the early 2000s, and after that intermittently for another decade courtesy of tax-loss carryforwards, employee stock-based compensation deductions, etc. This is well documented and clearly depicted within their SEC-10K filings, which is to say all fully legal.

We note this as it relates to two broad themes: 1) the decades long diminution of corporate taxation as a % of GDP; and 2) the value in structuring AI token taxation as <u>output not income</u> based. We reiterate: no disparagement intended to Amazon, they simply exploited the tax avoidance opportunities available as well as any company in recent memory, albeit at a spectacular scale.

Token taxation aligns naturally with the dominant method of AI generation in the U.S. economy today—that is, Cognitive AI. As for taxation of Physical AI, we propose a registration-fee-based mechanism, analogous to registration fees for automobiles in America, where the consumer pays an initial fee along with an annual renewal fee over the vehicle's useful life. This will modestly supplement the primary token-based mechanism.

An explicit objective in the proposed taxation framework is that the actual tax paid, the rate of taxation itself is not onerous, and therefore not a deterrent to the adoption of AI. Therefore, taxation can and should be "tiered" in a manner to ensure that it is progressive—not regressive. In practice this means a free tier for normal household and student use, and progressively higher tiers for larger corporations with U.S. "big cap" companies (e.g., those with annual revenue above $100 billion per year) at the highest rate. But in our model even the top tier users would be "capped" such that taxation in no case exceeds 1.5% of annual revenue, at least for the demand or consumption-side.

Cognitive AI: The Bi-lateral Token Taxation Framework

We break our token taxation framework into two parts: demand-side (consumption) and supply-side (output). Demand-side is the myriad array of users, from individuals to mega-cap U.S. companies. Supply-side is the companies that actually generate AI — that create the output. In concept these are two mirror images: every command or query is answered with a response; the query being demand-side, the response being supply-side — hence, bi-lateral. All of it is automatically metered as it is transmitted via the supply-side API (application programming interface), the mechanism by which software programs communicate, resident within every internet or AI company.

We further break supply-side into two parts, as both—while complementary —are fundamentally different: a) the AI models themselves, and b) what are referred to as hyperscalers. The AI model universe includes the big three frontier models — ChatGPT (OpenAI), Claude (Anthropic), and Gemini (Google) — along with notable others such as Meta's Llama and xAI's Grok. Most users interact directly with the AI model of their choosing, and the model provides everything—the interface, the intelligence, the billing, and the compute—so the user has a cohesive and seamless experience.

The reality is that—certainly for OpenAI and Anthropic—they do not perform the majority of compute themselves; it is handled by an underlying hyperscaler partner, typically Microsoft Azure for OpenAI and Amazon's AWS for Anthropic. Google is an exception, operating a frontier model and generating its own compute from its own "stack"; others, such as Meta and xAI, fit this category to some current or future extent. Hyperscalers are increasingly known for operating large data centers (DCs) across the U.S. outfitted with racks of GPUs or TPUs, typically part of the cloud-services business units of large technology companies such as Amazon, Microsoft, and Google.

This three-party structure—demand-side users, supply-side AI models, and supply-side hyperscalers—is the foundation of the cognitive taxation framework. Token usage is measured based on demand from U.S.-located APIs, and from foreign-based APIs tokens serving the U.S. as an end-destination market. The demand-side pays half of the applicable tax; the supply-side pays the other half, shared equally between the AI models and their hyperscaler partners. We refer to this as the 50/25/25 allocation.

All AI taxation proposed would be at the federal level, under the authority of Congress and the jurisdiction of the IRS—agencies that collectively hold all authority necessary for both legislation and compliance. Taxation would apply to all token generation and consumption within the U.S. (via U.S. APIs), and to tokens generated by companies of any foreign tax domicile for use in the U.S. market as the end destination—a cross-border transaction type we address below.

Cognitive AI: How the token tax is measured and collected

Having established the bi-lateral structure, we turn to how the tax is measured and collected. This mechanism applies to cognitive AI consumption based on tokens, measured in millions and charged on a cost-per-million basis (CPMM), as consumed by the user and as generated by the ASP (AI Service Provider—typically the AI model company). The user and the ASP are the two required participants in every AI interaction: the user poses the query, task, or project, and the AI model — hosted by the ASP or its hyperscaler partner— provides the cognition to complete it.

Most AI interactions have three parts: 1) input of a query, command, or data; 2) processing—or "compute"—by the model within the data center, also known as "inference"; and 3) generation of "cognitive output" in response. The compute is metered in both directions, input and output, by tokens. This framework applies to the vast majority of cognitive AI generation and consumption. (Physical AI and "edge" AI compute differ, as we will discuss shortly; for now, the key point is that the majority of U.S.-based AI generation at present is cognitive and thus DC located.)

Under this mechanism, users pay their token tax to their "AI utility"— typically the model of their choice—based on monthly consumption, at a CPMM rate set by their taxation tier. The ASP is entrusted with monitoring and collecting the tax and forwarding it to Treasury, as is the case in countless other instances in today's economy. Some consumers may use third-party resellers of AI models, selecting from American or even downloaded Chinese or French models; the same taxation process applies, since it attaches to token consumption in the U.S. market (as end-destination) regardless of the model's origin.

Operationally, taxation of tokens consumed can be accomplished via a simple and scalable framework:

1. Each ASP already measures token consumption via its API portals; most consumer plans and pricing already operate within token-consumption budgets.
2. Those who self-host (chapter 16) can be obligated, courtesy of the IRS, to install and operate an OpenTelemetry (OTel) observability framework—an industry-standard instrumentation layer that certifiably and immutably measures token consumption at the model level.

3. There is currently not a federal mandate requiring OTel adoption for tax purposes, but observability and audit-logging requirements are already standard across federal cybersecurity frameworks, industry compliance regimes, and cyber-insurance underwriting—meaning immutable transparency of computational workloads is already a familiar regulatory practice.
4. Mandating OTel instrumentation for tax-reporting purposes on self-hosted AI workloads is therefore well within the normal rule-making capabilities of Congress and Treasury—requiring extension of standard procedure, not invention of a new protocol.

With respect to token generation from offshore APIs: our government can assert that token consumption and use within the U.S. as an end destination is taxable in all cases. Mandating and enforcing this is well within the scope of Congressional authority. Our IRS and Congress have enforcement tactics to match their authorities. Cross-border digital taxation is not a new problem, and the enforcement architecture already exists.

Taxation of offshore-generated, U.S.-consumed tokens

The proposed token tax framework is "destination-based": it applies to tokens consumed in service of the US market, regardless of where the compute originates. We can portray the approach in plain English, leveraging existing precedent and law, with the expectation that—assuming the mechanism is adopted —Congress would bring their expertise and authority to bear to ensure compliance. The main point to communicate is that cross-border tax compliance is not a new topic, and can be managed via existing architecture, including:

U.S.-domiciled companies would self-assess and remit on all AI inputs, including those sourced offshore, with a Token-Tax Receipt required as a condition of the corresponding corporate-tax deduction — an enforcement model this cohort would already recognize from cross-border VAT reverse-charge and US state use tax.

Foreign AI providers with significant US market presence—defined by revenue and user-count thresholds—would register with the IRS and remit on US-attributable token consumption, following the OECD Pillar One / Digital Services Tax model.

U.S.-domiciled financial intermediaries (payment processors, app stores, cloud-billing platforms) would withhold the tax on cross-border payments where the foreign provider has not directly registered—an enforcement architecture analogous to the cross-border remittance withholding already enacted under OBBBA.

The requirement that token-logs include a verified destination stamp at the API level, drawing on metadata already captured by the major hyperscalers (AWS, Azure, Google Cloud).

Any workloads shifted to non-associated offshore affiliates would be captured by existing US transfer-pricing law, authorizing the IRS to reallocate income between related entities to prevent tax evasion. This would be supplemented by a safe-harbor provision treating AI consumption in service of end destination US revenue as domestically domiciled for token tax purposes.

None of these proposed mechanisms are novel. This framework simply adapts existing U.S. and international tax practice to a new asset class, with implementation and enforcement overseen by the qualified, authorized parties— Congress and IRS agencies—with whom that responsibility resides.

Does economic theory suggest this is the right time to implement AI taxation?

The optimal window of opportunity to enact the AI taxation framework is now—before the rate of change accelerates further. Importantly, doing so would establish the proposed AI token taxation framework as the "new normal", which all participants could regard as the baseline as they build out their implementation of token-based business development, both demand and supply-sides.

Acting now embeds AI taxation into the American economy, presenting perhaps the most seamless opportunity we will encounter, before AI potentially snowballs into becoming the backbone of economic activity. Equally, implementing a protective layer of taxation will help to shield our country from detrimental fiscal fallout from potential disruption in tax revenue during the AI transition period, therefore helping to prevent our fiscal instability from metamorphosing into fiscal peril.

From an economic theory perspective, we are in a moment of both rapid growth and price volatility in the adoption of AI. All reports are that demand for compute—and therefore token generation—dramatically exceeds supply. If anything, the rate of demand is reportedly increasing at an accelerating rate as Agentic AI is more widely deployed—even 24/7 in some use cases. Therefore, "now" is likely the exact right time, while we are in a phase of apparent price-inelasticity.

Conversely, the cost of token generation has been declining, due to increased efficiencies across multiple aspects of the generation process—from semiconductor efficiencies to algorithm efficiencies to model training and inference efficiencies, etc. A new dynamic has emerged in which GPUs—heretofore the stars of AI compute—are not being deployed for all use cases, as multi-modal generalist models are not optimal nor efficient in all cases. This is Agentic-driven inference routing, which orchestrates workloads across a range of chips—from CPUs to LPUs or GPUs, etc., being used based on the use case, and whether it is text only or multi-modal. In simple economic terms, we are at a moment with a significant supply-demand imbalance—but one in which inference is beginning to self-optimize—presenting a near optimal moment to implement such a tax, with the likelihood that it would have a *de minimis* effect on demand. In fact, it is <u>probably the exact right moment</u> for our Congress to act.

In the spirit of fairness, we have modeled a taxation framework that asks the demand-side and the supply-side to *share* this taxation expense. The scale of taxation envisaged is such that the impact felt by the majority of users would be nil—and would include a substantial "no charge" cohort, with AI taxation as a percent of annual revenue for most cohorts a fraction of 1%.

Alternatively, if AI related job dislocation does strain our "social safety net" the sums collected via AI taxation would in theory be more than offset by the expense reduction savings at the enterprise level of those which might reduce employment levels due to AI.

The fiscal—even political—perspective of "why now?"

It is reasonable to estimate that—due to the various features of our tax code—following wholly legal processes, AI model companies and hyperscalers are not likely to pay any tax on their AI compute or model operations for the foreseeable future, at the same time they might be facilitating AI-related job dislocation and disruption.

Depreciation of their considerable capital expenditures will likely result in a delay in recognizing net income, and therefore tax revenue contribution by this cadre of companies. We may therefore encounter a period of both employment and tax revenue disruption in which the architects of said disruption (AI model companies and hyperscalers) may be "tax immune" due to their depreciation of capex. All of which would simply be a matter of how our system works. An output-based tax countermands such an eventuality.

Is our view on the adoption of AI positive or negative?

Our view is overwhelmingly positive.

To be clear, our assessment is that AI, after a potentially bumpy transition and perhaps protracted period of creative disruption, will net, net lead to accelerating economic growth, a higher standard of living, as well as growth in employment. But the duration of this theoretical transition, and the depth of its potential disruption, is currently unknown.

Our Constitution stipulates all taxation is under the purview of Congress

These taxation mechanisms and their fee structures would need model verification, and confirmation and approval according to respective Congressional committees charged with its codification—presumably the House Ways and Means and Senate Finance committees. Implementing such a policy could (and should) serve as a non-partisan, apolitical, non-interfering mechanism (i.e., largely unobtrusive and invisible) to address the taxation deficit that we can expect to uniquely be caused by job loss (or, likely in many cases, "virtual" in lieu of human job creation) we are about to experience—and indeed are in the early stages of experiencing, per countless press releases. An "AI-era taxation policy", such as that which we illustrate, responds to the inflection point we are living while letting AI develop as a constructive economic force without further jeopardizing our fiscal well-being.

At present there are reports of taxation on power consumption by AI data centers being considered by Congress. While power consumption for AI is significant, and growing rapidly (chapter 19), we can simply say while we have no opposition to any such proposals, we suggest that such a strategy uses far too narrow of a lens, and would capture only a sliver of the potential impact of AI on our economy. We submit that AI token consumption and generation taxation would capture nearly all (even exponential) usage and output, and importantly would scale in synchrony with cognitive AI usage—even to its IUB, in a manner that taxation of electricity consumption—or other linearly calculated taxation solutions—simply could not approach.

From cognitive, to physical to edge AI

In this study, we have focused thus far on cognitive and physical AI. These are the two principal manifestations of AI in America today, with cognitive vastly outweighing physical. There is also a third dimension, which we pick up in chapter 17 known as Edge AI. Edge AI refers to compute that happens on the "edge" of our internet or Wi-Fi or intracompany networks. Its closest analog is mobile, and mobile's relation to the internet. In between DC (data center) AI and Edge AI, we also have hybrid DC/Edge AI.

The majority of AI consumption in the U.S. for now is office or home based, with factory and AV usage gradually increasing. The compute supporting this type of AI is generally DC generated, through what Jensen Huang refers to as "AI factories". Edge compute implies a remote device, even handheld, that likely contains its own model for compute, likely miniaturized in capability and in battery capacity. The current application use-case for this is limited (but growing). (When most of us use AI on our mobiles, we generally do so via the mobile app of our AI model of choice, with the compute occurring via the model's DC.) The notion of hybrid DC/Edge is a more prevalent use case, with AVs leading the way. AVs today, generally rely heavily upon communication back and forth with their network AI model located at a DC, but rely upon local compute (located within the edge device—such as an AV) for instances where low latency or zero latency is required. (Zero latency meaning immediacy of response.)

Implementation of token-based cognitive AI taxation means that we will be fully able today to capture most if not all cognitive compute consumption and generation. In the case of DC/Edge our ability to accurately capture this data is diminished—thus we offer a separate method of taxation for physical AI (below). For pure Edge AI, this is an emerging category, and accordingly we leave this to be determined later—but not too much later, as the channels and manifestations of this functionality becomes clearer. The expectation is that we will be able to identify a native mechanism that equally scales as usage scales. Mobile networks, and their related ecosystem are already able to capture rich amounts of data, thus the prospect of this objective becoming reality is highly realistic. .

AI token and physical AI taxation implementation framework and forecasts

In order to illustrate our taxation proposal for both token-based and physical AI, in the following pages we present the following:

1. Proposed token taxation tiers per user type and size;
2. Estimated token consumption and therefore taxation from 2025 - 2030;
3. Summary of combined demand-side and supply-side token taxation by year;
4. Projected "consumption" of physical AI from 2025 - 2030 with purchase registrations fee and renewal fee estimates by type; and
5. Summary of all taxation mechanisms: cognitive token taxation and physical registration fee taxation.

Let us state the obvious upfront, which is that since AI is early-stage, with a limited and fragmented variety of data sets available, stated trends and forecasts are dynamic and therefore evolving real-time. Our sources for these forecasts are a combination of publicly available data, press releases, industry (domain specific and financial) forecasts, along with a variety of platforms that collect and report estimates, etc. Therefore, these are best estimates, purely for the purpose of illustrating the proposed scope and implementation of our taxation mechanism, not specific and exact forecasts or final taxation recommendations. Were our Congress to take up this endeavor they of course have the prerogative to request all necessary information, and thereby verify all necessary metrics.

The need for credible Federal reporting on an agreed set of AI metrics for purposes of understanding, guiding and planning our AI-era economy quickly becomes evident. In the physical world, entities such as BLS and BEA perform highly beneficial roles via the credible and consistent frame of data they provide on a monthly basis. They will soon need to broaden their scope and include the appropriate set of AI metrics.

For this study, we asked two AI frontier models to formulate specific token consumption and output growth estimates for the 2025 – 2030 period, and have used their aggregated data and inputs, as a method of attempted triangulation towards best available consensus. Our focus has been on token generation and consumption forecasts, and secondarily on consumption rates of physical AI. For our projections below we are using the midpoint of their estimates, which we additionally reduced out of conservatism. (Our data sets cover the 2025 – 2030 time-frame, with 2025 obviously history and 2026 in process. We include this broader time spectrum in order to best depict the growth rate trajectory of AI adoption.)

In our opinion, even allowing for the inevitable variance in actual vs. estimated data, these illustrations provide an adequately sufficient use case forecast for our proposed cognitive and physical AI taxation mechanisms to offer draft illustrations. We include estimated government token consumption (of approximately 17.6% of total) in order to accurately reflect AI output in our economy for budgetary purposes, as ultimately, like all government services this will be taxpayer financed. (In the case of government agencies, any expected headcount reductions courtesy of AI would very possibly more than offset their added token consumption expense.)

Progressive Token Taxation Framework Overview

The token tax applies a cost per million tokens (CPMM) rate determined by the consuming (demand-side) entity's annual revenue tier. The structure is progressive, meaning each tier pays a higher rate than the tier below it, both in absolute CPMM terms and as a percentage of revenue. At the top end entities pay the lesser of their CPMM calculation or their tier max burden of 1.5% as a percentage of annual revenue. An output taxation mechanism—as opposed to income-based—is used to ensure visibility of compliance. (We note that since CPMM rates are fixed in nominal terms — not indexed to inflation or GDP — the real unit charge naturally erodes over time, leaving future re-evaluation of each fixed rate to future Congressional review.)

We allocate token demand taxation on a 50/25/25 basis to both demand-side and supply-side companies, with demand-side capped at 1.5% of revenue and supply-side taxation capped at 10%. This is done out of recognition of the fact that the supply-side companies represent a much smaller portion of the overall economy, and since broadly speaking, they are the ones driving—and benefitting from—AI disruption. Any doctrine of fairness therefore necessitates they pay their share.

We begin with demand side forecasts—the enterprises directly consuming AI—as the driver and most broadly applicable component of the framework.

Six-Tier Progressive Token Taxation Structure – Demand-side

Demand-side enterprises pay 50% of the full token tax as assessed per their tier. The remaining 50% is split equally between supply-side model companies (25%) and hyperscalers (25%)—analogous to FICA payroll tax shared between employee and employer.

Token-based Taxation Tier Introduction per 2025 Data

Tier	Revenue threshold	CPMM rate	Demand-side tax rate	Est. tax % rev. (2025)	Tier framework
Tier 0 Exempt	Under $10M annual revenue	$0.000/M	$0.000/M	0.000%	Students, nonprofits, startups. 94% of US businesses pay zero via this framework.
Tier 1	$10M – $100M annual revenue	$4.00/M	$2.00/M	~0.020%	SME universe. $50M-revenue entity pays approximately $10,000 annually.
Tier 2	$100M – $1B annual revenue	$6.00/M	$3.00/M	~0.030%	Mid-market enterprise. $500M entity pays approximately $150,000 annually.
Tier 3	$1B – $10B annual revenue	$8.00/M	$4.00/M	~0.033%	Large enterprise. Typical $6B entity pays approximately $2 million annually, or 0.033% rev.
Gov. Tier	All federal + state/local agencies	$8.00/M	$4.00/M	~0.029% of $7T budget	Government charged at Tier 3 CPMM rate.

Tier 4	$10B – $100B annual rev.	$10.00/M	$5.00/M	~0.071%	Major corporations. $38B entity pays $27 million; 0.071% rev
Tier 5	$100B+ annual revenue	$12.50/M	$6.25/M	~0.177%	Mega-cap corporations. $177B entity contributes $312.5 million, or 0.177% rev

Table 5: The Six -Tier Demand-side Token Taxation Framework

Note: Demand-side effective rate = 50% of CPMM per tier, reflecting the demand-side / supply-side split of the token tax. % of revenue figures are 2025 estimates based on representative entities and average token volumes. In practice every company's effective rate will differ based on actual consumption and revenue.

Government tier taxation—design intent

It is unusual to subject government entities to taxation, however we do so for the following reasons. The first principle is the notion that effective oversight of government spending is best served through transparency, which implies consistent and visible allocation of expenses. Placing AI consumption inside agency budget lines may help to increase expenditure visibility. If a department deploys AI at scale, it must account for the token tax cost within its existing budget parameters—similar to any other operating expense (OpEx). Conversely, any savings generated by AI-driven staff reductions would likely more than offset the added expense.

Demand-Side: Consumption-based (50% share of) taxation of AI 2025 – 2030

Each cell shows projected tax revenue per year and percent to revenue for a typical company. In years 2028 – 2030 Tier 5 maxes out at 1.5% of revenue taxation cap for demand-side, with tier 4 maxing out in 2030.

Tier	CPM M	2025 B % rev	2026 B % rev	2027 B % rev	2028 B % rev	2029 B % rev	2030 $B % rev
T0	$0.000	$0 / exempt	$0 / exempt	$0 / exempt	$0 / exempt	$0 / exempt	$0 / exempt
T1	$4.00/ M	$600/ 0.020%	$1.8B/ 0.056%	$4.5B/ 0.128%	$9.0B / 0.238%	$15.2/ 0.374%	$22.9B/ 0.518%
T2	$6.00/ M	$1.2B/ 0.030%	$3.6B/ 0.083%	$9.0B/ 0.192%	$18.0/ 0.357%	$30.5/ 0.560%	$45.7B/ 0.778%
T3	$8.00/ M	$2.5B/ 0.033%	$7.5B/ 0.093%	$18.8/ 0.214%	$37.5/ 0.397%	$63.5/ 0.623%	$95.3B/ 0.864%
Gov *	$8.00/ M	$2.0B/ 0.029%	$6.0B/ 0.083%	$15.0/ 0.199%	$30.0/ 0.383%	$50.8/ 0.625%	$76.2B/ 0.904%
T4	$10.00 /M	$8.8B/ 0.071%	$26.3/ 0.198%	$65.6/ 0.458%	$131./ 0.850%	$222./ 1.334%	$270.1/ 1.500%
T5	$12.50 /M	$5.6B/ 0.177%	$16.9/ 0.490%	$42.2/ 1.132%	$60.2/ 1.500%	$65.0/ 1.500%	$70.3B/ 1.500%
Tot B	—	$20.7B	$62.0B	$155.1	$286.0	$447.3	$580.4B

Table 6: Demand-side Taxation Revenue Forecasts 2025 - 2030

Note: % of revenue figures are model estimates based on representative entities and average token volumes. In practice every company's effective rate will differ based on actual consumption and actual revenue. The Gov tier depicts token tax as a nil % of revenue, this is in contrast to the $7T government agencies budget.

AI Model Company Supply-side (25%) Share of Taxation 2025–2030

AI Model companies pay 25% of the full token tax generated by their tier's demand. Capped at 10% of AI revenue. Each cell depicts tax ($B) / % of model company's own AI revenue.

Tier	Representative entity / revenue	2025 $B / % rev	2026 $B / % rev	2027 $B / % rev	2028 $B / % rev	2029 $B / % rev	2030 $B / % rev
T0	*Exempt*	$0 / exempt	$0 / exempt	$0 / exempt	$0 / exempt	$0 / exempt	$0 / exempt

T1	Boutique providers ~$10B AI rev +15% yoy	$300M 3.000%	$900M 7.826%	$1.3B 10.000 %	$1.5B / 10.000 %	$1.7B / 10.000 %	$2.0B / 10.000 %
T2	Mistral / Groq-type ~$7.5B AI rev + 20% yoy	$600M 8.000%	$900M 10.000 % ⌐	$1.1B / 10.000 % ⌐	$1.3B / 10.000 % ⌐	$1.6B / 10.000 % ⌐	$1.9B / 10.000 % ⌐
T3	Anthropic-type ~$24B AI rev +40% yoy	$1.3B / 5.208%	$3.4B / 10.000 %	$4.7B / 10.000 %	$6.6B / 10.000 %	$9.2B / 10.000 %	$12.9B 10.000 %
Gov	All Gov AI demand via hyperscalers	$0K / -	$0K / -	$0K / -	$0K / -	$0K / -	$0K / -
T4	OpenAI-type ~$40B AI rev +50% yoy	$4.0B / 10.000 %	$8.0B / 10.000 %	$15.0B 10.000 %	$22.0B 10.000 %	$30.0B 10.000 %	$37.5B 10.000 %
T5	Google Cloud / Gemini API ~$48B cloud rev +28% yoy	$2.8B / 5.859%	$6.2B / 10.000 %	$8.1B / 10.000 %	$10.5B 10.000 %	$13.7B 10.000 %	$17.8B 10.000 %
Tot	All tiers	$9.0B	$19.4B	$30.2B	$41.9B	$56.2B	$72.1B

Table 7: AI Model (supply-side) share of Token Taxation 2025 - 2030

Note: AI Token Taxation capped at 10% of annual revenue. Government usage taxation represented in hyperscaler component of supply-side.

Hyperscaler Supply-side Share (25%) 2025–2030

Hyperscalers pay 25% of the full token tax for compute infrastructure provided. Capped at 10% of their cloud/AI revenue. Each cell: tax ($B) / % of hyperscaler cloud revenue, as distinct from percent of parent company revenue.

Tier	Representative entity / revenue	2025 $B / % rev	2026 $B / % rev	2027 $B / % rev	2028 $B / % rev	2029 $B / % rev	2030 $B / % rev
T0	*Exempt*	$0	$0	$0	$0	$0	$0
T1	Small cloud providers ~$10B +15%	$300M 3.000 %	$900M 7.826 %	$1.3B 10.000 %	$1.5B 10.000 %	$1.7B 10.000 %	$2.0B 10.000 %
T2	CoreWeave / Lambda Labs ~$7.5B +20%	$600M / 8.000 %	$900M 10.000 %	$1.1B 10.000 %	$1.3B 10.000 %	$1.6B 10.000 %	$1.9B 10.000 %
T3	AWS - Anthropic partner ~$115B AI rev + 19%	$1.25B 1.087 %	$3.8B 2.737 %	$9.4B 5.752 %	$18.8B 9.665 %	$23.1B 10.000 %	$27.5B 10.000 %
Gov *	All hyperscaler serve Gov compute	$2.0B	$6.0B	$15.0B	$30.0B	$50.8B	$76.2B
T4	Azure OpenAI partner ~$100B AI rev +25%	$4.4B 4.375 %	$12.5B 10.000 %	$15.6B 10.000 %	$19.5B 10.000 %	$24.4B 10.000 %	$30.5B 10.000 %
T5	Google Cloud Tier 5 inference ~$48B AI rev + 28%	$2.8B 5.859 %	$6.2B 10.000 %	$8.1B 10.000 %	$10.5B 10.000 %	$13.7B 10.000 %	$17.8B 10.000 %
Tot B	*All tiers*	$11.3B	$30.3B	$50.5B	$81.6B	$115.3	$155.9

Table 8: Hyperscaler (supply-side) share Proposed Token Tax 2025 - 2030

Note: Government tax is uncapped as this expense applies to their compute providers Azure Government and AWS GovCloud. Reference to Government "revenue" pertains to department "budgets". Taxation cap of 10% applies to hyperscaler business unit only within large Cloud and related technology companies

Combined Token Tax: All Three Components – the 50/25/25 Framework

Summary of demand-side, supply-side AI model and hyperscaler taxation

Party — share	2025	2026	2027	2028	2029	2030
Enterprise — demand side (50% | 1.5% cap)	$20.7B	$62.0B	$155.1B	$286.0B	$447.3B	$580.4B
AI Model cos. Supply-side (25% | 10% cap)	$9.0B	$19.4B	$30.2B	$41.9B	$56.2B	$72.1B
Hyperscalers, supply-side (25% | 10% cap)	$11.3B	$30.3B	$50.5B	$81.6B	$115.3B	$155.9B
Annual Total	$41.0B	$111.6B	$235.7B	$409.4B	$618.8B	$808.3B

Table 9: Token Taxation Revenue Combined Demand and Supply-side 2025 - 2030

Note: Years 2025, 2026 for context purposes only. Captures Cognitive AI taxation.

Physical AI Taxation Overview

Cognitive and Physical AI operate in distinctly different environments, follow different protocols and therefore require different taxation mechanisms. Physical AI may operate remotely—on the Edge—or it may operate in a factory. Accordingly, its AI compute needs are met differently, with cognitive readily aligning with token taxation while physical—both due to its processing differences as well as physical location, not aligning well with token taxation at all. Therefore, we propose a registration fee and renewal-based mechanism of taxation.

The direct analog for this is the system used for automobile registration fees in the U.S., which we adopt for physical AI.

Unit sales estimates are largely drawn from the International Federation of Robots annual reports, public company deployment targets, and author estimates for emerging categories. As this broad category is the least developed in the U.S., we qualify these forecasts as best estimates used for directional and illustrative purposes.

Humanoid robots for example: The 500,000-unit 2030 forecast is appropriately conservative. Tesla Optimus has publicly targeted 1 million units by 2027; however, this category is currently pre-revenue and unsubstantiated. At Tesla's stated targets, 2030 registration fee revenue from humanoids alone would approximately double the total physical AI tax revenue.

As is the case with the token taxation framework, we implement a hard cap on a percent of transaction basis—in this case 5% of transaction price—to allow for a meaningful degree of taxation at a level that does not deter adoption. In this sector, broadly speaking, these entities represent at least a direct one-to-one replacement for human taxpayers and in some cases—such as those with potentially 24/7 operations—they potentially represent a three-to-one replacement.

Physical AI Registration Fee Structure

Every commercial physical AI unit would be required to possess a unique AI registration number (AIRN). Registration fees to be paid at time of purchase with renewal fees paid annually per expected operating life. Unregistered units would be illegal to operate commercially.

Physical AI Category	Avg. Unit Price	Registration Fee	Annual Renewal Fee	Useful Life
Autonomous vehicles (Waymo / Cybercab / Zoox)	~$100,000	$5,000 (5%)	$2,500/yr	10 yrs
Factory robots (industrial robotic arm)	~$50,000	$2,500 (5%)	$750/yr	12 yrs

Physical AI Category	Avg. Unit Price	Registration Fee	Annual Renewal Fee	Useful Life
Humanoid robots (Tesla Optimus / Figure / 1X)	~$75,000	$3,750 (5%)	$1,500/yr	8 yrs
Farm machinery (John Deere autonomous tractor)	~$250,000	$12,500 (5%)	$2,000/yr	15 yrs
Robotic surgery (da Vinci / Intuitive Surgical)	~$1,500,000	$45,000 (3%)	$15,000/yr	10 yrs
AI kiosks (fast food / retail / banking)	~$20,000	$1,000 (5%)	$200/yr	7 yrs
Distribution center robots (Amazon Kiva)	~$40,000	$2,000 (5%)	$600/yr	7 yrs
Mining robots (autonomous)	~$1,500,000	$45,000 (3%)	$7,500/yr	15 yrs
Delivery robots / drones (Starship / Wing / Zipline)	~$15,000	$750 (5%)	$150/yr	5 yrs

Table 10: Physical AI Proposed Registration Fee Structure

Note: 5% cap on expense relative to purchase price, exemptions granted to 3% for Surgical and Mining

Physical AI Registration Fee Revenue Estimates 2025–2030

Registration fee revenue; paid at purchase, with renewal revenue per annual fee on accumulated deployed fleet. Renewal revenue grows as fleet matures—by 2030, 24% of total registration revenue from renewals.

Year	Registration	Renewal	Annual Total	Cumulative	Physical AI Type
2025	~$756M	$0	~$756M	~$756M	Kiosks, factory robots, distribution centers
2026	~$1.17B	~$164M	~$1.33B	~$2.09B	AV, factory, kiosks
2027	~$2.02B	~$440M	~$2.46B	~$4.54B	AV, factory, humanoid
2028	~$3.63B	~$1.02B	~$4.65B	~$9.20B	Humanoid, factory, AV at scale
2029	~$6.58B	~$1.94B	~$8.52B	~$17.7B	Humanoid, delivery robot, mining, agr.
2030	~$11.47B	~$3.57B	~$15.04B	~$32.8B	Humanoid + AV + delivery + kiosks

Table 11: Physical AI registration and renewal fees; 2025 - 2030

Note: Registration fee revenue paid at purchase. Renewal revenue per annual fee on accumulated deployed fleet. By 2030, approximately 24% of total annual revenue from renewals.

Combined Total: All Taxation Mechanisms 2025–2030

All three parts of the AI taxation framework: 1) demand-side token tax (50%), 2) supply-side model company token tax (25%), supply-side hyperscaler token tax (25%), and 3) physical AI tax.

Mechanism	2025	2026	2027	2028	2029	2030	Cum. 2025–30
Part 1 — Demand-side token tax 50%	$20.B	$62.0	$155.B	$286.B	$447.B	$580.B	$1.6T
Part 2A — Model company token tax 25%	$9.0B	$19.4	$30.2B	$41.9B	$56.2B	$72.1B	$228.B
Part 2B — Hyperscale token tax 25%	$11.B	$30.3	$50.5B	$81.6B	$115.B	$155.B	$444.B
Token tax subtotal (Parts 1+2A+2B)	$41.B	$111.	$235.B	$409.B	$618.B	$808.B	$2.22T
Part 3 — Physical AI Registratio n tax + renewal	$756	$1.33	$2.46B	$4.65B	$8.52B	$15.0B	$32.8B
Total — All Mechanism	$42.B	$113.	$238.B	$414.B	$627.B	$823.B	$2.26T

Table 12: Combined all AI taxation mechanisms 2025 - 2030

Note: Sum of best estimates for directional and illustrative purposes. Author specification.

Proposed AI Taxation Policy Summary

Output-based, not income-based taxation: None of the proposed instruments can be minimized through accelerated depreciation. Tokens are generated or consumed, units are registered, or they are not.

Universal and progressive: Approximately 94% of American businesses would pay no tax. The burden falls on medium and large enterprises with the scale to bear it, as indicated in the token tax tier table with progressive CPMM rates. Physical AI registration fee capped at 5%—below most state sales tax rates on durable goods.

Bilateral and fair: The token tax applies equally to those who consume AI and those who produce it. A $50M small-scale GPU cloud provider and a $50M regional insurance broker sit in the same Tier 1 at the same rate. Scale determines the CPMM rate; the principle is universally applied.

Self-adjusting to scale: As entities grow in revenue, they migrate to higher token taxation tiers automatically. As token volumes grow, revenue grows without rate increases. As the physical AI fleet accumulates, renewal revenue grows without new legislation. The framework scales in synchrony with the AI economy.

The New Math: AI as the Fourth Pillar of Federal Revenue

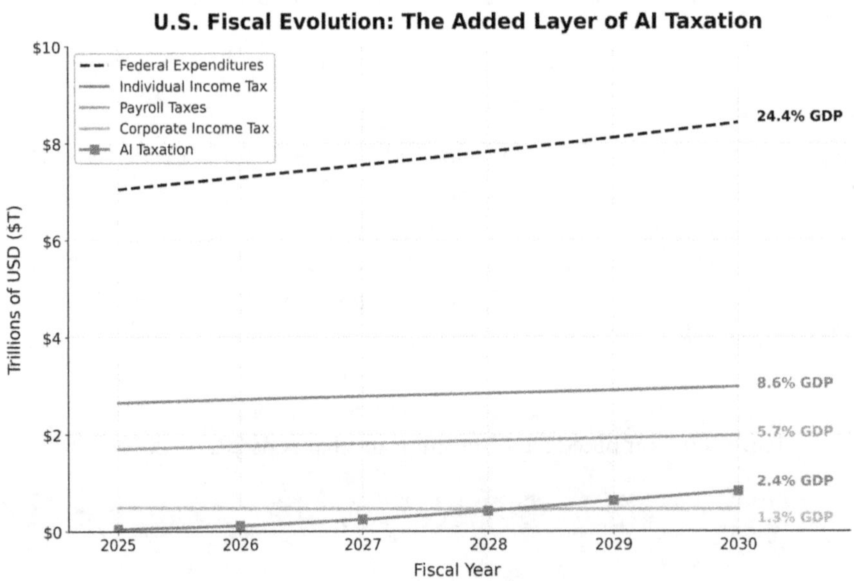

Figure 23: CBO forecast federal spending / taxation data with added 4th layer of AI taxation; Payroll taxation presented as unique line as links 100% to the individual

Note: Baseline federal revenue & expenditure trajectories from CBO 10-Year Economic Outlook (2025–2030), CBO Monthly review October 2025. Corp & individual taxation forecasts reflect OBBBA expensing provisions. AI Tax revenues per Author forecasts.

Summary of 2030 percentage of GDP for each of the five lines for fiscal forecast above (figure 23) based on CBO estimated GDP of roughly $34.5 Trillion:

- Total Federal Expenditure: 24.4% of GDP (includes annual public debt service)
- Corporate Income Tax (Ex. Payroll): 1.3% of GDP
- Individual Income Tax (Ex. Payroll): 8.6% of GDP
- Total Payroll Tax: 5.7% of GDP
- Total AI Tax Revenue (All 3 Sources): 2.4% of GDP
- Not included: misc. excise, custom, tariff revenue, per CBO projections about 1.8-2.0% per year—surprisingly greater than corporate income taxation.

As the above chart illustrates, even with the addition of AI taxation, by 2030, per current CBO forecasts we are at a level of total government expenditures totaling 24.4% of GDP, while all sources of taxation sum to 20.0% of GDP vs. 24.4% for expenses. As a country, fiscally-speaking, there is a lot of work to be done.

9. How to Enforce AI Taxation – defeating the Defeaters

History shows there is an established tradition of companies—and individuals—using a variety of tactics to defeat taxation mechanisms in America. Indeed, our own tax code provides multiple opportunities for this to take place. We have no issue with those who employ legal mechanisms to do so, and continue to believe that Americans and American companies are fundamentally honest, do not engage in corruption and in general recognize that rule of law is an important part of what enables our tremendous success as a country and as a people.

However, so as not to leave compliance to chance, or the good intentions of others, there are existing protocols that can be implemented to ensure broad-based compliance of AI taxation measures as implemented by Congressional legislation. We summarize those we find directly relevant below (in doing so we underline key points made in the previous chapter and emphasize additional tactics).

In theory, the compliance mechanisms available to our Congress, Treasury, and the IRS are more than capable of managing attempts to undermine the token-based AI taxation mechanism. There is little in the proposed token taxation mechanism that would be fundamentally new to our IRS compliance agencies. Additionally, we believe that American companies would exhibit a bias for a) obeying the law, and b) doing their part in stabilizing our country's fiscal position. Further, although all parties in a business transaction innately want the lowest possible price, as noted earlier, we are in a moment of apparent price-inelasticity, meaning the consequence of the proposed taxation mechanisms should be relatively *de minimis* all around.

What are the most likely avenues of tax avoidance to be utilized?

1. Token generation and consumption concealment;
2. Use of offshore API hosting;
3. On premise or "on-prem" private hosting; and
4. Use of offshore legal entities to "shelter" cost of token generation or consumption.

How can these attempted measures to defeat AI taxation themselves be defeated?

Token concealment:

Attempts at concealing tokens, token amounts, token units of measure—via compression, encryption or other protocols—can be countermanded via two main steps:

First, is establishing a legal definition of what constitutes a token, such as a standard token unit (STU), defined as a fixed baseline of semantic text weight (e.g., a standard byte-pair encoding mapping whereby one token averages four bytes of data) or is indexed to a baseline of raw computational output, such as a fixed number of floating-point operations (FLOPs) required during the model's output to the demand-side user. (FLOPs can be thought of as unconcealable units of measure of computational work and hardware output.)

Second is obligating all hyperscalers, all AI models, all supply-side companies to install an open telemetry framework (OTeL), an immutable system of measurement that would reside within the application runtime environment and container orchestration layer of each API (hyperscaler, AI model, offshore API, etc.).

In simple terms, this measures the exact volume of digital throughput and hardware resource consumption in synchronicity with all token generation. This becomes the universally recognized fair and objective data source for token generation and transmission for monthly usage and billing purposes.

API level installation could make use of open source OTeL frameworks, but would require resident engineering expertise to properly install, store data and oversee the mechanism's operation.

Offshore APIs:

First, taxation legislation would assert that taxation is premised on the "destination-end use market", meaning within the U.S. for enterprise (and other designated entities) purposes within the U.S., regardless of token API origin.

Second, is via the legislative stipulation that the Destination-Based Border-Tax Adjustment (BTA) is in effect. This is an existing protocol, an OECD standard, used routinely in the U.S. and in the EU for cross-border commerce.

And third, is securing IRS definition that only token expense by U.S. companies paid to an entity with U.S. tax registry compliance (along with OTeL generated consumption receipts) would constitute an allowable tax deduction in filing of entity net income tax reports. In other words, token payments to non-compliant entities would not be allowable as tax deductions in a corporation's quarterly or YE IRS filings.

On-prem hosting:

While an early-stage phenomena, on-prem hosting will likely grow in application for data security (a.k.a. data sovereignty) considerations. Once considered an option only for the corporations of considerable size and resources—involving dedicated servers, qualified staffing and an "air-gapped" environment, this increasingly can be accomplished on a private scale via properly configured home devices. Nonetheless, the following steps would effectively countermand this:

First, requisite installation of OTel as previously described.

Second, an additional OTeL configuration can then be integrated directly into the hardware management library and driver layer (such as NVML) in order to track raw processing cycles, core temperatures, and computational floating-point operations (FLOPs) as token generation evidence back-up.

Third, the IRS requirement of validated, OTel-generated consumption receipts—coupled with the strict rejection of tax deductions for un-instrument-verified or non-compliant compute expenses—effectively defeats any incentive an enterprise might have to hide or under-report their private, on-premise computational throughput.

Tax shelters:

There is only one step needed to defeat any claim that token consumption or generation expense occurred within an offshore entity tax domicile, and is therefore immune from taxation and that is as follows: the first declaration made in the AI taxation proposal is that AI taxation will be "output" not "income" based. Thus, the IRS is disinterested in business expense generation in an offshore tax domicile, as for the purpose of AI taxation it measures and taxes based on output, not net income.

There is always a plan B

Finally, as with any imperative, there is always a "plan B". Plan B in these cases—in additional to the implicit threat of the full weight of deployment of American criminal law proceedings for those choosing to violate U.S. tax law, would include the following, which could be construed as alternative means of taxation.

Option 1: taxation of training at the AI model and hyperscaler level. This is currently not specified or modeled within the proposed token taxation framework and is left outside of the scope of taxation as it is presently being viewed as a cost-of-goods (COG) expense, and importantly as an AI frontier development expense, and thus respected as such. This is, we believe, an important premise to leave this expense "off-limits" as this act, this process of model training and development at or over the frontier constitutes an almost sacred competitive imperative of American AI model companies, which among others, we want to see protected.

Option 2: expansion of taxation of instruments of physical AI, such as inclusion of GPUs, CPUs, LPUs, etc., in the registration and renewal fee taxation mechanism. Again, these were left "off-limits" as they again fall into the broad category of AI frontier development, where we among others wish to see all legal advantages given to American companies.

Reality check

As noted in chapter 8, it is important—at least in the court of public opinion—to keep in mind that it is highly unlikely that, under existing U.S. tax law, any members of the cohort of U.S. based AI model and AI hyperscaler companies will pay any income tax on their AI related activities for years to come. This is based purely on the concept of net income, which is simply operating profits less deduction of allowable expenses. And since capex by this cohort is of epic magnitude, we can expect their date with net income tax due is safely in the distant future.

We can only hope that this cohort remains mindful of this fact with respect to the assessment of token taxation. Indeed, one frontier model has previously acknowledged the likelihood of such an event.

10. *Agentification – the Teammates no one saw coming*

Over the past few decades, any fear that may have existed regarding workplace automation likely had to do with the roll-out of robots. While this was somewhat understandable, at present the US could charitably be called 2nd tier in terms of implementation of robotics in the workforce (far behind S. Korea, Japan and China). Instead, workplace automation will more likely be the result of the faster moving yet less visible threat of Agentic AI, and broadly speaking cognitive AI. It is their implicit threat of automated or augmented workflow, and to a much lesser extent Physical or robotic AI, that is poised to most severely impact our workforce—and influence our economy, at least in the near-term.

American management consultancy McKinsey was early to recognize the potential of Agentic AI, creating its own terminology, "Agentification", to describe the fast-forward adoption of AI in *both* augmentation and automation roles, and equally in "virtual job creation". Exactly what is Agentic AI, what is "Agentification" and why does this phenomenon likely represent the fastest growing "headcount" sector in the American labor force?

For most users in the early days of 2024 – 2025 our interaction with AI might have been called "command and response", meaning we could "prompt" it with a question or a command, even give it commands of an astonishingly wide variety, and we would presto get a "response" (hence the terminology "generative AI"). The relevance, even accuracy of said response being predicated on the breadth, depth and quality of its "training", and of course based on the specificity of said prompt. We, the users were, via sequential prompts, driving the interaction, defining the topic, the scope and nature of output.

This once-simple dynamic has now changed, and is evolving rapidly, beginning at scale in 2025 in what can be called the "Agentic era." As McKinsey describes the shift, AI systems have evolved to act more like co-workers — capable of identifying needs, setting objectives, autonomously orchestrating actions, and interacting continuously with the world via data, APIs and other systems. Agentic capacity can simplistically be viewed as an OS (operating system) added to an LLM that grants said LLM expansive capabilities, among which may include addition of use case or domain specific applications.

Agentic AI systems themselves—instances of which McKinsey terms "Agentification"—are typically characterized by five core capabilities: 1) autonomy to pursue objectives within defined parameters, 2) memory that enables learning and context retention ("state") across interactions, 3) access to data sources and APIs for environmental awareness, 4) the capacity to observe, analyze, orchestrate, and execute actions toward goal achievement and 5) the ability as an OS to integrate applications, thus dramatically expanding its capabilities.

They can function 24/7, as independently as they might be configured, or with parameters that serve as guardrails. They can be—and so increasingly are—integrated into a work process or workflow or analytical teams, like your newest, nerdy, super-quantitative and productive teammate. "Agentification" deployment can be as internal-facing team members, or client facing. An AI "agent" can act as a supervisor for a pre-determined set of outcomes, it can monitor and manage a collection of robots or workflow operations, it could accomplish financial analysis and posit recommendations, it could engage in autonomous customer service activities.

Its main distinction from what has gone before is as opposed to a "command and response" or task-based mechanism, the LLM is "wrapped" in an agentic AI operating system (AIOS), endowing it with memory, perception, the ability to orchestrate and to execute, allowing it to function autonomously, to make decisions (to become a supervisory workflow mechanism), to benefit from reinforcement learning (RL) and ultimately recursive self-improvement, allowing it to autonomously improve. It therefore can in some senses behave as if it were a human "cousin", so-to-speak, meaning not exactly but offering glimpses of human-like characteristics. And it can work 24/7.

This endowment and embodiment of Agentic capability is premised on a series of innovations that have occurred since the emergence of LLMs and Generative AI. These include not just the Agentic OS itself, but RL, first with "human in the loop feedback" (RLHF) and then with "machine in the loop" virtual feedback (verifiable rewards—RLVR) which can therefore enable "recursive self-instruction", or continuous and autonomous self-improvement, such as via the LADDER protocol described earlier. All of which gives Agentic AI the ability to supervise, to analyze, to course-correct, to initiate or schedule outcomes, and to even revise its objectives (all of which should occur within predetermined parameters or guardrails). Agentic capabilities are increasingly being paired or coupled with other capabilities—such as Analytic AI and Agentic Process Automation, or over in Physical AI, Agentic AI can assume a supervisory capacity for smart factory robotic manufacturing.

McKinsey, the legendary American consultancy agency, was early in engaging AI to augment and ultimately automate many of its work functions, ultimately deeply integrating it into many of their work processes. In 2015 (in an impressive act of foresight) they acquired London based QuantumBlack (QB), which had a fearsome reputation for their advanced use of data analytics and AI within the domain of F1 racing. This acquisition apparently helped fuel McKinsey's adoption and integration of AI best practices into their consulting operations.

Their approach seems to have been architected internally by the QB team, and features an approach known as *agentic AI mesh architecture*, which generally includes "active" and "warm" AI agents; active meaning those currently deployed on a project, warm meaning those that are "pre-instantiated", that is pre-programmed and ready to go. This approach may differ from a Generative AI provider which may instantiate, meaning bring to life and specify objectives, access, functionality as needed, not operate with a "warm" bench.

The expression "exponential" is often used to describe both the growth of AI's compute capacity and performance manifestations. The example of McKinsey's "active and warm AI Agents" reads like a user's manual of how to bring this to life, and it suggests a well-architected and agile deployment strategy.

In software, an "instance" refers to a specific, operative copy of a software application, object, or service. Each instance operates independently with its own memory, configuration, and data, even if multiple instances are running the same underlying code or program. An "active" instance would be those which are deployed and in-the-game, a "warm" instance would be those which are pre-instantiated and therefore "on the bench" and ready to enter the game as needed.

We refer to the perspective provided by an August 4, 2025, WSJ article on McKinsey in the modern era of AI, and what this portends for them.

"AI Is Coming for the Consultants. Inside McKinsey, 'This Is Existential'"

The headline of the article suggests that AI could be near life-threatening for McKinsey—or, broadly speaking to management consulting companies as a genre, but the article goes on to portray a completely different picture, one of a company that is using AI to its advantage, taking the "bull by the horns" so to speak. Highlights of this article read as follows:

"…McKinsey is trying to steer through its own existential transformation. Artificial Intelligence can increasingly do the work done by the firm's highly paid consultants, often within minutes."

"That reality is pushing the firm to rewire its business. AI is now a topic of conversation at every meeting of McKinsey's board, said Bob Sternfels, the firm's global managing partner. The technology is changing the ways McKinsey works with clients, how it hires and even what projects it takes on."

McKinsey is rapidly expanding the ranks of its Agentic team members. "These Agents now assist consultants in building PowerPoint decks, taking notes and summing up interviews and research documents for clients. The most-used ones help employees write in a classic 'McKinsey tone of voice'—language the firm describes as sharp, concise and clear. Another popular agent checks the logic of a consultant's arguments, verifying the flow of reasoning makes sense."

Sternfels said (in the August 4, 2025, WSJ article) he sees a day in the not-too-distant future when McKinsey has one AI agent for every human it employs. "We're going to continue to hire, but we're also going to continue to build agents".

Already, the shape of the company is shifting. The firm has reduced its head count from about 45,000 people in 2023 to 40,000 through layoffs and attrition, in part to correct for an aggressive post-pandemic hiring spree. It has since also rolled out roughly 12,000 AI agents." If we take Mr. Sternfels (Global Managing Partner) comments literally, McKinsey envisions taking its "workforce" to 80,000 of which 50% would be human and 50% would be Agentic, per his visualization of a 1:1 human to Agentic AI ratio.

In their March 2025 white paper on workforce automation, *AI-Driven Agentification of Work: Impact on Jobs (2024–2030),* they refer to this process as "Agentification".

If one objectively thinks about this new era of ubiquitous AI and one asks, how should I approach this for my company…an oft-heard recommendation is to engage a consultant for their ideas, which one presumes will be reflective of current "best-practices". If a consultant's own action is repopulating a portion of their workforce with Agentic AI, then this speaks louder than words.

A 1:1 Vision - "McKinsey-fication" of Agentification

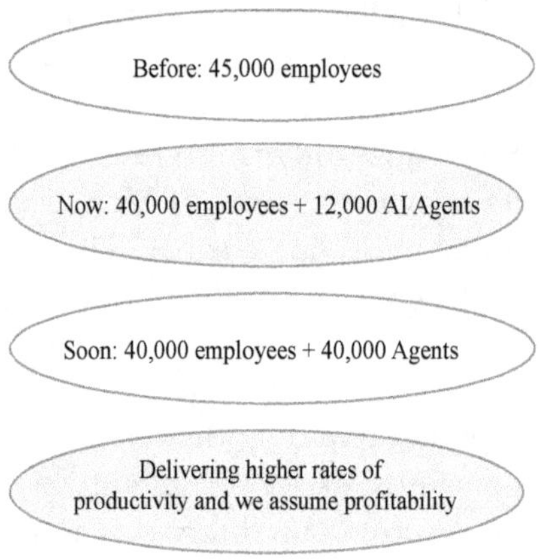

Figure 24: McKinsey "Agentification" vision, Author specification

The above is but one scenario. It is predicated upon McKinsey's own statements of intent with respect to its plans and its vision. Very likely it supports a high growth, high profitability future for the company, as is their right as a private company. It likely also—barring Mr. Gates' notion of taxation of robots coming to life, implies a company and an economy with a shrinking tax base. In sum: great for McKinsey, not so great for our country's fiscal solvency.

To be clear, there is absolutely nothing wrong with what McKinsey is doing, in fact it is tremendously clever (which is what we should expect from them). To be still further clear, this phenomenon is not limited to McKinsey, but their validation (courtesy of their actions) is significant, and they are graciously being forthright about their strategy and tactics (they actively publish on this very topic).

2025 was often termed the year of Agentic AI, of Agentification, and their numbers deployed are, we can safely assume, growing each day. Satisfied "employers" of Agentic AI team members can instantly clone them or make subtle modifications to further align them to a new or more nuanced role, leveraging the ability to ramp up their deployment quite rapidly. From the perspective of a business operator, one can innately recognize the value of having teammates who follow direction and are attentive to their scope of responsibility precisely, and who work

24/7. Their contributions are likely impressive, suggesting a "bright future" for the new virtual workforce. **However, the contributions of Agentic AI instances will of course become more fully realized once they become taxpaying members of our labor force.**

One could draw parallels between the potential impact of Agentic AI and the impact of globalization on our labor force in the latter part of the 20th century. At a very high-level globalization resulted in job loss concurrent with new job creation within America. Some industry sub-sectors decreased or disappeared while others were created or increased in numbers. Overall, total employment increased—inclusive of the continuing job shift out of manufacturing and into services, per capita GDP increased, but inequality widened.

The difference with Agentic AI is that the historical pattern of job creation offsetting job loss assumed labor input was still required somewhere in the production process—albeit even in a different country. With agents that can be cloned at near-zero additional cost and deployed near instantly, that assumption does not apply. The inherent capacity or deployable potential of Agentic AI appears to be near infinite (hence the IUB reference earlier). Agentic AI represents the ultimate "capital light" expansion of productive capacity — near-zero new capital required, near-immediate instantiation. This is unprecedented in economic history, and it will drive change.

11. The Reincarnation of Henry Ford...Dark Factories, where L = 0

In the history of the evolution of manufacturing, Henry Ford and his Highland Park continuously moving assembly line in 1913 marked the dawn of mass production. He reinvented manufacturing, effectively exploiting Adam Smith's concept of specialization to the *n*th degree, creating an inflection point that came to define the 20th century. Though countless innovations since have pushed along successive evolution and best practices in manufacturing, one can now easily imagine that the dawn of the "dark factory" era marks yet another such inflection point.

There is surprisingly little discussion regarding this recent phenomenon, surprisingly little acclaim, at least in the US, but it would not be hyperbole to view the advent of "dark factories" as transformational. To channel Eric Schmidt: dark factories are probably being under-hyped.

To be fair, dark factories aren't for everyone or for every manufacturing application. The capex (level of capital expenditures) necessary to create such a facility requires tremendous scale in output, and is best suited for mass production, meaning high unit volumes with a high level of repetitive tasks. It does however provide very predictable quality control and accuracy along with lower unit production costs. In that it is predicated upon an "Industrial Internet of Things" (IIoT) manufacturing environment, various smart factory applications and presumed Agentic AI production monitoring and supervision, it currently represents the apex of digital manufacturing. It also looks to be a modern-day manifestation of fierce competition.

A factory with 24/7 output of low cost of production, high quality products would have a good chance of becoming a global quality and price leader. While both German and American automobile factories are purportedly well along in their development and application of "smart factory" techniques, the specter of Xiaomi or BYD (in China) exporting dark factory produced EVs is likely a terrifying prospect.

By its current definition, a dark factory implies robotic production, robotic assembly lines, agentic supervision and quality control, operating 24/7 with "lights out", meaning no human presence is necessary. These factories are not necessarily populated with "humanoid" style robots, moreover mostly with stationary 4 or 6 axes robots along assembly lines and conveyors, much like modern world factories except at each point on the production line it is a robotic mechanism performing the specific, high-precision task needed, repeatedly, 24/7.

We can characterize somewhat "old school" but definitively productive 4- and 6-axis robotics, which are presently the workhorses of most factory robotic installations, as follows:

4-axis: highly specialized for high-speed, horizontal (X-Y plane) movements, with one controlled vertical (Z-axis) motion and a final rotation. Their design supports speed and accuracy.

6-axis: offers increased dexterity and flexibility, mimicking the range of motion of a human arm. It has six degrees of freedom, allowing the end-tool or manipulator to reach any point in its workspace at any angle or orientation.

How does this relate to the topic at hand of diminution of the US labor force and coincident structural decline in tax revenue? It relates in three ways: 1) the demographically induced decline in our labor force will likely leave us with a shortage of qualified factory workers, 2) absence of robotics in American factories will likely represent a cost *disadvantage*, since the all-in cost of a robot (over a robot's lifespan) is generally less than for a human worker, plus a robot can work 3 shifts a day, suggesting greater than a 3:1 cost advantage; and 3) the need to scale-up our development and production of factory robots links *again* to our need for a strong (and well-populated) STEM workforce.

This latest manifestation of "Physical AI", the impact of robotics in manufacturing, was reported in Vietnamese journal VN Express, in their July 30, 2025 article *"No lights, no workers: AI-powered 'dark factories' are reshaping China's manufacturing."*

Which reports…" China is accelerating the rollout of fully automated "dark factories", where production continues non-stop without lighting, human workers or shift changes."

In 2024, Chinese tech firm Xiaomi launched an 81,000-square-meter facility, about the size of 11 football fields, that operates 24/7 without any human presence. The plant, which cost 2.4 billion yuan (US$330 million), has the capacity to produce 10 million smartphones annually. The factory is part of Xiaomi's HyperIMP smart manufacturing platform, which uses an AI-driven ecosystem that allows machines to think, adapt and optimize independently. Xiaomi CEO and founder Lei Jun said in a video clip shared on social media: "There are 11 production lines. 100% of the key processes are automated. We developed our entire production and manufacturing software to achieve this."

The AI software capability described in the VN Express article implies deployment of agentic AI systems with recursive learning—continuously refining operational strategies through real-world feedback loops. As we review in chapter 15, Xiaomi's AI model development ability is now among the top-tier in China, thus their ability to conceptualize and structure the complex agentic robotic environment facilitating dark factory operation. Manufacturing environments like Xiaomi's dark factory can help optimize production processes through iterative learning from operational data, representing a sophisticated level of industrial AI implementation. China's progress in applied AI, particularly in manufacturing automation, demonstrates relative competitive advancement and implies that in manufacturing applications of AI, they may be well-ahead of the US.

Figure 25: The IIoT Stack, enabling the Dark Factory, Author specification.

Infrequently discussed but foundationally enabling, the Industrial Internet of Things (IIoT) is considered the necessary platform for automated and smart factories. Its origins go back to the late 20th century, but it really came to prominence via the emergence of the cloud platform, permitting intra-company connectivity, in about 2012.

Xiaomi also has a 720,000-square-meter (178 acre) electric vehicle factory in the Beijing Economic-Technological Development Area, also known as Beijing E-Town. The facility, built in 2023, produces the SU7 electric sedan. "A new vehicle rolls off the production line every 76 seconds with over 700 robots operating around the clock", according to *China Daily*. "Robotic arms perform high-precision tasks with few workers in sight."

Some takeaways from this are that robots can work 24/7, suggesting a unique ROI (return on investment), and that like in the US, top ideas attract capital for investment. While Chinese capital markets are certainly different and smaller compared to their U.S. counterparts, one interesting characteristic is that since often meaningful funding may come from the province level, this can create an interesting home-market competitive dynamic until the losers' face extinction or consolidation. Dark factories may indeed prove to be a "killer app". The US will have to reckon with this sooner than later when it comes to cost competitiveness and possibly even consistency in quality of manufactured goods. Note that this scenario implies an Agentic AI entity supervising a robotic "labor force".

The Xiaomi story serves to illustrate the competitive landscape of modern global manufacturing and pose the obvious question: are we (America) ready? Our current ranking of 8th globally in robot density in manufacturing cannot remain unchanged if manufacturing is to thrive once again in the U.S. Logically, this is what bringing manufacturing back to America might entail, as we certainly *do not* have an abundance of potential low-cost, or semi-skilled, or even skilled factory workers, and many that we do have will be retiring in the very near future as described in our demographic overview. Thus, for both demographic and competitive reasons, we need increased competency in robotic manufacturing.

American Factory Workers Age Up and Out of the Labor Force

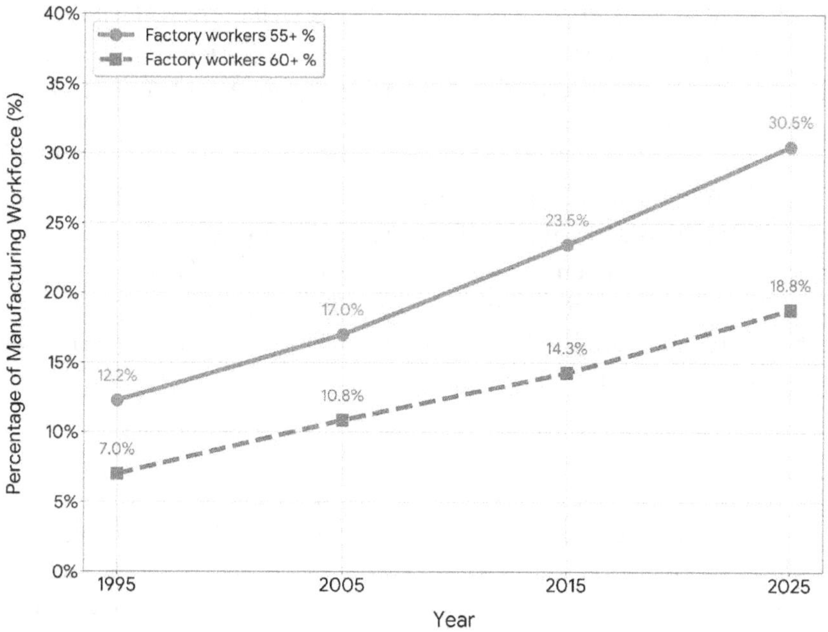

Figure 26: U.S. factory workers age 55+ and 60+ cohort percent of total

Note: Data sources BLS 2025, BEA 2025, OMB 2025, McKinsey 2024, OMB 2025.

For now, Xiaomi's dark factory enters history as a 21st century equivalent of the 20th century's "Sputnik moment".

Xiaomi, the company highlighted in this article and Lei Jun, its founder and CEO, were once—among other promising companies—considered the "Apple of China" due to their smart phone (Android based) development and marketing—with their Apple-esque retail presence, and their core competencies of software development and design. Apple was previously mooted to be developing an "Apple EV". Xiaomi has just brought this very notion to life, launching its new "YU7" EV - SUV at a special showing in Beijing in June 2025, receiving 200,000 orders within 3 minutes. As they were obliged to quote one year for delivery due to the unexpected demand for their product, they are likely now all-in on expanding capacity presumably via additional "dark factories".

In chapter 6 we reviewed the chronology of production functions, and the arc of human input dropping from 100% to something much, much less. Dark factories arguably introduce an even further evolution—even a hard re-set—in the production function, one in which potentially $L = 0$. We present this as a figurative end-point to our Arc of the Production Function (chapter 6) in which the Agrarian-era production function was $Y = L$, with the opposite side of the arc resulting in $L = 0$.

We previously updated the production function to reflect the impact of AI, by introducing the four-factor AI-era production function. Logically, when the input of L transitions to *0*, courtesy of the arrival of dark factories, it necessitates a further update still. We therefore introduce the Dark Factory-era production function, reflecting the transition of L to 0.

$$Y = A(t) \cdot K^{\alpha} \cdot (AI)^{\gamma} \text{ (where } \alpha + \gamma > 1)$$

In which case "beta", and in effect, Labor, or L as an input is equivalent to zero, and thus absent from the equation. In which case output continues, likely even increases—courtesy of the IUB of AI, but without human input or human share of income.

Which therefore poses the **fiscal policy version of an existential question: "Now, whom do we tax?"**

12. *Creative Destruction Redux: AI as a Change Accelerant*

We agree with those who have said that 2025 was the year of "Agentic AI" and will posit that 2026 will be the year of "Creative Destruction", courtesy of AI.

The simplest way to look at AI and its related workforce automation is that at its core, AI is Austrian economist Schumpeter's theory of creative destruction (1942) brought back to life in a "turbocharged" manifestation. We are living, real-time, a somewhat accelerated version of it compared to the history of this concept. Perhaps it is therefore fitting that the recently announced (Q4 2025) Nobel Prize in Economics recognized research in the impact of "innovation-driven economic growth," with specifically the theory of sustained growth through "creative destruction".

The recipients' (Professors Mokyr, Aghion and Howitt) research broadly focused on "innovation-driven economic growth," with specific recognition for the theory of sustained growth through creative destruction. Dr. Mokyr, in an acceptance speech, pays specific credit to the fact that innovation is cumulative, that technologists and their innovations today build upon the insights of those before them. This notion of course broadly applies to near all of mankind's march of progress and innovation and AI certainly manifests this.

In Schumpeter's 1942 *Capitalism, Socialism and Democracy*, which introduces his concept of creative destruction, he wrote...

"The fundamental impulse that sets and keeps the capitalist engine in motion comes from the new consumers' goods, the new methods of production or transportation, the new markets, the new forms of industrial organization that capitalist enterprise create…illustrate the same process of industrial mutation …that incessantly revolutionizes the economic structure from within, incessantly destroying the old one, incessantly creating a new one. This process of Creative Destruction is the essential fact about capitalism."

A simplistic way to view AI is that we are now about to enter the 3rd phase of its development, which will mark the beginning of its presumably vast commercialization, deployment and adoption.

Phase 1 was the period of research and development of its concept and its potential—from early pioneers such as Alan Turing to Marvin Minsky to latter day ones such as Geoffrey Hinton, and the computer science related innovations and foundations, such as machine learning, deep learning, neural network discovery upon which AI is predicated.

Phase 2 marks the recent Generative AI era in which "AI factories", as Jensen Huang calls them, are being built. This includes everything we are increasingly surrounded by today…from GPUs to CUDA networking software, to transformer architecture, to foundational models such as LLMs and the data centers and the companies that bring all of this to life, from Google Deep Mind to Open AI, to Anthropic, to Meta to Deep Seek, etc. It has also been the age of creation of AI as a platform.

Phase 3 will commence the vast commercialization of AI, leveraging AI as a new platform with applications and manifestations that we can both imagine and not possibly imagine at this date. The presumably rapid-fire sequence of these new applications coming online and replacing existing ones will cause us to experience an accelerated, 21st century version of "creative destruction". We've arrived at the inflection point where the AI platform is robust enough for new applications (both AI-Native and AI enhanced versions of existing applications) to emerge, in which many will likely prosper and some come to dominate their "verticals".

What the AI-era will mean is that there will not only be the workforce disruption we have discussed thus far but also disruption at the company level, meaning some existing companies will be "destroyed" and new ones will be "created", with likely every imaginable metamorphosis in between. Drivers of this will perhaps be **most robust in the AI Application sector as AI-Native applications emerge** and inevitably replace or outmuscle existing functional applications. Logically, many existing applications will make a successful transition from pre-AI to the new AI rich environment protect their market share while enhancing their functionality, but it is likely the newly emergent cohort of AI-native companies will prove to be the most disruptive.

The following "AI Applications Stack" depiction is intended to illustrate the sequence of events and fundamental accomplishments and building blocks that have brought us to this point, as well as to suggest the near-term next steps in the commercial evolution of AI.

Figure 27: The AI Application Stack 2026, Author specification

These new applications and processes may be innovations from existing companies or from new "AI-Native" companies. Many of these are already emerging. Many are already demonstrating tremendous promise, even at these early days, with we can expect more to come.

In considering the internet era and the Internet Stack below we can see by comparison the foundational components that helped facilitate the growth, expansion and shape of the world we live and work within today. We can also see clearly that in terms of massive value creation, the application layer companies were the clear winners. (There are no guarantees that the presumed Application Layer will come to dominate the AI Stack, but it would be foolish to not consider this as an outcome given the prior events we can learn from via the emergence of the Internet Stack Application companies from over the last 1-3 decades.) We can assess that as far as development today we are in the realm of the top two stacks in the above graphic: AI-enhanced applications are increasingly prevalent and AI-Native applications are in early-stage emergence.

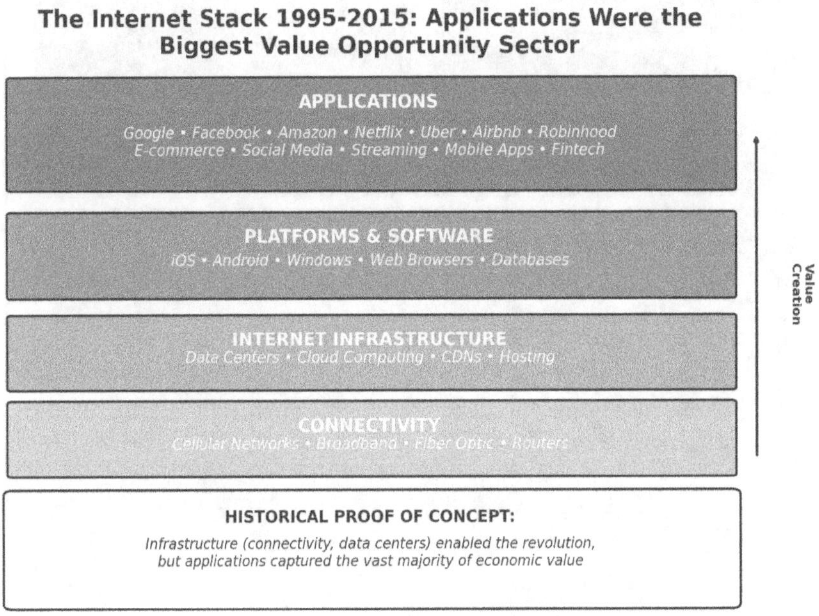

Figure 28: The Internet Stack, Author specification

Does the "old stack" give way to the "new stack"? History suggests "yes". History also affirms that this is what creative destruction is all about.

In considering lessons from the recent history of the internet transformation to better understand the potential transformative impact of AI, one can assume the emergence of AI as a platform—and that this would enable a new generation of applications and access to new functionalities.

Three decades ago, in the "client-server-based" software era, large corporations would purchase software (licenses) and install it on their own servers and distribute it to their internal users, each with their own desktop. Allowing company wide use of the specific software or operating system in this model could be characterized as capital intensive and even cumbersome. Companies needed IT departments and capex budgets up to the scale of this task. Although Salesforce, founded by former Oracle VP Marc Benioff in 1999, was the first notable SaaS (software as a service) company, one could say it was the advent of IaaS (infrastructure as a service) a.k.a. "cloud computing" as a platform, pioneered by Amazon's AWS (Amazon Web Services) in 2006 that facilitated the eventual large-scale adoption of subscription-based (SaaS) software.

This led to a momentous transition in how software was purchased and distributed. Its innovation was allowing smaller companies, often start-ups, to acquire use of software formerly off-limits to them due to the up-front costs involved. This, along with the innovation of "cloud computing" proved seismic, and so-to-speak "democratized" access to technology, to software, to computation and storage in a heretofore off-limits manner, a transition which was logically beneficial to productivity, and aided in the process of new company formation.

There is thusly an argument to be made that AI as a platform ("AIaaS" or AI-powered SaaS) will prove to be similarly "enabling" in creation of a new generation of applications, Native AI or others that will dominate this new era.

The other expected feature of our near future economy will be of increased rates of productivity. Businesses and entrepreneurs discover new uses for AI, new applications, new solutions to old challenges…as our media reminds us on a near daily basis. Our media seems to convey non-stop stories from business leaders regarding the output generated by a handful of Agentic instances they have engaged for specific projects or in specific domains. This is fundamentally creative destruction at its core: new technologies and processes and business entities emerging that are more efficient, more productive, more cost-effective and feature-rich relative to those from the last cycle.

Logically, some of the new iterations will prosper and the less relevant, less efficient will suffer and often simply cease to exist. AI, as a change accelerant, will accelerate this process. The good thing about creative destruction, at least as evident from prior history, is that the "create" part of the equation far outweighs the "destruct" part. Meaning, net of a sometimes-jagged transition, we have come out ahead in each instance, at least cumulatively.

Qualified spokespeople, such as Stanford's Andrew Ng, Adjunct Professor for CS and AI and more, speak to this acceleration and remark how quickly, by leveraging AI, one can develop prototypes of new applications, new business concepts. His point, in so many words is: develop the new business idea quickly, "vet" it, and then either decide to kill it or modify it if it fails or launch it if shows promise. Most importantly, there is no need to drag out the development process. His message in so many words is: don't wait, use these new tools to accelerate the business development process (which is likely both a brilliant and insightful message).

The above-described encapsulation of creative destruction has been "bench tested" by the human experience over centuries. One can imagine the road ahead may be bumpy for some, exhilarating for others and likely accelerated for all. But, if history is our guide, a promising outcome is around the corner.

One domain which is highly anticipated to experience (the benefits of) creative destruction is medical research and health care in general. Health diagnosis is expected to experience augmentation and, in some cases, automated discovery of new treatments, heightened accuracy and diminution of errors via robotic surgery and AI-tech augmenting bio-tech drug discovery are some of the imagined advances, some of which are likely to be realized.

In a November 16, 2025, interview with CNN's Anderson Cooper, Dario Amodei (CEO Anthropic) posited the following regarding his vision of a "compressed 21st century", which summarizes the potential medical impact of AI, and impact of AI in general on critical scientific and medical research, in an inspiring manner. "The idea would be, at the point that we can get the AI systems to this level of power where they're able to work with the best human scientists, could we get 10 times the rate of progress and therefore compress all the medical progress that was going to happen throughout the entire 21st century in five or 10 years?" And accordingly, "bring forward" medical revelations that would occur over the course of the entire 21st century into the present decade. (We must compliment Mr. Amodei for describing nothing short of an inspiring vision.)

The secret behind rapid development and commercialization of new ideas will be that AI makes it easy, requires fewer human staff, and therefore costs less on the front end. It can be said to reduce "friction". These phenomena—collectively, will result in an acceleration of new business creation and a lower development cost per instance. In so doing AI will amplify leverage: one person, a small team, a lean company will be able to do more with less. In which case, the amplified leverage enabled by AI will amplify productivity.

Productivity increases bring mostly good news. The creative destruction part—of job loss or the unpredictability of job transformation, company closures, all in their way suggest a difficult transition, with potential pain being felt by those directly affected. It will also bring, again using a narrow economic lens, increased profitability for companies experiencing increased productivity, which will bring increased earnings retention, which will bring increased investment, which will bring additional new company formation, and increased demand.

Productivity increases, just like new business development, generally occur overtime, increment by increment, quarter by quarter, not overnight. Equally, one must keep in mind that a very "real" part of the creative destruction process is that today's leaders may not be tomorrow's winners. The internet era taught us this; regardless of capital deployment company by company. From an investor perspective, risk management 101 reminds us that a diversified set of holdings—even within the same industry sector—is generally a more prudent bet than a concentrated bet. In the U.S., as in China, the early-stage era is often characterized as a crowded competitive field. With the best ideas, best companies, most-promising industry sectors usually finding success.

In the AI industry, it may look like the leaders are clear, that market share and functional lines are by now clearly drawn. We beg to differ, and suggest that history teaches us the contrary: that some current leaders will prevail, some may slip slightly, others may be subsumed by newer "creations" that renders them obsolete, other AI-Natives, not yet known to us, will likely emerge. Beneath the seemingly calm surface, there is likely fierce competition, segment by segment, with perhaps semi-seismic events still to occur with regularity. The amount of invested capital at stake makes it even more captivating. We are witnessing accelerated creative destruction real-time, often with high levels of incongruity and unexpected disruption.

We review below two examples of creative destruction that each came from wholly unexpected origins, or followed unexpected paths to market—each seemingly more academic or theoretical than commercial in origin—and explore the incongruities and disruption in product development they brought to bear.

In 2017 the Google Brain team released the research paper on the training and inference concept known as MoE (chapter 15) *Outrageously Large Neural Networks: The Sparsely-Gated Mixture-of-Experts*

Layer (January 2017). Apparently, this bit of genius was overlooked until—when years later—French AI company Mistral embedded this approach (MoE) into their "Mixtral" model, released late 2023. It was one year later (late 2024) when Chinese model DeepSeek shook the AI world with their V-3 model, exhibiting rapid inference with a much lower training budget, premised on—among other factors—Google's MoE.

Fast-forward a few years to late 2025 and Chinese MoE based models enjoy a growing U.S. market (chapter 17). This is occurring both through Chinese-based APIs and US-based resellers of the big four Chinese MoE models (Qwen, DeepSeek, Kimi, and MiniMax), via US-located resellers using private or 3rd party data centers, in each case offering a lower cost product. Thus, in the case of MoE as a driver of "creative destruction" it travelled across not only time (6 years) but also geography, as it was a uniquely U.S. innovation exploited first by a French and secondarily Chinese companies.

In Q1 2026, we have seen—premised on the recent Agentic AI revolution—the introduction by Austrian Peter Steinberger, of an open source, downloadable "personal agent" known as "OpenClaw" that—in its early days broke all prior download and adoption records. Its unique attribute is that it can, in almost any environment, even on one's own personal computer (assuming certain memory and processor capacities), mobile phone or within your downloaded model—or even via your closed model's OpenClaw application, exhibit an Agentic supervisory role. One can communicate with it directly through one's WhatsApp or WeChat account—a channel that not only provides ease of access but allows the user to maintain "state" 24/7.

It brings with it certain "security risks" as it is given access to everything on your computer. No matter: its rate of end-user adoption has quickly broken all precedents, including those set by ChatGPT. At Nvidia's GTC event in March 2026, when Jensen Huang was introducing their extension of "NemoClaw" he posited that it is now incumbent upon every CEO to ask and understand what their company's OpenClaw strategy is. By all accounts, OpenClaw came entirely "out-of-the blue", a "textbook" example of the relenting and disruptive nature of creative destruction.

It has long been said, that necessity is the "mother of invention". This was evident in multiple instances of innovation in the Industrial Revolution. A hallmark of creative destruction, however, has also been that innovation often comes from quarters—or participants—from which we least expect it. Several of the examples noted above are all examples of this. The genius within the Google Brain papers we refer to were apparently left on the drawing room floor for five and six years respectively until they were brought to market by individual "geniuses" who saw their value. As for OpenClaw: before December 2025 Peter Steinberger was an independent IOS entrepreneur working in Austria; not a possibly pivotal figure in AI evolution. Since its release, not only does it have very high adoption rates, but within a few weeks after its release it has been integrated or added to numerous models and applications, with more in progress. In other words, many may choose to react to this sliver of genius; whereas other may feel "forced to react" to protect their relevance and share.

A final point: February 25, 2026 saw the introduction by Nous Research of the Hermes Agent, which contains several notable advancements relative to` OpenClaw. These enhancements are fundamental improvements: the ability of the agent to implement recursive self-improvement and the ability to maintain "state". A vivid, near real-time example of creative destruction.

This is what technology industry incumbents and existing AI leaders must always be cognizant of: Who's next, or what's next? Meaning, what company or what product may be about to come after my company's market share? We are about to enter the thick of AI-era creative destruction; in fact, it is still very early days. It is instructive to keep in mind that in the earlier internet era Yahoo once was the *de facto* search leader; then Google happened.

13. AI-related gains in Productivity will be Disinflationary

Although U.S. productivity has shown meaningful increases the past several quarters, as of yet there is little empirical evidence affirming the linkage between AI adoption and productivity, and between AI and disinflation. The Fed and macroeconomists, the BLS and BEA are—we can expect—following these developments closely. The following commentary is therefore based on applying simple economic theory to the observable forces at this time.

To explain this phenomenon of AI as a driver of disinflation we will lean into what we will call "reverse-Friedman" logic. Nobel Laureate Milton Friedman was a master of the economic school of thought known as "monetarism", with the majority of his breakthrough studies occurring in the 1960's. He famously defined inflation as "always and everywhere a monetary phenomenon", a more definitive framing than prior characterizations of inflation as a result of "too much money chasing too few goods." These remain two of the most intuitive explanations to this day, if one visualizes an equilibrium of supply and demand, with a perfect balance resulting in price stability. Supply, demand and price factor equally into understanding this equilibrium.

When supply and demand are in balance (in equilibrium) we have price stability. If demand is greater than supply, then the price of said good will increase as a method of "re-equilibrating"; if supply is greater than demand, then price also re-equilibrates, but downward, as the price becomes lower. This is the simple law of supply and demand, with price as the change agent that enables re-equilibration.

But there is also another mechanism in cases of supply-demand imbalance by which to restore equilibrium, and that is by changes in either supply or demand, as the mechanism by which to re-equilibrate. Economic history is full of cases of price changes as a result of increases or decreases in supply, in fact, in economics inflation is often described as being either "supply-side" or "demand-side" driven.

During the early stages of Russia's war on Ukraine, blockades or embargoes on Russian oil exports caused supply shortages resulting in global increases in the price of oil. Ukraine's inability to export wheat resulted in global supply shortages of wheat and related price increases.

(We refer to empirical research on this topic by Ben Bernanke and Olivier Blanchard in their 2023, *What Caused the Pandemic Era Inflation?* which demonstrated this cause and effect and in large part explains the Covid-era inflation that swept the world.)

Today's AI-productivity-driven disinflationary impulses are premised on what we refer to as 1) "reverse-Friedman" logic and 2) changes in the production function, as described in the work of Nobel Laureate Robert Solow (who was a contemporary of Friedman). Friedman's belief that inflation is always and everywhere a result of the supply of money (M2) directly translates into M2 increases facilitating increased consumption, and M2 decreases facilitating decreased consumption—the former being inflationary, the latter disinflationary. This is often characterized as "demand-side" inflation, influenced by the macro level stimulative or contractionary impact on demand by changes in money supply.

Much of Friedman's work was influenced by the Quantity Theory of Money, dating back to 16th, 18th and 19th century economists. By demonstrating turnover (velocity) of money was generally stable, he was able to explain the impact of changes in M2 on inflation, with price as the change agent. The intuitively equal but opposite side of his framework was the impact of changes in supply on inflation, again via price as the change agent. In Econ, this is often expressed by Irving Fisher's 1911 MV=PQ (money supply, velocity, price level, output) framework.

In the AI-era, reverse-Friedman logic refers to changes in inflation or disinflation that are driven by changes in the supply-side (not the demand-side) via the production function, influencing output or "supply". If output grows or contracts due to evolution of the production function, as exhibited by changes in the contributions of labor, capital, Solow's TFP residual or AI—assuming constancy in size and in velocity of M2, then equilibration comes from the opposite side of the framework than Friedman emphasized—from changes in "supply", not changes in demand.

In chapter 6 we refer to Solow's theory of the production function and the concept of Total Factor Productivity (TFP), which says increases in output unattributable to increases in capital and or labor are a) less readily apparent and thus captured as a residual, and b) are the result of technological improvements categorized as gains in TFP. Equally, we refer to our introduction of the AI-era four-factor production function, in which AI as a cognitive input factor gradually supplants L—and drives increasing returns to scale.

Thus, **the impact of AI on inflation will be via the production function**, which given the expected trendline of the adoption of cognitive AI should become a structural feature of the economy, and should exhibit an accelerating disinflationary impact over time. While the direct driver of this change will be the production function, the mechanism of equilibration will remain price, as all else being equal, price will decrease as increases in supply impact the supply and demand dynamic.

There is emerging data depicting AI-related Productivity increases

Q3 BLS Productivity Report: Output +5.4%; Labor input +0.5%

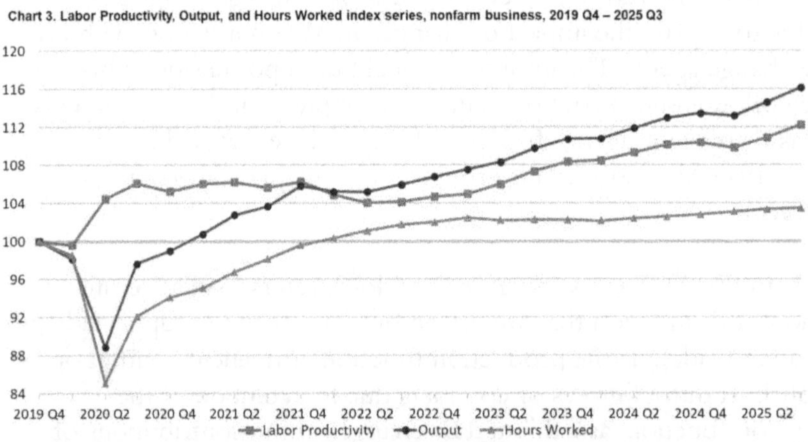

Figure 29: BLS data depicting productivity trends, released January 29, 2026

Note: BLS release showing nonfarm business sector labor productivity increased 4.9 percent Q3, output increased 5.4%, hours worked increased 0.5%.

The graph above depicting productivity increases does not assert causation, rather it depicts correlation of output vs. inputs, which per our supply vs. demand reference previously, is tantamount to either an inflationary or disinflationary impulse. (The price mechanism of re-equilibration is affected by a variety of inputs thus we cannot assert that productivity alone is disinflationary, but that it contributes to a disinflationary outcome—hence the terminology "impulse".)

A more granular perspective from BLS shows perhaps an even more impressive productivity rate trend, but with footnotes. In the graph below, the increases in Q2 and Q3 productivity (measured in output-blue bar) show sequential strength in Q2 and Q3 2025, whereas Q4 2024 shows a softer rate of growth, which economists attribute to the Boeing strike, with the Q1 2025 output dip attributed to massive imports to front-run Trump imposition of Tariffs.

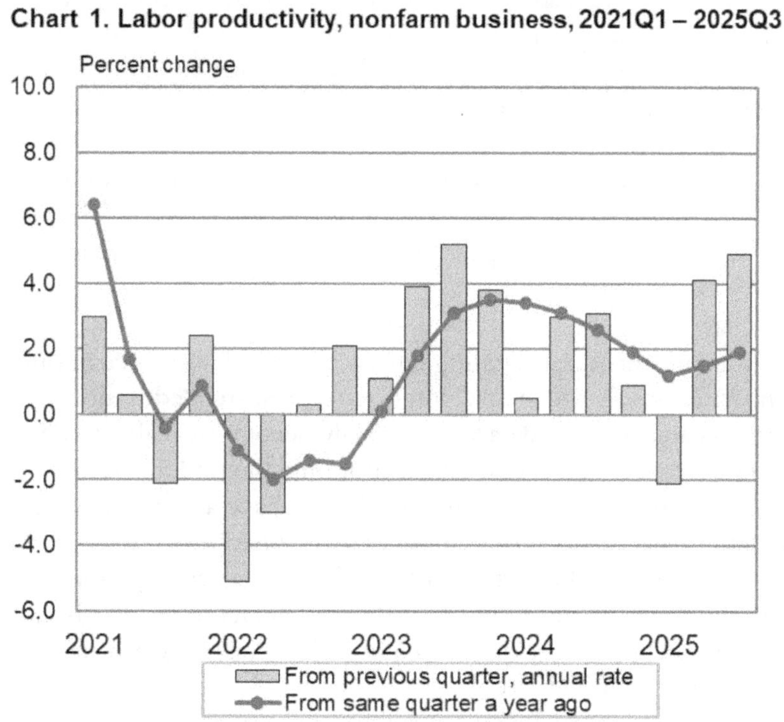

Figure 30: BLS depiction of productivity change vs. prior quarter and vs. LY; January 2026

Note: Source = BLS, their release showing nonfarm business sector labor productivity growth on a quarterly basis and in contrast to the prior year.

Thus, without these exogenous factors, productivity increases would show impressive sequential increases for 6 consecutive quarters. Therefore, absent specific attribution of causation, we can clearly observe something is beneficially affecting US rate of productivity, as the data suggests marked improvement.

Federal Reserve Vice-Chair Philip Jefferson recently reported on the growing disinflationary impact of supply-side dynamics in his February 6, 2026 presentation to the Brookings Institution *Economic Outlook and Supply-side (dis)Inflation Dynamics*, from which we present the following excerpts:

"One important development in recent years is … productivity growth in the United States … a key component of aggregate supply in the economy, appears to be notably above the growth rates observed in the decade before the pandemic. Productivity growth… is reported to have increased at an average annual rate of 2.2 percent from the start of 2020 to the third quarter of last year, notably faster than the 1.5 percent pace over the previous business cycle."

He continued "… integration of AI into production and the workplace may already be having some early effects on productivity, although most economists expect that the bulk of … productivity gains due to AI are yet to come."

The presumed accelerating emergence of AI as a force in our economy suggests that high level intelligence, research, education, solution sets and relevant data will gradually become available to an increasingly broader set of individuals, not only the traditionally privileged groups (academic, commercial) who have access today. This would definitively broaden or democratize the distribution of knowledge, similar to the impact of Solow's residual, as an enabler of growth. But it will be the addition of the fourth factor in our AI-era production function—that is AI—that will likely have the greatest influence, simply due to its IUB.

Abundance of cognition, courtesy of its commoditization, should—all other things being equal—singularly become an outsize driver of growth of productivity and therefore disinflationary impulses. The role of AI as the fourth factor in our AI-era production function will increasingly impact output, contributing without constraint due to its infinite upper bound, exponentially driving future returns to scale in the dynamic of output vs. inputs. Thus, AI cognition, by contributing to increases in the supply component of the supply demand equilibrium, as manifested by change in price, will become a structural driver of disinflation.

AI will broadly be held to be positive for gains in productivity via either a) increased output—as described above or b) via decreased employment—by virtue of job augmentation or substitution, or both. One can therefore conclude that even with a "fixed or static level of inputs" that output derived from fixed inputs will in theory increase. Therefore, like any supply-demand relationship, an increase in output and therefore supply (assuming static demand) places downward pressure on pricing, as supply would in theory exceed demand.

To visualize the impact of the commoditization of cognition on output, one can look back to the industrial revolution and recall that technological innovation resulted in the commoditization and amplification of human labor as growth in machine capacity (*K*) exponentially supplanted human output (*L*). At its core, as a transformational force, AI shares this characteristic, except that it commoditizes cognition—human thought and analysis, even human action impulses, as opposed to labor.

We can ask, over time, which has proven to generate higher value…labor or cognition? And which in theory would therefore have a greater impact on productivity, commoditization of labor or cognition?

The answer to the above rhetorical question is obvious: in the developed world, cognitive output commands far higher wages than physical labor because it generates greater value.

The **commoditization of cognition therefore represents a productivity shock of greater potential magnitude than the Industrial Revolution's commoditization of physical labor**—with greater disinflationary potential.

Therefore, a key breakthrough (perhaps *the* key breakthrough) of AI will prove to be the IUB in the generation and application of cognition via what Jensen Huang astutely refers to as "AI factories". Cognition is the primary output of these factories, with inputs of energy and compute such that advanced cognitive output—with tokens of output as the unit of measure—results in a relationship whereby *static input levels of* L + K + *A(t) along with increased levels of cognition (AI)* = *increased output.* By any definition—and in theory—this would equate to an increased rate of productivity, and increasing returns to scale.

If history is our guide, as described in our chapter on Creative Destruction, the increasingly pervasive and theoretically infinite capacity of artificial cognition will enable and indeed power the emerging layer of

AI-Native applications. These may come to manifest the greatest potential for workplace disruption, as well as disruption of the cloud-based layer of applications that have preceded them.

AI-driven reduction in the cost of intelligence (cognition) may very well prove to be the most powerful structural disinflationary force in modern history. However, as we have described throughout, **the consequence of this dynamic** will likely be that **the tax revenue from human intelligent labor is vastly reduced**, as a simple and direct consequence of AI increasingly supplanting *L*.

An historic perspective is depicted by the graph below from Federal Reserve data showing the inverse correlation between gains in productivity (rate of change vs. prior year = green line) vs. the rate of inflation (rate of change vs. prior year = blue line) over the last 65 years.

Were recent upticks in productivity to be sustained—or even increase due to AI-induced gains, with a consequence of stable or reducing rates of inflation, this would be unambiguously positive for our country's GDP growth and likely beneficial to interest rate stability or even suggest potential decreases.

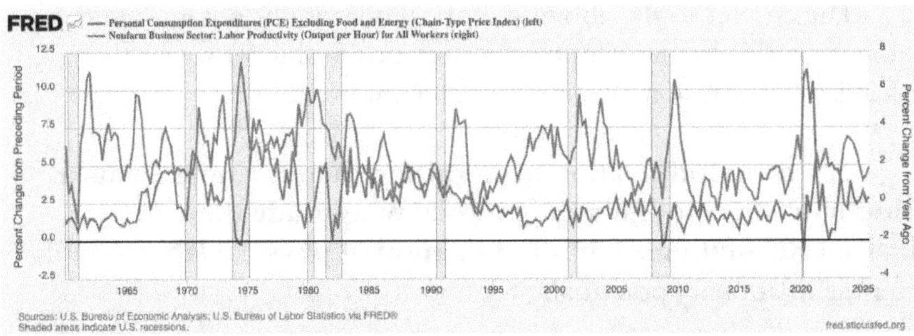

Figure 31: Gains in productivity vs. change in rate of inflation; 1960-2025, Federal Reserve data and chart. Higher productivity inversely correlated to inflation, on average.

It is easy to imagine that AI-driven reduction in the cost of intelligence and resultant productivity efficiencies should prove to be a powerful structural disinflationary factor. Such an outcome would correlate to our depiction of the arc of the production function over time, depicting the minimization of *L* as an input, from when $L = Y$ to where in the foreseeable future (rhetorically speaking) *L* will = *0*. **The evolving production function therefore becomes a proxy for the arc of modern economic history**.

As illustrated on multiple occasions, the consequence of the directionally apparent evolution of the arc of the production function will be that the tax revenue from human intelligence will be further impaired, in synchrony with the reduction of human effort as an input, with a near zero terminal point. **Which presents a macroeconomic paradox: an era of potential abundance in output concurrent to a collapsing public-sector tax base**. The implicit call to action for our Congress—whether they align our system of taxation with the economic reality of the AI era, or "kick the can down the road"—will be legacy defining.

14. *Will the Advent of AI increase Income Inequality?*

The question above could be re-stated as "do new, industry changing innovations generally lead to the accrual of disproportionate benefits to early adopters and to capital?" History suggests "yes".

Prior research has explored income inequality through various lenses: the disparity between capital returns and economic growth (Thomas Piketty), the shifting production function and capital's increasing share of output (Robert Solow and Joseph Stiglitz), and the role of interest rates (Bank of England). Benefitting from this, we focus on the now-accelerating shift in the production function as we enter the AI era (per our four-factor AI-era production function). Specifically, we examine how this shift impacts income inequality when it encounters our legacy taxation mechanism. As a result of this juxtaposition, this line of discourse offers a new way of understanding income inequality in the modern era.

To briefly recount the historical evolution (post-industrial revolution) of inequality, one could say that technological advances have favored early adopters, and that equally in terms of classical economic thought that the owners of capital disproportionately benefit. This line of reasoning goes back to 18th and 19th century economists such as Adam Smith, David Ricardo, and Karl Marx who characterized economic output as a function of the inputs of *K* and *L* (K for capital, L for labor). This was simply stated as $Y = f(K+L)$, meaning output was a function of the inputs of capital and labor. Their masterpieces, respectively *Wealth of Nations*, *Principles of Political Economy* and *Das Kapital* characterized contemporary thought as far as productivity, its inputs and the insight that wealth increasingly accrued to the owners of capital (*K*) not labor (*L*), laying the foundation for our understanding of inequality.

In the 1920s this was updated by the Cobb-Douglas function (positing that the effect of both *K* and *L* was non-linear) and then more triumphantly by MIT economist and Nobel Laureate Robert Solow who in 1957 demonstrated that allowing for advances in and application of technology provided a more accurate picture of increasingly dramatic improvements in output. This came to be known as Solow's "A" ("*A*" being a term within his production function) or Solow's "residual", with his concept of TFP (total factor productivity), representing the benefits of (heretofore unmeasurable) accrued technology in addition to *K+L*, becoming pivotal in the evolution of economic thought. What these had in common was that they demonstrated the reduction in the share of output attributable to *L*, and therefore the reduction in the share of income received by *L*. What they did not do was correlate this shift to changes in share of taxation.

Therefore, what these production function-focused studies illuminate— including our own in chapter 6—is the protracted diminishment of the share of *L* in output, juxtaposed to the increasing tax burden levied against *L*, and what this reveals about the structural drivers of income inequality. This fundamental incongruity can only be interpreted as the diminishing retained earnings or wealth which accrued to *L*. As we cite earlier in our Arc of the Production Function (chapter 6) and as we now correlate specifically to income inequality, the consequence of this incongruous outcome is cumulatively consequential and under-recognized in policy discourse. Further, courtesy of the role of AI, as noted in our "AI era four-factor production function" this disparity is set to widen, not narrow—certainly not stabilize.

These divergent, protracted trendlines—diminishment in share of income allocated to *L* vs. increase in tax burden levied against *L*—are helpful in understanding not just our present fiscal fragility but in understanding income inequality. To illustrate this theme of the impact over time of the divergence of these trendlines we insert below a histogram depicting their juxtaposition taken from our chapter 6, Arc of the Production Function.

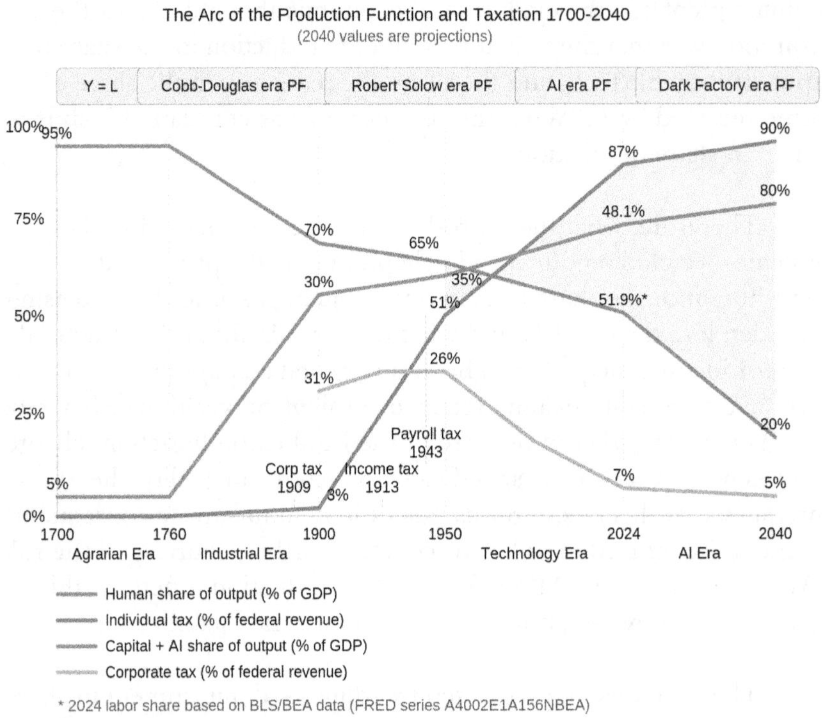

Figure 32: The Arc of the Production Function juxtaposed to the Arc of Taxation in America

Note: Data from multiple government sources: BLS, BEA, IRS, Federal Reserve, compiled per author specification for illustration purposes, depicting best-estimate output vs taxation history.

The cautionary tale that should be evident to all is that no one in our country, no one in our government, should be "caught off-guard" by the potential for adverse social impacts stemming from the AI revolution, its economic transformation and the implicit prospect of increased income inequality. We can ask, as a consequence of projected job dislocation 1) will unemployment, even transitionally, increase? 2) will job dislocation and transformation occur, creating an imperative for workers to broaden their skill set, including retraining for new careers, and 3) will income inequality increase? The answers to the above, it seems safe to say are "yes", "yes" and "most likely".

While not a treatise on income inequality there are a set of historically persistent occurrences within the U.S. that correlate to shifts in inequality. For example, it is evident that periods of slow economic growth generally correlate to income inequality increases, whereas periods of above trend rate of GDP growth correlate to periods of decline in inequality. (Inequality is typically measured via the Gini coefficient index—since about 1963 the universally recognized unit of measure—plotted along a "Lorenz" curve against a theoretical line of perfect equality.) The graph below depicts the inverse relationship between increase in growth and increase in inequality.

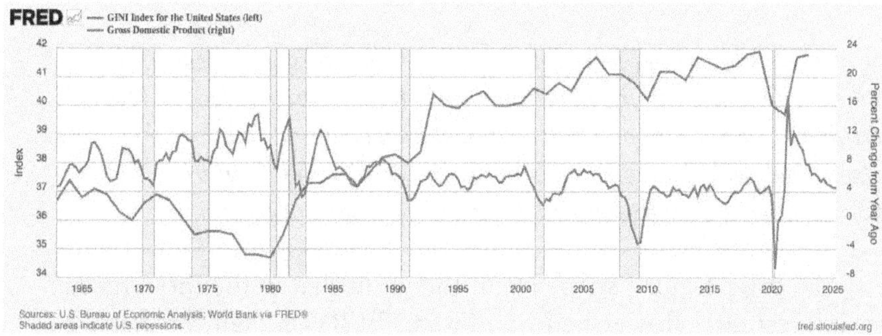

Figure 33: Gini index vs GDP, Federal Reserve Chart, Author's specification

Note. Data sourced and aggregated via the Federal Reserve Economic Data (FRED) platform. GDP data from the U.S. Bureau of Economic Analysis (BEA); Gini Index data from the BEA and World Bank.

Although it is difficult to generalize with respect to drivers of inequality, we can observe that changes in the U.S. tax code over the last 4 decades have facilitated the emergence of an "ownership class", those who do vs. those who do not own assets. Data suggests—by correlation—that owners of assets seem to disproportionately benefit by periods of low interest rates (as seen frequently in the 21st century, post 9/11, post GFC, post Covid). Low interest rates have a history of uniformly correlating to increases in asset valuations (see NPV below) which generally correlate to periods of low GDP growth.

In the U.S., a reduction in the "capital gains" tax rate (for assets held longer than one year) to 20% in 1997 (Taxpayer Relief Act) has been instrumental in allowing the "ownership class" to enjoy higher rates of compounding on their investments relative to non-asset owning American taxpayers, thereby exacerbating income inequality. Without asserting causality, we can unreservedly cite the obvious correlation between the advent of lower tax rates for capital gains in the U.S. with the era of dramatic widening of income inequality, post the brief economic recession of 1990, per the Federal Reserve depiction above.

This mechanism is direct: when capital gains are taxed at 20% vs labor income rates reaching 37%, our tax code rewards wealth accumulation over wages concurrent to the protracted shift in economic returns from *L* to *K*, as evident in the evolution of the production function. For decades, *L* increasingly received less in income yet paid a higher relative statutory taxation rate than *K*.

The author wishes to acknowledge that he has personally benefitted from capital gains taxation and from participation in the "ownership class". Thus, the perspective regarding the impact of the misallocation of our tax burden on our fiscal situation is not borne from personal grievance or "class unrest" but from simple analysis illuminating the fiscally destabilizing role of our tax policy.

To offer a quick snapshot of the point that in the modern-era, lower interest rates (lower Fed Fund Rates FFR) generally correlate to increases in asset values, with the opposite also holding true, we include data from our Federal Reserve to broadly illustrate this. As is well known, our Fed typically lowers FFR in times of sluggish or negative economic growth and raises them in periods of strength. This also in part explains why income inequality has grown in times of slow economic growth, as lower interest rates correlate to elevated asset prices, thereby benefitting the "ownership class".

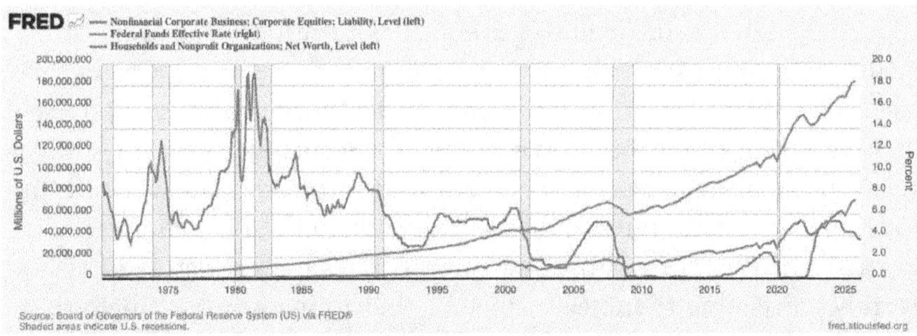

Figure 34: FFR (green) and its inverse relation to asset valuations (red, blue)

Note: FRED Federal Reserve data and graph creation.

The other, more orthodox way to understand the relationship between lower interest rates and higher asset valuations is via basic finance, and the concept of "net present value" (NPV)—as briefly referenced above. NPV—a fundamental asset modeling tool from basic finance—holds that decreases in interest rates imply an increase in future cash flows from any given asset, validating a higher valuation with dynamic asset markets responding in near real time. This rapid reaction by asset markets to changes in interest rates is mirrored by changes in home valuations, for example, as lower interest rates allow buyers to afford "more" house, exhibiting upward pressure on home valuations. This relationship was center-stage during the recent pandemic, as interest rates decreased, home valuations famously escalated.

Income inequality has received substantial scholarly attention over the past seven decades. Our contribution, as noted above, is to connect three distinct phenomena: analysis related to the evolution of the production function, the declining share of income enjoyed by *L*, and the wholly divergent trend of the increasing share of taxation levied against *L*. The consequence of which has clearly been lower "retained earnings" (after-tax income) by the individual taxpayer and higher retained earnings by the "ownership class" and by (owners of capital) corporations.

There is in some quarters significant optimism surrounding the emergence of AI as it relates to a so-called "Abundance Hypothesis". This line of optimism—that AI will lead to widespread abundance—has been articulated by AI "thought leaders" such as Sam Altman, Peter Diamandis and in 2026 by the Milken Institute Review, "AI and Abundance". In a recent conference in Saudi Arabia, FII9 (October 2025) featuring notable AI figures Fei-Fei Li of Stanford and Eric Schmidt, formerly of Google, addressed the topic of abundance by saying that although AI would be" democratizing". Mr. Schmidt added that there was significant precedent for the benefits or rewards of technology breakthroughs not being broadly distributed.

"Abundance hypothesis" holds that the benefits of AI will lead to productivity increases such *that mankind broadly speaking realizes these benefits in terms of access to necessary goods, increased leisure time, and that reducing the marginal cost of intelligence-based work will dramatically reduce the need for work requiring human intelligence, that is diminished need for human input.*

The abundance hypothesis could be said to present a somewhat utopian, or at least unproven, view of the future—where the marginal cost of intelligence reduces to near zero, unlocking unprecedented medical, scientific, and material wealth. However, as Eric Schmidt—and historical precedent—both caution, capitalism does not natively distribute the benefits of innovation evenly. Left to its own devices, this new abundance will logically continue to flow to the owners of capital and compute infrastructure (correlating to our updated production function), driving the Gini coefficient higher as the input of human labor and intelligence is diminished, with the corresponding human share of output also reduced.

Thus, to answer the question we pose to open this chapter: Will the advent of AI increase income inequality? After consideration of the evolution of the production function, which illustrates that AI will further diminish both human input and share of output, alongside a review of our legacy system of taxation which persistently advantages our corporate sector while disadvantaging the individual taxpayer, barring legislation that reverses our misallocation of the tax burden, we see no other outcome than continued increases in income inequality.

Abundance alone does not guarantee wisdom or sensible policy. The Industrial Revolution led to unprecedented material abundance—yet also helped to create the inequality that inspired an era of social division and unrest. AI may unlock abundance, but absent policy intervention, the legacy tax foundation that influences wealth distribution will only continue to weaken our fiscal status, and allow income inequality to widen, at our peril.

15. The Tipping Point - Human vs. Machine in the Loop

As acceleration in the development of AI models plays out, each day brings us closer to a metaphorical "bridge" we will one day cross. This "bridge" on the horizon signifies the transition from the currently prevalent "human in the loop" (HITL) protocol to a "machine in the loop" (MITL) one.

In HITL systems, humans approve key decisions; in MITL systems, machines evaluate and refine their own outputs without waiting for human approval at each stage. This transition is inevitable in domains where speed is paramount, and it represents another vector by which human cognitive labor becomes practically and economically obsolete, or simply second choice.

This shift in protocol may not occur in all domains, in all applications, but certainly will become a strong candidate to occur in domains and applications in which high speed decision making is an important determinant in positive outcomes, and in cases in which human latency in decision making is undesirable. It may very likely become a competitive advantage of sorts, at both the operative or company level, as well as at the country level.

What does this mean? What are these protocols and why would we care? Specifically, it means the following:

> **Human in the loop** (HITL) means humans supervise critical decision points in AI systems - approve outputs, guide training, and provide oversight. This provides presumed safety and accountability but introduces a fundamental human constraint: latency. Humans deliberate slowly, require sleep, and may create bottlenecks in time-sensitive decisions.

1. Human judgment in supervisory oversight of course predates AI.
2. AI models have therefore uniformly been trained with human oversight.
3. Inference output has followed and adhered to this training.

4. As critical decision points have been reached, a human has generally been in a position of sign-off, as if a "gating" factor in moving forward.
5. Human latency means delays in response time, delaying the next step.
6. In time-critical decisions, this delay can hinder the decision process, can hinder accelerated learning on the part of the model, and can create delays that at times could become problematic.

In the HITL architecture era humans have supervised critical stages of training, evaluation, and decision-making. A human is often in the loop at key points to approve or guide output, but human review slows decision cycles. In many applications—particularly those requiring real-time responses—this delay becomes a limiting factor. Thus, the benefit of HITL vs MITL varies by application.

Machine in the loop (MITL) removes human checkpoints, allowing AI systems to evaluate and refine their output at machine speed—milliseconds not minutes or hours—operating 24/7. The system becomes both decision-maker and reviewer. It allows recursive self-improvement to naturally occur, whereas HITL structurally prohibits it.

1. Recursive self-improvement, refers to the ability of a model or an agent to learn independently, step-by-step, self-augmenting its training.
2. This is often an active part in advanced problem-solving techniques, such as "laddering", "scaling" or "chain of thought reasoning" (analogous to "horizontal laddering"), whereby problems can be broken into steps, solved, knowledge augmented, enhancing the ability to solve the next problem from a premise of increased "knowledge".
3. Machine decision making is natively infinitely faster than human.
4. Given the commoditization of cognition—along with the IUB, its rate of learning becomes unhindered; it may race ahead, offering a competitive contrast to HITL systems.
5. Its advantage will be amplified by the fact that HITL requires breaks for humans to sleep; MITL does not…and can thus provide 24/7 monitoring of critical outputs. MITL—courtesy of the IUB—can scale near infinitely.

Examples of this distinction include autonomous vehicles, in which navigation decisions in complex environments can be made real-time with observations reverting back to the central system, thereby improving the knowledge base for all future instances to benefit from.

In airplane flight, AI sensor mechanisms may monitor and optimize what types and proportion of instrument controls (flap settings, airspeed, airflow attack angles, close-in weather analysis of phenomenon such as micro-bursts or wind shear) enhance flight safety and comfort, and internalize these findings for future flights to benefit from. MITL in theory could operate at levels beyond what existing auto-pilot systems can offer, courtesy of their capacity for unlimited accelerated learning and implicitly high-level, real-time problem solving.

In warfare, during real-time battle situations, it would be difficult to imagine that an HITL system could outperform a MITL system. MITL would overwhelmingly be expected to make the quickest risk assessments and predictions, most quickly identify targeting windows and initiate active response or pre-emptive action. The presumed difference in capability would in theory not even be close, the question becomes one of governing objectives and developing effective safeguards, and when or whether one is ready to hand-off decision making of this nature.

The hypothetical of AI adjudicated termination of a perceived enemy crosses several ethical and legal red-lines. Future potential risk types and scenarios must be mapped out in advance, relevant "decision trees" must be analyzed, gamed and solved in advance, with respect to even theoretical operational decisions. We in no way advocate extra-judicial termination. We cite this type of scenario to identify potential future MITL applications and risks, such as if an enemy deploys MITL weapons against us.

Will MITL come to be preferred to HITL?

As artificial intelligence dynamically develops, the balance of cases in which MITL will presume to be preferred to HITL will increasingly come to the fore. One can expect social and public safety concerns to be identified, while equally the use cases for MITL will inevitably increase. While this is at present conjecture, the trajectory or improvement of MITL efficacy will require serious consideration, especially—we suspect—in cases in which competitive outcomes become critical.

Somewhat counterintuitively, use cases will emerge in which public safety may "argue" for increased application of MITL. An easy-to-understand example of this will be the AV category. In the U.S., there are presently three main participants—Robotaxis, Waymo and Zoox—with each using slightly different AI protocols, and all to some extent still use HITL. Data increasingly suggests that AVs are far safer modes of transportation than manned vehicles, thus along this trajectory, the day will come in which pressure mounts—for safety purposes—for a shift to AV over manned vehicles. This may therefore coincide with the inevitable shift from partial HITL to zero HITL for AVs.

This supposition, although still unproven, is not difficult to imagine, as among the big three, Waymo already has earned L4 fully autonomous accreditation, with the others certainly believing they can in time acquire this as well. (Waymo released data in Q1 2026 affirming that for 170 million customer miles the rate of injury-causing crashes involving Waymo vehicles was 82% lower compared to manned vehicles.)

In the emerging MITL architecture era, AI models will increasingly evaluate and refine their own outputs without waiting for human approval at every stage. The machine would thus become the initiator and the reviewer of its own decisions. The reason for this transition is the benefit of enhanced speed, as well as—in some cases—the benefits of 24/7 MITL monitoring of operations.

In domains in which speed of decision and action can be paramount, such as financial markets, autonomous vehicles, aviation, and defense, the trade-off is one of human oversight versus machine speed. MITL architectures allow artificial cognition to function and to be additionally interjected as agentic AI supervision deems beneficial, while conversely HITL systems would become structurally disadvantaged due to their inherent latency. An MITL architecture may allow for—even facilitate—recursive self-improvement or at least reinforcement learning.

Eric Schmidt has throughout 2025 spoken of the phenomenon of recursive self-improvement, of its growing impact, suggesting it results in non-linear acceleration in domain and application specific expertise. In simple terms, this constitutes a process by which Agentic AI iterations can help train themselves, even advance their learning at a rate beyond which humans could guide them

A simplistic way to understand what this entails for AI entities, Agentic AI for example, is that "we" (man) have given it via its training an inference capability along with a GPU—or such processor type along with a model type. In this scenario, humans were "in the loop" each step of the way...we give it tasks, even objectives, and it accomplishes these as directed or as trained. The "in the loop" part means that a human gave it guidance at each critical juncture of training or decision and action.

"Machine in the loop" means absence of human step-by-step guidance or supervision, because the entity has become well-enough informed, with sufficient reasoning ability, to provide its own feedback, and do so without latency, and self-determine its answers, augment its training and independently decide in future contexts. This "in the loop" fork in the road offers a choice between existing, somewhat predictable human guided behavior and next generation, partially or fully autonomous behavior, one which benefits from accelerated learning and one in which AI can operate at machine speed.

Is it inevitable that the bridge from HITL to MITL will be crossed?

During a July 17, 2025 interview on the *Moonshots* podcast, Eric Schmidt offered the following observations and thought-process regarding the state of AI and model development for enterprise applications:

"AI is a learning machine. In network-effect businesses, when the learning machine learns faster, everything accelerates. It accelerates to its natural limit. The natural limit is electricity." This implies accelerated learning for MITL vs. HITL.

Mr. Schmidt continues... "Recursive self-improvement is the term for computers continuing to learn. We've already crossed that... systems are learning from what they think, within limited functions. When does the system have the ability to generate its own objective and its own question...we do not have that today."

He makes the analogy..."is it possible to have a teacher watching a student that is smarter than the teacher?" He adds "it appears that we can".

An implicit, but unspoken take-away is that if one country or company develops highly recursive MITL AI systems, their models would improve faster than their competitors. Anthropic's Dario Amodei, in nearly every 2025 interview seems highly cognizant of the competitive environment for AI development that exists—specifically inter-country—and uniformly encourages a high level of vigilance in this respect. From which one can easily deduce that a shift in emphasis to MITL protocol is in our future, if for no other reason than geopolitical optionality. We ask rhetorically, what country would not seize such a competitive advantage, given the opportunity?

To summarize the likely influence of MITL, given that AI models are learning machines, constrained—in theory—only by electricity, suggests a world in which innovation velocity becomes a competitive variable, leading to enhanced technological discovery, economic optimization, cyber defense and offense as well as enhanced weapons development. In such cases, virtually no alternative would exist in a competitive world but for the metaphorical "bridge" from HITL to MITL to gradually be crossed, at least in select sectors.

Arguably, the simplest way to understand the implication of HITL is that it prohibits AI from reaching its potential development and application, whereas MITL allows for AI to learn at machine speed, which clearly would be non-linear.

There are several domains—many of which we have referenced—that are natural candidates for this transition. These all share the characteristic of having either a high level of autonomy or a high-dependency on real-time decision making. Equally, as edge applications grow and proliferate, each one of these is to some extent a "decision waiting to be made" due to their implicit remoteness from a central data center or instruction set, and although decision-tree type response paths will be embedded in their training, invariably they will encounter new circumstances in which the edge device will need to decide. All of which will serve to update the master "data base" for the benefit of future instances.

Will it become a disadvantage to default to HITL?

The consequence of this fork in the road, application by application, is that it credibly presents cases wherein AI would be more effective without step-by-step human sign-off. The impact of this on our taxpaying labor force—MITL supplanting HITL—obviously represents another vector of human salary and tax revenue reduction, and may also represent cases in which public safety would be enhanced via absence of latency in a dynamic decision process. To be clear, any large-scale adoption of MITL, even for purposes of improvement of AI competitive stature, explicitly accelerates job disruption.

Such a change will also represent a **handover of control, from human to machine**. Humans will do their best to integrate guardrails to govern independent actions, but this transition can be said to be both in process and inevitable.

Although this topic can be viewed as being "technical", in practice, a shift from HITL to MITL is likely to be accompanied by social debate, along with the impact on employment and loss of taxation derived from the individual. In theory, HITL protocol stands in the way of AI reaching next level functionality, via migrating to MITL. HITL prevents non-linear growth in learning that MITL will facilitate. This is the simplest way to frame it, in which case for competitive reasons—including defense of our country—we posit it is inevitable we will gradually cross this bridge.

16. *The Open-Weight movement, Data Sovereignty and China*

There are several topics that are becoming fundamental to the adoption of AI within the U.S. but remain relatively "off the radar screen". We therefore introduce: the vibrant "open-weight" movement, the concept of "data sovereignty", and the role of Chinese AI models in America—which is likely already much deeper than is broadly recognized.

We have heretofore been discussing what can be considered "closed" models—most famously ChatGPT, Gemini and Claude, in which the inner workings or "weightings" of each model are proprietary and private. These are the famous cadre of "frontier" models. We the users generally pay for this service and interact with these models based on GPU (or TPU, etc.) clusters premised within the AI service provider's (ASP) data centers or "clouds"—or more specifically, often within their hyperscaler partners DCs or clouds. Most everyone—broadly speaking, seems delighted with this relationship, if demand for said product is any indication, with fee structures that are generally predicated upon "token" usage for both input and output (i.e., query or command vs. response). As users we seem to trust that our data, our information, our conversations are secure. So far, so good.

There are however, cohorts—such as banks, departments of defense, nuclear industry, for example, for whom data security, "data sovereignty" is an absolute non-negotiable, zero-potential-risk-tolerated scenario. These cohorts, increasingly have a different set of options available to them. Their common requirement is absolute guarantee of data sovereignty.

The two attributes they must typically consider in achieving data security or "sovereignty" will be: 1) the type of AI model they use, and 2) the nature or configuration of model hosting to ensure absolute data security.

As for model type, these can be categorized (albeit simplistically) as "closed", proprietary models or as "open", typically known as "open-weight" (OW) models, which can be downloaded and "configured" to meet the user's requirements. ("Open-weight" means the model's "weightings" or internal parameters are made publicly visible, allowing customization, while the underlying code and training data remain confidential). This harkens back to server based operating systems of past decades when proprietary systems prevailed until Linux (an open-source approximation of Unix which went on—due to low cost and openness—to become the backbone of the internet) became a viable option.

As for the configuration necessary to achieve data sovereignty, there are two typical solutions available. First and simplest, is employing a virtual private cloud (VPC) through a qualified U.S. domiciled hyperscaler. The second option is one of going "on prem", meaning their servers are on their own premises, necessitating a thresh hold level of security competency, etc.

If a bank, as an example, decides it wants to only use an AI model that is located within their premises, on their servers—thereby precluding any potential data leakage, they may opt to buy rights to or download and use an "open" model, likely customize it, and locate it within their on-prem data center. In a scenario such as this, their data never leaves their premise, it exists only within their closed environment; they likely use a secure conveyance mechanism to import or export data, or, as needed, "batched" model updates. Their data, by definition, would therefore be highly secure—exhibiting "data sovereignty". This implies of course ownership of one's GPUs and servers, and the technical expertise and infrastructure this requires.

What the user gains in this case is absolute data security, what they give up may be use of state-of-the-art model processing capabilities, as evidence suggests most closed-models are evolving in near real time, whereas once an open model is downloaded and deployed its capabilities remain "fixed" per its state of evolution at time of download, as it will exist and operate within total (physical) isolation, often referred to as an "air gapped" server environment.

The other alternative is to use the closed model of their choice, and via their ASP use a virtual private cloud (VPC) with private routing, as offered by top hyperscalers. Typically, this involves using the data center's servers, GPUs (or TPUs) and overall infrastructure and expertise, using the AI model of the customer's choosing, which could be either an open or closed model. In cases such as this there are operational format distinctions that present strong to strongest data security, with most of the major data cloud providers such as Amazon's AWS, Microsoft's Azure, and Google's Vertex also having U.S. government certification for their multi-layer security protocol. (In some cases, this may still be deemed insufficiently secure, in which case the on-prem option is chosen, typically necessitating use of an OW model.)

As of Q4 2025, the highest market share providers of OW models in the U.S. were mostly Chinese—Qwen (from Alibaba), DeepSeek (founded by Chinese hedge fund "High Flyer Capital Management"), Kimi (from Moonshot AI, with Alibaba funding), MiniMax (Shanghai based; with Alibaba and TenCent funding) and Llama 3.1 (from Meta). Recent entrants include Xiaomi's MiMo V2-Flash, and Z.ai's GLM. Xiaomi and Z.ai are both Peking / Tsinghua University adjacent, and now publicly traded companies. All of this is early-stage, but results thus far show meaningful market share gains by Chinese OW models. Let's briefly dive into this cohort:

What are open-weight (OW) models, and why are they rapidly gaining market share?

A brief outline of developmental details and timeline:

1. Open-weight (OW) is different from "open-source" (technically known as open-source software OSS) and of course different from a "closed model". Open-source implies all technical details are visible; "open-weights" means that the model's training protocol and inner workings remain proprietary, but that its "weighting" or parameter configurations are public and therefore configurable and customizable by the user. This is what makes it suitable for downloading and use in a closed, domain specific, secure environment. Closed models are of course completely proprietary, and in almost all cases hosted and operated by the respective frontier model company or their hyperscaler partners.

2. The operational genius of Chinese OW models: allowing fast, direct inference even while using older, less advanced GPUs is often attributed to a problem-solving architecture known as "mixture of experts" or MoE, meaning all training parameters are not brought to bear in each instance, but only those deemed most relevant for that specific instance. (Qwen, and others, also use a protocol known as "Quantization"—among others—which is a form of file size compression—via bit reduction, previously developed and broadly in use in many arenas.) As new innovations come to

the fore, the Chinese OW models and Mistral (French) have been quick to adopt them—such as "Mamba", first released by American-based researchers Gu and Dao in 2023.

3. Accordingly, the token and therefore power consumption—less so for training but specifically for inference—in each instance is less, often far less, than a typical closed model, due to use of MoE.

4. Of note, MoE's provenance is not Chinese but was first announced in a Google Brain research paper in 2017 titled "Outrageously Large Neural Networks: The Sparsely-Gated Mixture-of-Experts Layer" (we cover this earlier).

5. Instead, it was French AI company Mistral (founded by former Google Deep Mind and Meta executives) who first demonstrated the value of MoE in their "Mixtral" open-weight model released in 2023.

6. This innovation was followed by DeepSeek in 2024, and then Qwen in late 2024 with refined versions in 2025. (It is said the hedge fund behind DeepSeek had been using MoE to optimize its investment process.)

7. Thus, the AI model "breakthrough" known as the "DeepSeek moment" of January 2025, as it was referred in American media, was as much as anything else on the shoulders of Google's 2017 innovation of MoE, which facilitates a less dense, less expensive to build, to train and to operate model than the comparatively dense, expensive, yet more complex and comprehensive American closed models.

8. At the time, both OpenAI and Anthropic argued that DeepSeek's training "efficiency" was also a result of "distillation" of response downloads from Claude and ChatGPT via massive queries from Chinese proxy IP addresses. ("Distillation" as a technique being equivalent to acquiring the teacher's answers to study for the exam.)

9. OpenAI then in August 2025 released its own OW / MoE model GPT-OSS, ostensibly positioning itself for a role in government downloads for private data security environments.

10. In December 2025 the U.S. government proclaimed that Chinese models could not be used by U.S. government entities or their contractors, barring the door for the Chinese OW models from government work, and leaving a large, un-served market (ostensibly the 17% government share of the U.S. market to Llama 3.1 and Chat-OSS).

11. Nvidia however, released their Nemotron 3 Super (NM3S) model in March 2026. It is described as a Mamba-Transformer hybrid with MoE model, with Agentic programing and fully open source (OSS), not just OW. It is fully downloadable, configurable and suitable for the government contract sector.

The move, on March 11, 2026, by Nvidia in releasing its "Nemotron 3 Super" model—a fully open-source AI model with advanced agentic capabilities positions Nvidia to step into both the enterprise and government data sovereignty markets. A notably rapid reaction to the federal governments December 2025 decree.

Nemotron 3 Super (NM3S) is by any definition a highly unique, leading-edge model. It is described as hybrid Mamba-Transformer MoE model, with a one million token "context window" meaning that it combines three of most important model technologies spanning 2017 to 2026, with its immense context window allowing it to maintain "state" across complex problems. ("Mamba-2" technology allows use of space state modules (SSM)—which further amplifies the impact of Transformer architecture (similar functionality, different axis), along with MoE, making it highly up-to-date.

Five days later, by announcing "NemoClaw", Nvidia responded to arguably the biggest innovation of 2026 to date: "OpenClaw" (as discussed earlier in our chapter on Creative Destruction). The rapid pace of model iterations both by American and Chinese companies is reflective of a highly dynamic, highly competitive market. And clearly innovation in the world of OW models (which was initiated by non-U.S. model companies) presents a force to be reckoned with.

How important was Google's MoE to the emergence of Chinese AI models?

It is accepted wisdom that the larger, denser, more expensive closed models are more "brilliant" than OW models but also acknowledged that for many applications the OW / MoE models provide perfectly satisfactory results at a much lower cost, lower rates of power consumption, etc. Nvidia's new Mamba-Transformer hybrid with MoE should only contribute to this line of thought.

MoE premised models are less expensive top to bottom: they can operate on less expensive hardware configurations (servers and GPUs), cost less to train and less for compute. While their performance is considered a tier below the closed models, in some environments, some use-cases, cost can become the deciding factor—not to mention intended function—edge vs. DC deployment, and thus chip and battery size requirements. Hence the striking recent market share gains of the OW / MoE crowd.

Anecdotally, we note the somewhat ironic and recent trend among Chinese models to offer both OW and closed models: OW for market share gains and developer interaction—and potentially for edge applications—and closed, API-based models for revenue generation. Recently, DeepSeek, Qwen, Z.ai and Xiaomi have taken this path and announced closed, API-based models. (API-based means one can only use the model via the model's API, which of course generates token revenue for the host-model company.) Notably, Xiaomi's MiMo V2-Pro—a closed model—released in mid-March, quickly surged to a top ranking as far as the "OpenRouter" developer market traffic rankings—an implicit sign of approval with respect to its efficacy.

A useful metric for comparing AI infrastructure efficiency is tokens generated per kilowatt-hour (kWh). This efficiency measure, combined with regional electricity costs, helps explain differences in the cost of tokens across geographies. We assemble and present representative data below. An interesting datapoint that emerges when comparing AI in the U.S. vs. China is that of token generation by kilowatt-hour. Kilowatt-hours (kWh) are the standard unit of measure for electrical energy, in this case used to power AI compute.

Tokens per kWh estimates Q1 2026

Metric	China (Industrial Hubs)	USA (Hyperscaler Hubs)
Tokens per kWh (Est.)	~42,000 / kWh	~31,000 / kWh

Metric	China (Industrial Hubs)	USA (Hyperscaler Hubs)
Output Cost (per 1M tokens)	Low-tier	Mid-tier

Table 13: Tokens per kilowatt-hour contrast

Note: Tokens per kWh comparison. Industry analyst estimates synthesized from multiple sources; IEA Energy and AI 2025 report cited for broader energy context. Author specification.

The presumed cause of this purported advantage in tokens per kWh in China vs the U.S. is in theory based on architectural efficiency, meaning while U.S. GPUs and TPUs are more powerful—and hence consume more energy, China has—perhaps of necessity given U.S. export restrictions—architected their compute and inference processes differently, specifically by adopting MoE architecture, thus streamlining their operative software, resulting in models that are less kWh thirsty. There may be a fortuitous bias to the future edge or mobile deployment, which logically would be reliant on smaller, less powerful chips—or hybrid compute solutions—anyway.

With benefit of hindsight the adoption of MoE by Chinese AI model companies can be regarded as seizing a **transformational window of opportunity** that allowed them to develop effective AI models that could function satisfactorily on the restricted chip sets that were available to them. In other words: the **U.S. may have taken away Chinese access to top tier GPUs** but **allowed access to innovative AI model framework technology** (MoE); and the Chinese apparently "connected these dots"; or observed the French (Mistral) connect them and were accordingly inspired.

This—in large part—explains the "DeepSeek shock" of Q1 2025, when their V3 and R1 models demonstrated unexpected performance levels. Specifically, their R1 model reportedly achieved (OpenAI) GPT-4-level performance using fewer computational resources (GPUs) with vastly less training, indicating that algorithmic efficiency can in part compensate for hardware limitations.

The following is speculation on our part, but…it is not unlikely that the future will see development and proliferation of miniature AI applications for mobile and "edge" deployment. Very likely, MoE models—or variations thereof—with their smaller storage, compute and battery size requirements may be more naturally suited for these environments, a development that would be consistent with the "mobile-first" development focus displayed by Chinese companies throughout the last two decades. (More on this next chapter.)

What is the market share trajectory of Chinese models in the U.S.?

There is more still to the story of OW models of Chinese origin in the U.S. market. Presently, there are three ways in which U.S. individuals, companies or businesses may use Chinese OW models, as follows:

1. Visit the DeepSeek or Qwen (etc.) websites, domiciled in China, and use these via their Chinese data centers and APIs (your data resides in China);

2. Access it via a U.S. based company (a private "re-seller") that has downloaded these models and operates them within a U.S. based data center and API (in which case your data remains within the U.S.);

3. Or, if data security is required, download the model and use it via a VPC within a U.S. based ASP (your data remains in the U.S.), or "on prem" via your own (or your company's) DC set-up.

Beneath the radar, this "plan B" of U.S. based operators (or "resellers") of DeepSeek and Qwen (etc.) is alive, well and purportedly acquiring meaningful market share. To their consumers, these providers offer a suitable AI model at a low cost, or a vehicle for data privacy (government cohort excepted post December 2025).

This phenomenon of U.S. based operators of Chinese produced open-weight MoE AI models echoes two modern era precedents:

1. First, in our section on robotics we discuss how the now prevalent robotic arm for manufacturing originated in the Stanford AI Lab (SAIL) in 1969, was not commercialized in the U.S. but later dramatically so in Asia and in Europe; and

2. Second, it echoes the era of globalization wherein U.S. manufacturing jobs were lost to Chinese and SE Asian factories, except in this case **share gains by Chinese**

companies are occurring within the service sector, not the goods sector, as OW models take share from US closed models. (We note that token generation from Chinese OW models via U.S. based APIs still allows for ready taxation of token output per the bi-lateral, CPMM model described in chapter 8.)

For those who argue that it is in the U.S. interest that our AI protocols become the default global standard, one might ask is it the hardware (the GPU) that creates the standard or the application (the AI model protocol itself). We suggest this is open for debate but that it is likely it could be said to be both. The Chinese are certainly learning from the Americans (as noted via our discussion of MoE, Mamba and Transformer protocols) but likely the Americans are learning from the Chinese as well—perhaps in the edge domain. We have also seen how, despite American restrictions on Chinese access to top-end GPUs, their use of U.S. academic research—specifically MoE and of course Transformer Architecture—allowed them to develop models which handily worked-around this impediment.

The "U.S. Hosted Chinese model" share as referred to above is comprised of a cadre of companies ("re-sellers") that appear at least in part to target higher use customers or developers via their customizable configurations of a U.S. based API with Chinese open-weight models, as well as other (domestic, French) open and closed models. They may also simply target those who desire a lower token cost of AI access. Their model offerings, token pricing emphasis and often data security options suggest they collectively address a likely high-growth user segment. In the closed model segment, one may argue that Anthropic is (successfully) targeting enterprise customers, but upon examining the description of offerings on the US hosted Chinese models one must ask if the open-weight segment group is also discretely doing the same, but using "data security" as their point of competitive differentiation.

As of this date, market share data, token generation data and comparative metrics in general are exceptionally hard to come by. There are no central authorities domestically—at least at present—who are collecting this and disseminating it. Closed model companies protect their data, understandably for competitive purposes. The best one can do to estimate usage metrics is from independent reports or proxy data.

For now, the penetration of Chinese AI models into the American market is documented by three independent sources (that we are aware of) with institutional credibility.

First would be Stanford HAI's DigiChina Brief which reported that between August 2024 and August 2025, Chinese open-model developers accounted for 17.1% of all HuggingFace downloads — marginally exceeding U.S. developers at 15.8% — on what remains the world's dominant open-weight model repository. (HuggingFace is a U.S. based, model and country agnostic model download company, broadly deemed legitimate and among the best available sources of model download data. As for Stanford's HAI: first, it is Stanford, and next, Professor Fei Fei Li, who is highly regarded, is connected with its founding.)

Second, RAND Corporation, in a January 2026 report drawing on website traffic data across 135 countries from April 2024 through May 2025, found that traffic to China-based LLM endpoints (APIs) surged 460% in the two months following DeepSeek R1's January 2025 launch, with Chinese models' global share rising from 3% to 13%. RAND also noted that this growth did not represent a temporary spike — other Chinese models continued their upward trajectories throughout 2025 independent of DeepSeek, suggesting structural rather than event-driven penetration. U.S. models nonetheless retained approximately 93% of global LLM site visits as of August 2025. (We can frame this as: high rate of growth but from a small base.)

Third, San Francisco based OpenRouter's State of AI report, co-published with venture firm Andreessen Horowitz in Decemeber 2025 and based on analysis of over 100 trillion tokens, found Chinese open-source models reached nearly 30% of token volume on its platform by late 2025, rising from a negligible 1.2% base in late 2024.

(RAND is the well-known U.S. think-tank, often focusing on defense analysis. OpenRouter is a U.S.-based commercial API aggregation platform — allowing developers and companies to access multiple AI models through a single unified API. Thus, its data is self-reported user engagement.)

Each of these measures a distinct layer of the AI adoption stack. HuggingFace captures model downloads — a leading indicator of deployment intent, RAND captured actual traffic to Chinese model endpoints and OpenRouter captures token consumption among the developer and cost-optimization cohort that may set architectural patterns for broader enterprise adoption. They document not a single metric but a broad trend. Chinese AI models are—per these reports—achieving rapid, broad-based penetration into the American AI market at multiple layers of the adoption stack.

One other entry point into Chinese model share of the U.S. market is via mobile usage, for which some data insights are available. Sensor Tower is a U.S. based mobile data and analytics company, broadly used by the financial industry for operational metrics. From their publicly available data, we are able to construct the following, based on Apple and Android App store usage, giving us insight on mobile user trends in the U.S. market from January until July 2025, as a proxy for the broader universe. Thus, the following is representative only, but implies clear trends.

U.S. AI App Engagement — January to July 2025

U.S.-specific data as available; global figures noted with *; MAU = monthly active users

App	Origin	Jan 2025 min/day	Jul 2025 min/day	Growth	Notes
DeepSeek	China	6.8	15.5	+126%	U.S. data. Highest engagement growth of any LLM in this period. No platform integration advantage. Approx. 6 sessions/day.
ChatGPT	US	~10 (est.)	16.0	+67%	U.S. data. Dominant in absolute usage. Jan figure estimated from H1 average & reported growth rate. 59.5% U.S. consumer market share.
Gemini	US	—	—	+170% YoY change	*Global MAU only — U.S. min/day not publicly disclosed. 13.4% U.S. consumer share.

					Android OS integration provides distribution advantage.
Claude	US	—	—	+190% YoY change	*Global MAU only — U.S. min/day not publicly disclosed. 3.2% U.S. consumer share. Leads enterprise: 40% of U.S. enterprise LLM spend (Menlo Vent. 2025).
Perplexity	US	—	—	+370% YoY change	*Global MAU only — U.S. min/day not disclosed. 6.2% U.S. consumer share. Fastest MAU growth rate any U.S.-origin model globally for period.

Table 14: U.S. AI mobile app engagement, January–July 2025. Sources: Sensor Tower "Top ChatGPT Competitors" (Jan–Jul 2025); Sensor Tower State of AI Apps 2025; Views4You AI Usage Statistics 2025; Menlo Ventures State of Generative AI in the Enterprise 2025. Author specification.

Note: Min/day figures are U.S.-specific from Sensor Tower's "Top ChatGPT Competitors" report (Jan–Jul 2025). * YoY growth figures are global MAU from Sensor Tower Nov 2025 data — not U.S.-specific and not directly comparable to min/day metric. U.S. consumer share percentages from Views4You study; treat as indicative. Full U.S.-only data available via Sensor Tower enterprise license. All figures mobile app only.

In the above table, Chinese model DeepSeek is the star of the show. Much like Chat GPT in the U.S., they were the first in China to have a market-shaking event, in January 2025 with the launch of their R1 model. Thus, in spite of a field of highly capable domestic competitors, DeepSeek—at least as of this reporting date—remained the most popular Chinese model in the U.S. The above is but proxy data, but in aggregate it paints a clear directional picture of increasing share of Chinese AI in the U.S. market. It underlines that in spite of chip restrictions, they have and are finding framework workarounds, such as MoE, often provided to them via U.S. research.

The U.S. government's December 2025 prohibition of Chinese model use by federal contractors and their suppliers represents perhaps a corroboration of this trend — an implicit official acknowledgment that penetration is at a scale warranting legislative response. This prohibition immediately created a significant unserved market, as the government sector represents approximately 17% of U.S. AI consumption, a market now only open to domestic alternatives such as Meta's Llama, OpenAI's GPT-OSS, and Nvidia's NM3S

Highlights from this chapter include:

1. Rapid market share gains made by Chinese open-weight models using American APIs;
2. The cost reduction influence Chinese MoE models are having on token generation and therefore on the "commoditization of cognition";
3. OW success is largely premised on Google's MoE protocol innovation;
4. Data sovereignty considerations increasingly determine model type and deployment architectures;
5. Growing bifurcation of model types (OW vs. closed) appears to be under-reported by American media;
6. The market share gains by Chinese OW models are striking and significant; and
7. Chinese gains in AI market share indicate an expansion of inroads by Chinese companies into the U.S. service sector, as opposed to the goods sector, as has primarily been the case heretofore.

A final point: We are in a moment in which U.S. hyperscalers are committing significant capital to the AI infrastructure buildout, which financially of course, only works if the necessary revenue and profit flow is ultimately derived from it. Based on all available evidence, we can surmise that results are meeting expectations, as demand is vastly and exponentially exceeding supply. However, the fact that Chinese OW models are showing significant market share gains via lower cost of token generation and lower cost of token pricing at the API level bears watching. At times in recent history—such as in the globalization era—dynamics such as this have led to margin erosion on the part of the incumbent, coincident with loss of market share. Not an expression of concern, but likely a framework relevant CFOs are keeping on their dashboards.

17. AI moves to the Edge: Advantage China?

The mobile-first focus of many Chinese developers is well-established, simply consider their early development and high domestic adoption rates of Alipay, WeChat Pay, short form video, the vast suite of mobile applications developed by Shenzhen based Tencent, and of course in recent years the penetration of TikTok, Shein, Temu, et al. in the U.S. market. There was a common refrain in the days of decades past of increasing market share gains in the U.S. market by Japanese electrical consumer goods companies that those who survived the "cauldron" of the intensely competitive Japanese domestic market were well prepared to take on American rivals. The same argument could increasingly be made with respect to many Chinese companies across multiple sectors today—from factory robotics, to EVs to now humanoid robotics—which first face-off against multiple domestic rivals, often funded by rival provinces, before entry into the U.S. market.

Today, a mobile-first strategy means the end AI products will often reside on the "edge" or employ a hybrid DC/Edge compute strategy, and likely have a consumer focus. Of the recent generation of Chinese AI model developers, perhaps MiniMax (MM) is uniquely focused on smaller format applications (their "M2" and "Hailuo") that are structurally optimized for mobile, in such sectors as fast, low-latency video, translation, and short-form music clip generation. In some cases, they are purportedly providing the "back-end" for US developed apps, to side-step the potential "Chinese app" stigma. MiniMax's "Talkie" brand is said to be targeting an AI version of Character.ai, and from the start uses Singapore as its data storage domain to side-step "is my data being stored in China" concerns, even though MM itself is headquartered in Shanghai.

We have heretofore largely framed our discussion in terms of cognitive vs. physical AI. In doing so, it is clear that cognitive AI relies mostly on DC compute, whereas physical may be based on DC compute—for stationary physical AI manifestations—but that it also significantly implies edge compute, or hybrid DC/Edge. As edge AI applications proliferate, even consumer edge apps, we will see edge compute necessarily follow. Conversely, we can say that as AI compute can be further miniaturized, this will enable development of iterations—even generations—of edge compute devices. Until someone invents a better vehicle for this (which we should expect) mobile devices will use AI apps pushed out to them.

Jensen Huang, in a Q4 2025 Mayfield podcast describes migration of AI to the Edge as following two fundamental paths. First, is via sensory detection from the physical world, with this detection being sent back to the DC-based model for compute. The second is a matter of AI leaving the digital world and entering the physical world, where it must understand not merely text and vision, but the broader properties of the physical world—how objects behave, how forces interact, and how to anticipate the next state in a dynamic environment. This obviously suggests a different dynamic, requiring different processing of a wider variety of multimodal sensory inputs—preferably with low to no latency. In his first "path" data from the edge is pushed to the DC, in the second instance, compute is pushed to the edge. Another expression for this physical world of AI (as used by Nvidia) is the AI of Things (AIoT).

One can view this transition as similar to the transition earlier in the 21st century from internet to mobile. Consider the vast array of mobile-native applications developed; it is clear in hindsight, the iPhone app store was like Helen of Troy: "the face that launched a thousand ships", with the application developer community benefitting greatly. We expect a re-invention of this, but with a broader radius of impact given the greater potential for integration inherent to AI. Will AI launch a thousand edge applications? Easily, given its pervasive platform.

Presently in the U.S., DC located cognitive AI dominates, whereas edge applications are early stage and therefore just beginning to emerge. In fact, we could say that both physical AI edge and consumer edge are both early-stage. Whereas in China, for a variety of reasons—perhaps chiefly their focus and history of success of their mobile-first thesis, the physical AI and consumer AI (both edge) sectors are more developed than in the U.S. This "status" aligns well with most observations regarding Chinese research focus, Chinese patent application focus, even Chinese industrial focus, which has a tradition of being application-focused, and for the past two decades, mobile-focused.

China's long-standing "mobile-first" focus, as evident by their innovations and wide spread adoption of mobile applications presents another example of American developed technology or platforms (i.e., the smart phone, Android) commercially exploited by non-Americans. One could say that the U.S. invented the smart phone, and developed it to great lengths, simply consider the success of both Apple and Android phones, along with Facebook, WhatsApp, and IG. But the U.S. has nothing that rivals the adoption rates of Chinese payment apps, such as Alipay or WeChat Pay, which are used not just for person-to-person payments but also broadly in the SME sector.

We can now add to this China's leadership in EVs and robotics—both factory and humanoid. The ubiquity of both of these physical AI applications (technically, EVs are DC/Edge hybrid) also exhibits the respective engineering focus and component manufacturing capability to support these sectors. A generation ago, Harvard Business School Professor Michael Porter, in his *Competitive Advantage of Nations* (1990) characterized this as "industry clusters" in which specific geographic regions become centers of expertise for specific industries, lending them an enduring competitive advantage—at least until the next disruption.

The relative absence of clusters of expertise in both EVs and robotics manufacturing in the U.S. regrettably depicts a sharp contrast. There are singular companies doing great work in these domains, such as Tesla in EVs and in robotics and Amazon in distribution center robotics (along with other humanoid robotics focused start-ups), but on an aggregated basis, the U.S. is behind. We may lack not only the sub-sector technical expertise, but also the available manufacturing staff to step in and scale up should we so desire.

The U.S. can look backwards and claim initial leadership in both of these sectors: factory robotics were an American invention (the "Stanford Arm" – chapter 4) and EVs, while not invented in the U.S. were famously commercialized by Elon Musk's Tesla. We have since fallen down the ranks as far as global leadership in both of these sectors. There are few if any clusters of expertise—to use Porter's terminology—in the U.S. The U.S. is fighting its way back in these sectors, with the most visible example being the AV category. Tesla's Cybercab, along with Google and Amazon's AVs, each of which uses a slightly different autonomous driving "stack" along the spectrum of "edge heavy" (Tesla) to DC/Edge hybrid (Waymo) with Zoox in between. Clearly Cybercab (Texas Giga factory) is building their own vehicle, Zoox is having its vehicles built in Hayward, CA in a former bus assembly plant, and Waymo is transitioning from Jaguars to Chinese (Geely) built Zeekr EVs; in aggregate running counter to Porter's concept of clusters of expertise.

In robotics for manufacturing, the U.S. for now is principally relying on factory robotics made by U.S. domiciled Joint Venture (JV) companies with foreign manufacturers, or simply by importing said factory robots. A dramatic reversal for the inventor of the category.

With respect to consumer or even cognitive Edge AI, this is a sector which is likely very much in play as far as near-term development. Increasingly we see Edge AI models embedded in smart phones and laptops. In the U.S. we hear of medical applications where a medical technician could have a tablet with a 1B parameter model embedded for purposes of medical imaging analysis, bringing diagnostic care to the edge, or benefitting from a more robust Edge hybrid model. Conversely, Chinese company MiniMax has their app "Talkie" in the hands of 150 million consumers today, using a hybrid model: DC based text LLM derived generation, sizeable (DC domiciled) memory with smart phone viewing and distribution. Talkie viewers reportedly engage in 90-minute average sessions. Are they inventing the next "addictive" application, based on emotional connections developed with the individual during simulated conversations, as opposed to Facebook-style algorithmic connections that chiefly respond to the content you view or search for? TBD.

Edge AI models will typically be smaller in every way: physical and therefore battery size, with vastly reduced training parameters—ranging from 1B to 28B for various cognitive and consumer (often hand-held) Edge models, vs. 400B to 1.6T for DC based models. (When one thinks of larger format, more mission critical Edge AI models, such as Cybercabs or robotic surgery units, these of course have higher parameter and processing capability. They have typically been use-case-engineered from the outset, with customized compute, code, and algorithms—as well as battery capacity, scaled to their mission.)

We outline variations between American vs. Chinese AI focus, by contrasting hardware types in use, respective models, applications, industrial vs. business adoption patterns, and overall focus in the spectrum from DC to edge, below.

A Contrast in Channels: Cognitive, Physical and Edge

	AI w American Characteristics	AI w Chinese Characteristics
Technical Ability	The U.S. is broadly considered in lead position – globally.	Chinese Universities are catching up quickly. Tsinghua THU, Peking

		PKU - Beijing, and Zhejiang ZJU - Hangzhou are all formidable in AI.
Capital Markets	Absolute competitive advantage. All other countries are in 3rd or 4th tier. The very definition of "American Exceptionalism".	3rd tier status capital markets, but… intense inter-province rivalries with funding flowing from "home" region and municipal sources.
GPU and Chip Design	Design leadership and high influence over TSMC and ASML export partners, a significant "gating" factor and advantage.	Persistent architectural "workarounds". Huawei (Ascend NPUs) and Moore Threads pursue domestic accelerators optimized for transformer and MoE workloads, partially offsetting the 7nm/5nm fabrication ceiling imposed by export restrictions.
AI Model Design	Leaders in "closed", high-end frontier AI models. Source country of nearly all pivotal AI research last decade: Transformer, MoE, Chat-GPT, Mamba, but with heavy leadership from foreign-born researchers, and often slow home market adoption.	Architectural efficiency masters, in context of GPU constraints. Leaders in application of USA pioneered breakthroughs: DeepSeek V-3 + MoE; Q1 2026 Xiaomi's MiMo-V2 architecture on their XRING chip (mfg. by TSMC). Robotic tech leadership.
Cognitive	All indicators suggest continuity in USA leadership, consistent with intensive, high-level DC compute capacity. AI Model superiority deep reasoning & coding.	Distillation and MoE intensive model construction yields efficient and capable models with cognitive skills below USA closed models, yet at a lower cost.
Physical	Several credible manifestations underway: robotic surgery, Waymo,	Mass application of robotic manufacturing. Pioneered dark factories.

	Amazon distribution centers, humanoids, but overall, in catch-up mode relative to China. Greater breadth in tech solutions for AVs vs China.	Apparent leader in humanoid robotics, strength in which said to follow from hyper competitive domestic EV market. Far more AVs deployed than US (3:1).
Edge Processing	US focus on security & privacy. Apple/Qualcomm 3nm chips focus on secure, local "Personal Intelligence" on phones and laptops. Increased focus on SLMs, Microsoft "Phi", Google's "Gemma". Meaningful chip evolution to NPUs, even SoCs for efficient edge compute.	China's MoE based models moving to DC / Edge hybrids and Agentic. Xiaomi xRING O1 and Huawei Kirin 10 focus on real-time, low-power "Car-Home-Phone" agentic responsiveness. MoE / Mamba melds DC / Edge processing. **China's GPU disadvantage diminishes in Edge AI**.
Edge Applications	Largely focused on applications as extensions of prevailing closed cognitive models. Kiosks are old news, but meaningful edge applications emerge: edge medical diagnostic tablets; in defense, Anduril's (Lattice) will likely revolutionize edge battlefield management.	China's mobile-first mind shift the last two decades evident. Integrated service agents, embedded into smart city infrastructure, the SU7 EV ecosystem, and WeChat-based service workflows. Exploiting hybrid potential.
Consumer Apps	For now, by all indications still dominated by centralized LLM portals (ChatGPT, Claude) and generative multimodal tools. AI-Native consumer (mobile) apps still to emerge. Microsoft's "Phi" and Google's "Gemma" are efforts to address this market, but app creation—apparently—thus far limited. Where is the AI	Agentic micro-agent embodiments are becoming ubiquitous. AI-driven short-video creation ("Talkie"). Xiaomi's Q1 2026 "XiaoAi" has become what Siri long promised: an agentic, multi-modal personal assistant that flows to home, car, office real-time. Last, China's embrace of "OpenClaw"

	equivalent of iPhone App Store?	is ruthless: days after release Xiaomi embedded in MiMo-V2-Pro; now a "rockstar" use-case for WeChat.
Management Consultants (a uniquely American propagation mechanism)	U.S. Management Consultant companies are tantamount to "management with American characteristics", generating $125B per year. Highly influential in business processes, and will "push" cognitive AI into American companies, becoming walking, breathing cognitive AI "use-case" generators. But U.S. consultants have little expertise in edge, thus little to contribute here, U.S. companies being the poorer for it.	Chinese Management Consultant businesses generate about $23B per year. In cognitive AI, Chinese companies will by default rely on province and government level best-practices and directives. Perhaps effective, but may exhibit inconsistent imagination and absence of incentive-based outcomes. However, Chinese app developers (also) never sleep, thus innovation will be incessant.

Table 15: It's an interconnected world, but different cultures deliver different outcomes.

Edge deployment will both drive and benefit from changes in chip design. We will likely see continued development of use case-designed chips, generating necessary compute but in a scale that matches said deployment characteristics. DC powered LLMs are by necessity multi-modal generalists, as supported by their chip sets, whereas edge AI devices will likely be more purpose-specific.

We know about GPUs, CUDA and all the application research and model development that has followed. We know that China—for a variety of reasons was severely limited in access to top flight chips. We can now see, that incredibly, American research innovations helped them create architectural work-arounds in many cases—such as papers by Google Brain on Transformers, MoE and then by Gu and Dao on Mamba. Applying these innovations allowed Chinese AI companies to develop highly suitable (for most uses-cases) models. These same structures, these same model approaches to efficiency, coincidentally lend themselves neatly to edge application. Thus, this transition means that **edge processing diminishes the Chinese GPU disadvantage,** simply because less dense models with lower parameter counts are often a better scale and therefore match for many AI edge applications, likely including consumer use cases.

Inevitably, chip evolution continues unabated. Perhaps this sector is more competitive than ever (how would you react if you were an industry participant and observed Nvidia's robust revenue and margins)?

Simplistically, we went from CPUs to GPUs and now to NPUs (neural processing units) and SoCs (systems on a chip), with LPUs (language processing units) now being championed by Nvidia—albeit for narrower use cases, such as accelerated language (text) processing, not image and video. What these new chips have in common—at least NPUs and SoCs—is that functionally they remain generalist but are sub-optimized for graphics. The heavy lifting required for graphics can be left to the GPUs. These smaller footprint chips can easily meet the processing needs of SLMs, are well suited for edge (lesser battery requirements), and are still quite strong (NPUs at least) for DC located inference. (Nvidia, masters of the GPU, recently acquired rights—for $20B—to Groq's LPU technology, ostensibly to countermand competitors such as Broadcom who are having success with customized, targeted chips for the DC. Jensen Huang also implied—at GTC March 2026—Nvidia's increased focus on Edge computing. The vision he voiced at GTC is one of inference running "everywhere at the edge".)

Does Xiaomi derive synergy by being both an AI model and AI application company?

Is there a concurrent explosion in edge applications and use-cases? Yes, but it goes beyond that. An example from Q1 2026 that those outside of China may not have noticed is Beijing-based Xiaomi's updated XiaoAi, which delivers what Siri long promised—agentic-like capability in a virtual assistant. XiaoAi is Xiaomi's persistent voice assistant (the interface layer), part of its new model MiMo-V2-Flash (the underlying edge model powering it) based on a 3nm (TSMC produced) xRING SoC of their design. XiaoAi accompanies the user from home to mobile to auto to office, in a way that is held to be ahead of any rival. This is a highly effective, integrated system running on their software and their hardware. Thus, Xiaomi has transitioned into not just an Edge and DC compute company, but an integrated ecosystem in which the user experience is seamless across devices or manifestations.

To accomplish this Xiaomi integrated two new models into their ecosystem, their MiMo-V2-Flash for edge devices and a denser, 1 million token context window, closed AI model, MiMo-V2-Pro for DC compute. (When first available for download, V2-Pro was anonymous in attribution, with most surmising it was the next gen DeepSeek). It is instead part of Xiaomi's broader, updated ecosystem, which as noted ranges from EVs, to mobile, to home, to office. XiaoAi, its version of Siri, accompanies the user throughout their day, from Edge to DC compute and back—while maintaining "state".

They have built their ecosystem on their own design 3nm xRING (system on a chip) SoC produced for them by TSMC. (Xiaomi is not on the U.S. "entity list", thus whereas other Chinese chip designers are restricted to 5nm product—both via external acquisition and in practice internally as well—as Chinese companies presently lack the ability to execute below 5 nm.) Xiaomi now powers its ecosystem using their xRING SoC, using a single chip version on edge devices (e.g., their EVs and mobiles) via their smaller MiMo-V2-Flash Edge AI model whereas their closed model, DC based cognitive AI MiMo-V2-Pro, uses an xRING cluster chip set.

Xiaomi's world thus spans Edge to DC AI, dynamically, courtesy of their proprietary integrated AI stack and hardware, making them an outlier in the world of AI, as of Q1 2026. In Xiaomi's ecosystem, when the user transitions from edge (mobile) to DC compute, the user's "state" (context memory retention) follows them, whereas top U.S. closed models employ a "siloed" state model, meaning when you transition devices your prior state remains in the prior device. ("State" referring to your conversation, your query history, your project status, etc., following you from device to device.) This is a small, but remarkable feature which no other model—anywhere—appears to presently match.

The biggest earthquake of Q1 2026 was the launch of OpenClaw, an open-source Agentic framework that becomes a personal agent residing on one's laptop or mobile, looking after your "needs" 24/7, thus operating as an agentic orchestration layer that coordinates your various inputs and outputs. It is early-stage, but it has been received with broad acclaim—both in China and in the U.S.—requiring virtually all players in the AI model sphere to respond; fairly quickly, most have. Xiaomi integrated this shortly after its release—as have other Chinese models, while in America Nvidia did so within days via NemoClaw, with Anthropic, Gemini and OpenAI also responding.

OpenClaw has quickly gained a reputation for being "token thirsty" because it is often on 24/7, performing its agentic role of supervising and orchestrating its affairs. By necessity this often pushes it to rely on DC compute, or DC/Edge, as most pure Edge devices may lack the battery power and token "budget" to satisfy its needs. Although in practice it is therefore a hybrid DC/Edge model, it is easily the Edge introduction of the year, thus far.

Shenzhen-based Huawei, in chip design, continues to push ahead with improved performance from its domestically produced 5nm chips. Its Ascend GPUs have been used for notable levels of training and inference, by among others, Z.ai, for use in both DC and Edge (via its GLM model). In training their GLM model, because Ascend's 5 nm GPU is lower output than western GPUs, Z.ai simply used more chips, but at a lower per unit cost, still netting out with a savings in training expense. This growing domestic ability, along with less dense models which make use of most modern inference innovations (MoE, Mamba) seems pointed to supporting both DC-based inference but also increased Edge applications.

The through-line in the increasing transition of AI to the edge is that while innovation itself is often unpredictable, what can be said to be predictable is change and evolution, and that new applications can and will easily upset well established business practices and even consumer norms. China's recent history of capitalizing on the internet's transition to mobile suggests there is greater than a non-zero chance this could repeat itself in AI. As noted above, China is easily the equal of the U.S. at present in Edge AI, arguably ahead. We suspect that two channels will lead Edge development:

1) Consumer application and product development, moreover than chip design (although chip evolution will be requisite to facilitate this). This presumes a proliferation of new consumer and edge use cases. History says we can count on this; and

2) The simple fact that the physical world offers a near endless "buffet" of manifestations to be optimized. The world we live in offers opportunities for modernization in sector after sector, from healthcare, to transportation, to education, to housing supply, to safety and security, to public health, ad infinitum. AI will inevitably bring change to most all of the broader physical world around us. As this occurs, it will no doubt be called "creative destruction".

Our AI taxation prescription, chapter 8—which is largely token based—is less suited for Edge AI than it is for Cognitive AI. We therefore conclude that the wiser course of action is of "strategic sequencing" and to let the future dominant manifestations of Edge AI emerge, and given that or those, determine the optimal Edge AI taxation sub-strategy to match the emerging sector in an equally native approach to our solution for cognitive AI. This will become clear in short order.

A final point: the tremendous success and proliferation of the iPhone in the mobile era was in part due to a) being recognized as the default leader and platform; and b) the introduction of the App Store as its dynamic engine of distribution and monetization. This synergy, provided by its platform and captive sales channel, provided a self-reinforcing vehicle for business development and expansion—not to mention created one of the most astute corporate "moats" ever.

In doing so, they took hold of a high-growth but nascent category—mobile and mobile apps—that was competitively-speaking, highly fragmented, and forged brand dominance. This was, in the annals of business history, a tremendous accomplishment that largely underpins their multi-trillion-dollar market valuation to this day.

Who, or what, will emerge as the default platform and distribution hub for Edge AI? Will it continue to be a mobile device? Will Apple leverage its sophisticated hardware strengths and emerge as the leader in this presumed new platform or will it be another entity altogether? This has yet to be revealed.

18. *Contrarian reports on AI Efficacy and Adoption*

It would be remiss to not acknowledge two recent and somewhat contrarian reports with respect to both adoption rates as well as the impact on employment relating to AI. To briefly review both: 1) one by three Stanford Professors, which has received quite a bit of press, and 2) from the opposite coast, one from an MIT based research laboratory, that has apparently received comparatively less attention. They are both worth exploring.

There have lately been reports (specifically an August 2025 research paper "*Canaries in the Coal Mine*" by three Stanford professors—Brynjolfsson, Chandar, Chen) concerning the difficulty for recent college graduates (the 22-25 age cohort) in finding jobs. Highlights included computer science graduates—a field that was up until recently considered an automatic ticket to fast, well-compensated employment, as well as in customer service jobs—and in general jobs vulnerable to automation as opposed to augmentation—where employment increased, with a lessened overall effect in jobs "less exposed" to the increasing capabilities of AI. Their account and conclusions were well-founded as they were based on data provided by payroll processing company ADP. The key take-away was the correlation—albeit early stage—between the rise of AI and the apparent emerging difficulty many fresh graduates (in the sectors noted in particular) in finding jobs.

In an interesting counterpoint to this story, Andrew Ng, Stanford Adjunct Professor in deep learning and related (computer science, AI) topics, in September 2025—that is, one month later than the aforementioned academic research—observed in a video-recording of his CS230 class that in his experience computer science graduates with AI specific skills were in high demand, those without were not. He further observed that job candidates with a good understanding of computer science fundamentals along with AI skills were especially valuable, specifically stating that perhaps some universities may not have kept their computer science programs current, by not covering the "connective" innovations of machine learning and deep learning, which represent the "bridge" curriculum between computer science and AI.

As is often said these days, "both, can be true", with both sets of Stanford professors providing complementary observations on today's job market for the fresh graduate cohort. Anecdotally, Jensen Huang in comments also made at Stanford, albeit on April 16, 2026 echoed Mr. Ng's observation that CS graduates with strong AI skills are indeed in high demand—and he is an employer, not academic.

Related to this topic, four months later on January 29, 2026 in a Forbes interview with David Rubenstein, Eric Schmidt was asked what could an average person do to prepare themselves for the AI world, and his response was, "…let me turn the question around and direct my response to MIT and Stanford…and say the most important class that you do not have is a freshman class on 'prompt engineering'". This response is both obviously highly pragmatic and speaks volumes with respect to the average employee (not just technical students) and their near-future relationship with the job market.

On this exact topic of the importance and potential of "prompt engineering" and AI-assisted code development, Professor Ng elaborates in his class—and elsewhere—on the speed of development AI enhanced programming brings. The point he makes clear is that it allows one to engage in test of concept rapidly, with concepts generating "green lights" being pursued and those receiving "red lights" summarily trashed or reworked. Further, that AI enabled programming speeds up development and testing and implicitly is a net positive in concept and business (or application) development. One can view his last point as implicitly "bullish" for new business formation as well as for creative destruction.

To identify a key take-away from this episode, one can agree the Stanford paper makes a timely point, with the counterpoint coming in the form of "encouragement" to ensure one is preparing themselves to take part and compete in our evolving economy.

AI adoption is still early stage, and results are purportedly uneven, but effort and investment seem indisputably "full throttle"

Along the continuum of adoption of AI and efficacy thereof, in a July 2025 report by MIT's NANDA "The GenAI Divide: State of AI in Business 2025" may have coined the expression "Gen AI divide", which implies exactly what it seems, that a divide has already emerged between those "equipped" to productively use AI and those who are not, or have not adopted these skills. (NANDA = MIT NANDA team - Networked Agents and Decentralized Architecture, led by R. Raskar, A. Challapally, C. Pease and P. Chari.)

As an intro, the executive summary of this report is as follows: "Despite $30–40 billion in enterprise investment into GenAI, this report uncovers a surprising result in that 95% of organizations are getting zero return. The outcomes are so starkly divided across both buyers (enterprises, mid-market, SMBs) and builders (startups, vendors, consultancies) that we call it the GenAI Divide. Just 5% of integrated AI pilots are extracting millions in value, while the vast majority remain stuck with no measurable P&L impact. This divide does not seem to be driven by model quality or regulation but seems to be determined by approach. Tools like ChatGPT and Copilot are widely adopted. Over 80 percent of organizations have explored or piloted them, and nearly 40 percent report deployment. But these tools primarily enhance individual productivity, not P&L performance. Meanwhile, enterprise grade systems, custom or vendor-sold, are being quietly rejected. Sixty percent of organizations evaluated such tools, but only 20 percent reached pilot stage and just 5 percent reached production. Most fail due to brittle workflows, lack of contextual learning, and misalignment with day-to-day operations."

While on face value a bit of a stunning report, one can also deduce it is not all bad news, one can fairly assume that deployment, adoption, training, success, configuration validation are all dynamic processes, with a steep learning curve. We note their expression that results thus far fall chiefly into productivity increases, which a) is broadly considered good news, almost always coming home to roost in one's P&L—perhaps even be-getting more investment, and b) fits into the half of the impact of AI characterized by nearly all observers as the "augmentation" side of the augment / automate divide.

One can also ask, if the results firms are experiencing are so low level, why all the buzz around vibe-coding? That is the act of generating functional code via a continuum of prompts to Claude Code or Codex. That this is wildly popular and itself a bit of a breakthrough is beyond dispute. But this fact matches well with other reports that acceptance of AI is in some cases powered by a" bottoms-up" phenomena wherein early adopters (read: younger cohorts) are adopting AI like crazy and this will in time become institutionalized…and exhibit "upward pressure". It also suggests a relative "fluency" among AI-Native companies in making full use of this new set of tools and capabilities, possibly giving them an advantage in future market-share competition.

Enter the consultants, the intermediaries, as the "buzz" surrounding AI is such that most enterprises will likely be gripped, if not already, with fear of missing out (FOMO) and spend accordingly to get up to speed. Specifically relevant to this point is the following quote in the MIT research: "Implementation advantage: External partnerships see twice the success rate of internal builds". This statement, attributed to MIT in July 2025, is every consultant's friend.

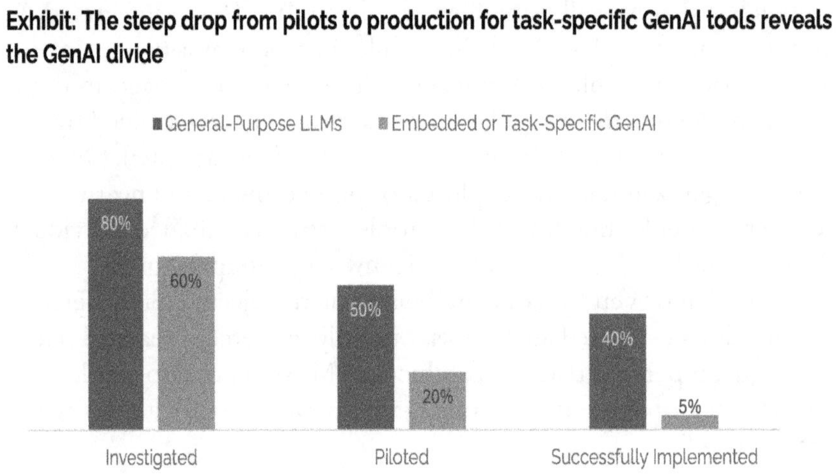

Figure 35: AI adoption rate, MIT NANDA

Perhaps the NANDA report is perfectly encapsulated, for this point in time, by their statement: "The biggest thing holding back AI is model quality, legal, data, risk → What's really holding it back is that most AI tools don't learn and don't integrate well into workflows." But then they offer the following: Behind the disappointing enterprise deployment numbers lies a surprising reality: "AI is already transforming work, just not through official channels. Our research uncovered a thriving "shadow AI economy" where employees use personal ChatGPT accounts, Claude subscriptions, and other consumer tools to automate significant portions of their jobs, often without IT knowledge or approval." This off-hand observation, which they characterize as the "Shadow AI Economy" is powerful stuff and suggests "ignore AI at your own peril…". To wit…they (MIT NANDA report) summarize as follows:

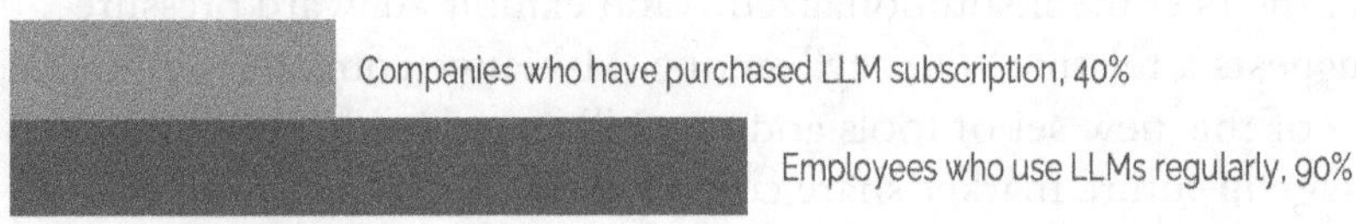

Figure 36: Company vs Employee AI usage, MIT NANDA

…which reveals the prospect of widespread, almost irrepressible productivity increases. (History does suggest, after all, that many successful "revolutions" start with the individual and work their way up.)

Note that a big caveat (quite surprisingly) in the MIT NANDA report is that they focused on LLM use at an individual and enterprise level, not Agentic AI. (This fact alone represents the rapid speed of evolution in the world of AI; last month's observation is akin to an "historical event".) Agentic AI purportedly solves many of the purported weaknesses they cite such as lack of memory, failure to learn and forgetting context. Agentic AI's strengths are purportedly, among others: persistent "state" and memory, continuous "recursive" learning, autonomous action, workflow adaptation, even supervisory course correction. Thus, taken as a consequence of the Gen AI vs. Agentic AI theme, there is an aspect of this report that demonstrates the limitation of Generative vs Agentic; with one model type being backward looking and the other forward.

Many profoundly impactful AI adoptions one reads of these days are with the combination of an LLM with Agentic capability added to it. Meaning, high level LLM reasoning with memory, recursive learning and self-improvement along with the supervisory or orchestration ability that Agentic AI brings. The supervisory and orchestration ability of Agentic AI allows digital inputs, via APIs, to become automatic or autonomous. This brings advantages to modern firms, and places many legacy business-process outsourcing (BPO) systems at risk of slow-motion obsolescence.

To reflect upon the MIT NANDA report, they raise points that cannot be ignored, but also acknowledge—via their admission that their research subjects were not using Agentic AI, that some of the issues raised seem to be in the process of being solved, such as addition of memory, and therefore retention of "state", the ability to become adaptive vs "brittle" and in particular the "bottoms up" adoption they report. One can hope that a follow up report appears in the next several months.

There are also companies following the opposite model of McKinsey…

Indeed, McKinsey's strategy (of internalizing Agentic AI development via its prior acquisition of QuantumBlack) is impressive…and seems to suit them perfectly, but others including other consultants, are and will adopt a partnership model. For example,

OpenAI and others have been very publicly active with expanding capacity partnerships, meaning expanded compute capacity arrangements with those who specialize in providing this, both from a GPU perspective and datacenter capacity perspective.

Others, seem to be quite active in terms of adoption, implementation and application partnerships, namely Anthropic, while also active in expanding capacity have also had a keen focus on building distribution and deployment agreements, specifically with the consulting community, and with it seems enterprise at large. A question every board, every management team must have been asking their CEOs these past quarters is… "what exactly is our AI strategy?" Which today is the same as asking what is our "go to market" or our "competitive strategy". It would be difficult to imagine a CEO that has not of late been focused on optimizing their company's AI strategy.

We cite below examples of what the MIT report itself hinted at, that in American corporations, business processing consultants hold tremendous sway, often with track records to back it up. To simply connect the dots between the statement in the MIT research output of "Implementation advantage: External partnerships see twice the success rate of internal builds", with the actual implementation mechanism typically provided by America's management consultants, such a strategy seems to help bridge this gap in a meaningful way.

To put this in sharper perspective, American "big cap companies" have a lot at stake simply due to their scale. Every significant step they take represents an opportunity to meaningfully upgrade or degrade their competitive posture. Few boards would sign off on a potentially material overhaul to internal or external facing process that are not well thought-out. What level of preparation do you want backing you up when you propose a transformative change to your board? Enter the consultants.

The WSJ on 4 November, 2025 announced Anthropic's recent partnership to this end with professional-services firm Cognizant, in which Cognizant would embed Anthropic's Claude into its products.

Anthropic reports… "The deal makes Cognizant one of Anthropic's three largest customers by total number of enterprise seats, the AI company said, and comes at a time when it is ramping up efforts to sell to corporate clients. Cognizant will roll out Claude to its 350,000 employees."

Further…" "All of our enterprise customers, they know what they want to do, but they're all looking for advice on how they accomplish it," said Paul Smith, Anthropic's chief commercial officer. "By coming together with Cognizant, we're making it easy for our enterprise customers to really drive the adoption of AI."

This last statement is a dead match with the comment made by MIT's NANDA above with respect to enterprise customers being predisposed to employ a consultant with the expertise to ensure their AI launch and integration occurs at a high level. A key take-away from the events of the day is that companies not properly prepared to exhibit competence or even excellence with respect to AI risk being on the *wrong side* of the creative destruction equation.

In select cases, Anthropic reportedly uses teams of what it calls forward-deployed engineers—or staff embedded within enterprises to teach them how to use AI—but it does not have the scale needed to reach all potential customers. Thus, a partnership such as that with Cognizant allows this approach to scale. This is a similar strategy to that used by leading AI government security and defense contractor Palantir, and on face value not terribly different from that used by IBM and its "systems engineers" in the '70's when it was rolling out the System 360.

The WSJ adds…"Anthropic last month reached a deal with International Business Machines, and announced that Deloitte's over 470,000 employees will use Anthropic models—representing its largest enterprise AI deployment so far."

AI roll-out and adoption is emphatically alive and well

The composite outtake from the above reports seems to be: 1) do not expect a straight line of expansion and implementation, in fact 2) expect a jagged path with hits and misses, epiphanies and setbacks, but for certain 3) expect this line to have an unrelenting steep trajectory. It seems easy to assess that a lot of impressive things are happening, and for those firms that are yet to feel they have conceptualized or are on the path to implementing a clear AI strategy, this is probably causing sleepless nights. As for our central thesis of the accelerating disruption of our labor force, and its disruption of our fiscal stability, none of the above causes us to change our view at all. The above sets of experiences simply provide insight into the actual process of transformation. And the anecdotes from the field, as well as direct conclusions from the NANDA report, underline the important role to be played by American consulting companies—a well-established mechanism within American business.

A final note on this topic and the potential for disruption in the post-college career development of our nation's youth: it would, if this becomes a sustained pattern, be something worth being significantly concerned about. We are reminded of research published by Larry Summers and Brad de Long more than a decade ago in their *Fiscal Policy in a Depressed Economy* (2012), in which they described the cumulative and substantial effects of what they termed the "long shadow of recessions", specifically leading to periods of prolonged youth unemployment, and the consequences on the careers, and the human capital development of those who had the misfortune to experience this effect. (While we are not predicting a recession, the potential similarity lies in an elevated risk of post-college periods of unemployment.) It is our hope that our nation's youth will be spared such an experience, and that if there is material reluctance to hire recent graduates during the forthcoming AI transition, that the matter is treated with urgency by all parties involved.

If a generation of college graduates has a stunted professional development and is delayed from reaching peak earning years, then not only is this a harsh outcome on an individual level, but the federal government is in theory deprived of one of its future highest-yielding individual income tax cohorts, with predictable consequences as described earlier.

19. *AI Data Centers – an Imperative in Search of a Solution*

AI data centers, in some communities, are popping up with unexpected frequency and consequence. They are—after all—the AI factories we have described, enabling the staggering rates of growth in AI adoption and transformation. But they've also—in adjacent communities, and ultimately in political circles—created considerable levels of conversation and controversy. At the community level, their sheer physical scale takes many by surprise, quickly followed by realization that their 24/7 white noise generation is there to stay.

As a purely economic event, the scale of investment being made by the private sector in data centers—and the AI infrastructure buildout in general, are completely unprecedented, dwarfing all other investment events in U.S. history barring the tremendous level of munitions production in WW2 (in the context of gross expenditure as a percent of GDP, WW2 munitions expenditures remain unparalleled). Equally, this funding has entirely come from corporate sector balance sheets, cash-flow and of course U.S. capital markets. In terms of sheer scale, it is captivating, however the wisdom thereof—ultimately defined as return on these investments, will not be confirmed for several years.

The AI Infrastructure *Estimated* Investment in Context

Project / Era	Peak	Expenditures (in adj. 2024 USD)	% of US GDP	Primary Funding
WWII Munitions	1940 – 1950	$4.2 Trillion	~38%	Government Debt
AI Infrastructure	2025 – 2034	$4.0 Trillion	~2.24 %	Private Sector Equity/Cash
Railroad Expansion	1880s	$1.2 Trillion	~6.0%	Private/Land Grants

Project / Era	Peak	Expenditures (in adj. 2024 USD)	% of US GDP	Primary Funding
Peak Auto Mfg (GM/Ford)	1950s	$700 Billion	~1.5%	Private
Interstate Highways	1956 – 1992	$620 Billion	~1.0%	Government
90s Fiber Optic	1995-2005	$450 Billion	~1.2%	Public companies / Private invest.
Apollo Space Program	1960s	$260 Billion	~0.4%	Space Race, Government

Table 16: AI infrastructure investment forecast 2025–2034 decade with historical context; "conservative" estimates.

Note: Data for AI infrastructure investment across 2025-2034 decade aggregated from multiple press releases with specific investment commitments, plus financial industry and other forecasts, then reduced 20% out of conservatism. (Press releases include: META, AWS, MSFT, GOOGL, Vantage/ADQ, BX and MU which sum to $1.69 T.) Fortune magazine April 2026 forecast U.S. utilities will spend $1.4 T over the next 5 years for system upgrades. Collectively, these commitments sum to $3.09 T for roughly half the decade—suggesting that our decade-long forecast is conservative. March 2026 JP Morgan estimated $5 T over the following decade for AI infrastructure and global grid development; a meaningful portion will occur in the U.S. market.

An important consideration to keep in mind is that we are still early-stage in the AI revolution. The investments in AI infrastructure made thus far, massive by any context, are in many respects—chiefly that of unmet demand for token output—viewed as insufficient. Thus, it will not be surprising to see a continuum of additional capital raises for expanded capacity.

On the supply-side, AI model companies are in full out invest mode, not profit-generation mode. The demand side, the actual end users of AI on the enterprise side, while generally expressing enthusiasm, expanding their internal investments and even reducing non-AI head count, are not yet consistently reporting growth in profitability attributable to AI. To be sure, profit forecasts for the cohort of SP500 companies are increasing sharply, and overall economy wide productivity metrics show promise, there is not yet clear broad-based linkage of AI investment to enterprise profitability. Nonetheless, nearly across the board, for both the demand-side and supply-side, capacity is being increased.

In the U.S., the supply-side continues to address our data center needs via a massive build-out, not necessarily adjacent to demand, but as best as possible in environments that are most hospitable to such projects. The characteristics of this "hospitality" may include a) available land, b) available energy, and c) state and local taxation policy. In some respects, this has resulted in data center density disparity, as our map below suggests. With, in fairness to those residents adjacent to these newly arrived data centers, there have been significant levels of complaint regarding the coincident a) noise, b) impact on electricity rates and c) "aesthetic contribution" of having a data center nearby.

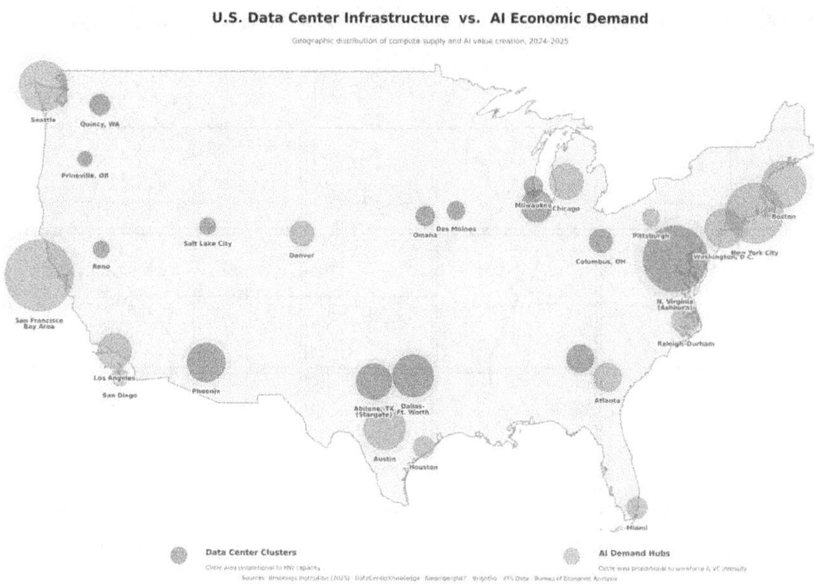

Figure 37: Approximate existing AI demand and data center locations, Q1, 2026; scaled to relative supply and demand.

Note: Brookings Institution (2025), VTS Data / Bureau of Economic Analysis (BEA), BloombergNEF (BNEF), best estimate data, author specification

However, existing capacity (in the U.S.) is near universally deemed inadequate, in particular with respect to power supply—as recognized by industry and U.S. Dept of Energy. Reports exist of GPUs "in hand" by leading ASPs but with an inability to operate them due to inadequate electricity supply. Additionally, several states and communities have complained of escalating power prices due to high levels of consumption by newly arrived data centers. There are accordingly numerous additional data centers committed to or under construction, along with increased power capacity.

This raises the coincident topic of sources of energy supply. The U.S. is said to suffer from neglect in expansion of its energy capacity in recent decades, as well as purported neglect of its transmission grid, perhaps in both cases due to regional management of these factors (decentralization of these components as opposed to a national strategy). The following table depicts energy by source for a selection of peer group countries, and demonstrates high levels of variance in energy sources:

Electricity Generation Source Comparison (Estimated 2025/2026)

Country	Nuclear	Renewable	Natural Gas	Coal	Profile
USA	18%	24%	42%	16%	Dominated by Natural Gas
Canada	14%	67%	16%	3%	Hydro-heavy (55% of total)
China	5%	37%	<5%	58%	World leader in *both* Coal and Solar

Country	Nuclea r	Renewabl e	Natur al Gas	Coal	Profile
France	68%	25%	5%	<1 %	Most decarbonize d major grid
German y	0%	56%	18%	24%	Ended Nuclear

Table 17: Approximate energy generation by source type, peer group countries, Q1, 2026

Note: Data adapted from Ember, *Global Electricity Review* and U.S. Energy Information Administration (EIA) International Energy Statistics. Table author specification.

One can readily see how energy strategies by respective countries affects their energy profile today. France and Germany are absolute contrasts given France's commitment decades back to nuclear, whereas Germany closed down their nuclear plants after Japan's Fukushima nuclear disaster of 2011 (which was the result of a tsunami as opposed to a plant process malfunction). The U.S. has built only two nuclear plants since its Three Mile Island meltdown in 1979, but has recently begun to develop additional nuclear capacity in size ranges from large to micro. In effect, the U.S. took nearly a four-decade break in nuclear energy construction, and related development. We know much more about the risks and benefits of nuclear power today, and have the long-term example of France as a reference. We also have the continuing accrual of fossil-fuel related climate change as a factor in our decision set.

As far as renewable energy, the U.S. has exhibited incongruous policies towards renewables under the last five presidential administrations, which has likely disadvantaged renewable energy development in the U.S., regardless of comparative cost of output. Forgetting political perspective on this topic, objectively this can only be viewed as forgone capacity.

The map below, following the template of the previous map depicting existing data centers and related power plants endeavors to show both new data centers and new power plants both committed to and under construction. The data is approximate, but it portrays a picture of attempted "catch-up" in addressing our energy shortfall.

Figure 38: Approximate AI demand and data center locations, Q1, 2026; scaled to relative supply / demand, plus committed but not completed new data centers and power plants

Note: Brookings Institution (2025), VTS Data / Bureau of Economic Analysis (BEA), Bloomberg NEF (BNEF), best estimate data, author specification

Pragmatically speaking, the single biggest question that surrounds this topic is how will we meet our rapidly accelerating energy needs, and do so in a manner that exhibits economic efficiency, environmental intelligence and respect for adjacent communities.

We await with enthusiasm more details from those who conceive of locating data centers in unconventional, even non-terrestrial venues. Should these prove to be cost-effective, energy-effective, and data transmission-effective, these concepts appear to offer exceptional opportunity. The physics of such endeavors seem daunting, but the benefits overwhelming positive.

20. *Simple Government Economics*

In their 18 October 2025 edition the *Economist* magazine Deputy Editor writes…" Each year we pick a theme—in 2024 it was America's powerhouse economy, in 2023 the dangerous economics of defending the homeland. This week we publish "Governments going broke", an in-depth look at the looming threat posed by rich countries' mounting debts. Rich-world public debt is already worth 110% of GDP. Barring the covid-19 pandemic, it has not been this high since the Napoleonic wars."

Objectively, that aptly introduces our predicament: our debt situation and the dynamics encompassing it are bad, and poised to get worse, even before the impact of our three forces. This is the same magazine, the world-renowned Economist which in 2024 proclaimed America's economy the wonder of the modern world.

Economic orthodoxy holds that periods of above trend economic growth should not result in increased public debt; the opposite should occur, as it did for example during the Clinton administration as well as partially during the post GFC and post Covid periods. Across the last four decades, unfunded tax cuts have on multiple occasions continued to fuel our deficit, thus our public debt trajectory continues unabated, despite overall solid economic conditions.

Clearly, governments fund themselves through taxation of their citizens and their domestically domiciled companies (and by taxation on profits generated within the U.S. by foreign companies). In an ideal situation, government expenditures would match incoming revenues for any given year, resulting in a balanced budget. This is a reasonable baseline assumption. Both taxation and spending—so called fiscal policy—are the exclusive purview of the US Congress, as specified in our Constitution, so the reality is, they have near complete control.

If a government decides to make an investment that it determines is in the country's best long-term interest, and doing so requires borrowing money to finance it, then so be it, as long as all assumptions—cost estimates, return on investment, ability to repay said loan—are credible. Businesses operate according to the same principles, only they are held accountable by their boards and shareholders for the sagacity of both their investments and financing decisions. In America, the government is responsible to the voters, which have apparently not met their responsibility of fiduciary oversight, otherwise the re-election rate in our country would be near nil—simply based on results, not the purported 90-98%.

If in times of emergency there is a clear need for expenditures above what revenues would normally permit, then money is again borrowed to see the country through the "tough patch". (Examples of such a scenario include outbreaks of war, or the recent Covid epidemic.) In cases such as this one would assume that as soon as recovery occurs that the loan would be repaid as the economy recovers. In times of plenty or above expected economic growth one might even imagine a government would run a surplus and put money in reserve for the needs of a potential future "rainy day".

The above describes the general theory of how democratically elected governments of market economies (so-called "liberal democracies") function and loosely aligns with what is known as Keynesian Economics, named after one of the founding fathers of modern economic theory, John Maynard Keynes (1883-1946).

We can see the modern history of taxation in America via the following graph, depicting all sources and blended total of taxation expressed as a percentage of GDP based on actual tax receipts, not statutory tax rates.

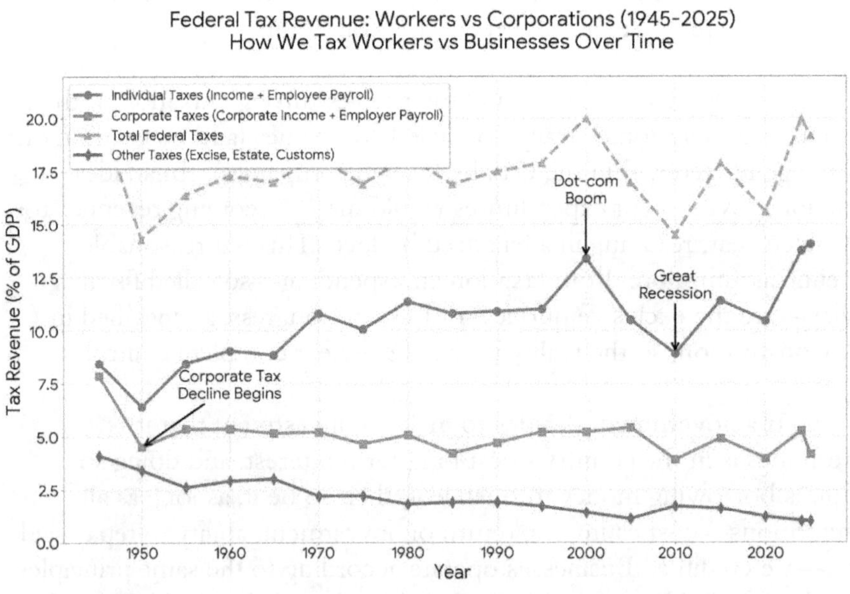

Figure 39: US Federal Taxation history % of GDP, Payroll tax allocated 50/50

Sources: U.S. Office of Management and Budget Historical Tables (Table 2.3), Congressional Budget Office, U.S. Treasury Department, Tax Policy Center

For the first time in our history, the 21st century evidenced the normalization of deficit expansion during periods of prosperity. This is completely anomalous and runs counter to any recognized economic theory: responsible governments simply do not run perpetual massive deficits in times of prosperity.

The President Bush 43 administration marked a turning point when they a) inherited a budget surplus and b) refused to increase taxes during wartime (as is our country's historic precedent) to offset the real-time cost of the Afghanistan and Iraq Wars. It was as if populist sentiment—and fear of political backlash over raising taxes, overtook reason, even principle. Famously, Senator John McCain in May 2003 challenged the administration on this failure, remarking that it did not seem right that the military, seemingly alone, was bearing a heavy burden during a time of war while the average American's life remained largely unaffected.

Four details to understand about the US deficit are the distinctions between:

1) primary deficit (which is the debt generated on a yearly basis per a given year's budget deficit),

2) the cumulative federal debt, or gross public debt (the sum of prior years' debt yet unpaid, plus added debt incurred to pay accumulated interest due on said debt over time),

3) the alternative definition of public debt used at times by Congress or Treasury known as "debt held by the public" which refers to gross public debt but subtracts from this figure prepayments (held by Treasury) for social security or Medicare via employee payroll taxes,

4) net interest outlays are debt service payments made each year on the total accumulated federal debt. Any unbudgeted and thus unfunded interest payments are simply added to the public debt total, adding to taxpayer's liability, therefore acting as an "autonomous tax increase".

The CBO chart below makes this distinction, on an annual basis, as it depicts the layers that figure into each year's total federal deficit—such as "primary deficit" plus the added layer of "net interest outlays" on existing public debt. This percent to GDP of 7.3% (which is debt added annually) is different than the cumulative federal or gross public debt of (now) $38 trillion, which is about 127% of our annual GDP.

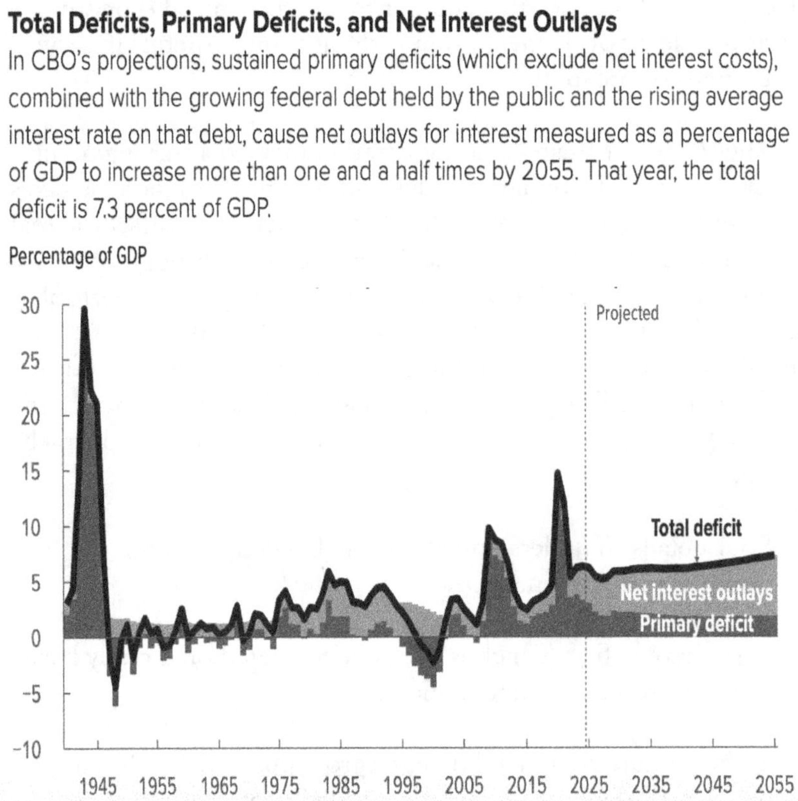

Figure 40: US Budget Primary Deficit + Net Interest (CBO)

Does Congressional oversight not ensure responsible fiscal management?

One might ask why our elected officials do not give the American voter a clear annual appraisal of our public debt—including its twin drivers of annual primary deficits and public debt service.

For example, in the "discussion" surrounding the July 2025 passage of the OBBBA (One Big Beautiful Bill Act) there was modest debate regarding the primary deficit impact over the next decade, portrayed as cumulatively about $4.1T (which was the cumulative sum of the projected primary deficits over the forecast decade).

However, there was apparently little debate regarding each year's obligatory annual debt service payments—over this same forecast horizon—which alone adds about $12.4T to our public debt over the forecast decade. (This $12.4 T figure was provided to Congress by our CBO – and their February 7, 2024, report, *The Budget and Economic Outlook: 2024 to 2034*.)

By using simple math one can see the OBBBA adds about $16.5T to our gross public debt, not the $4.1T advertised. This difference is purely due to the unfunded—yet obligatory—annual debt service payments, for which the American taxpayer is liable. It therefore incumbent upon those responsible for fiscal oversight—that is, our Congress—to account for these mandatory expenditures in the planning process, as not unlike entitlements, debt service payments are mandatory. From a taxpayer perspective, these are tantamount to stealth tax increases, as they will be liable for this expense year after year, regardless of what was disclosed in the OBBBA framework.

One could term this a $12.4 trillion error of omission, as the projected cost of unfunded interest payments had been provided by the CBO more than a year in advance of the OBBBA machinations.

As the table below summarizes, the One Big Beautiful Bill Act (OBBBA), signed into law on July 4, 2025, was presented with an addition to our public debt over the 2025-2034 decade of $4.1T. The difference between the presented price and the ultimate increased public debt is plainly evident—with even its claimed budget reductions being overwhelmed by tax cuts. The "Fast Track" budget reconciliation mechanism used, leading to the absence of the routine CBO generated "budget scoring mechanism", resulted in a "deficit" of data disclosed and debated.

The "Incomplete" Presentation of the OBBBA (July 2025)

Metric	Data Presented	Actual Liability – CBO data
Primary Deficit Impact	$4.1 Trillion	$4.1 Trillion
Unfunded Interest Debt Service 2025-2034	*Excluded from debate*	$12.4Trillion
Total 10-Year Increase in Public Debt	$4.1 Trillion	$16.5 Trillion

Table 18: Fractional View vs Full Disclosure of public debt impact of OBBBA

Note: Data July 2025 CBO Cost Estimate for the One Big Beautiful Bill Act, February 2024 CBO - The Budget and Economic Outlook: 2024 to 2034; author specification

Why does the above matter? How does this affect the narrative of our declining fiscal health, and of the accelerating impact of the "three forces" we are suddenly poised to experience?

It affects it in a hard-hitting manner, as this one episode depicts our need—in this author's opinion—for a procedural change that ensures an all-facts-on-the-table fiscal appraisal of our budgeting process. Doing so, in practice means abandoning the continuing resolution (CR) process, used repeatedly over the past four decades as a shortcut budget approval process. The OBBBA episode also illustrates why in 1974 Congress passed the Congressional Budget and Impoundment Control Act, requiring both houses of Congress as well as the President to follow a deliberative budget review and approval process. Congress is therefore, by using CRs to side-step a formal budget review and approval process, in continuing violation (CV) of its own legislation.

The chart below, courtesy of the CBO, shows cumulative total, not annually accumulated. federal or public debt after years of deficits plus compounding interest relative to GDP on left axis. In other words, it shows the consequence of our Congress's continuing difficulties in presiding over fiscal policy, and equally it presents the "opportunity" for Congress to take the initiative necessary to ensure its fiscal credibility is restored.

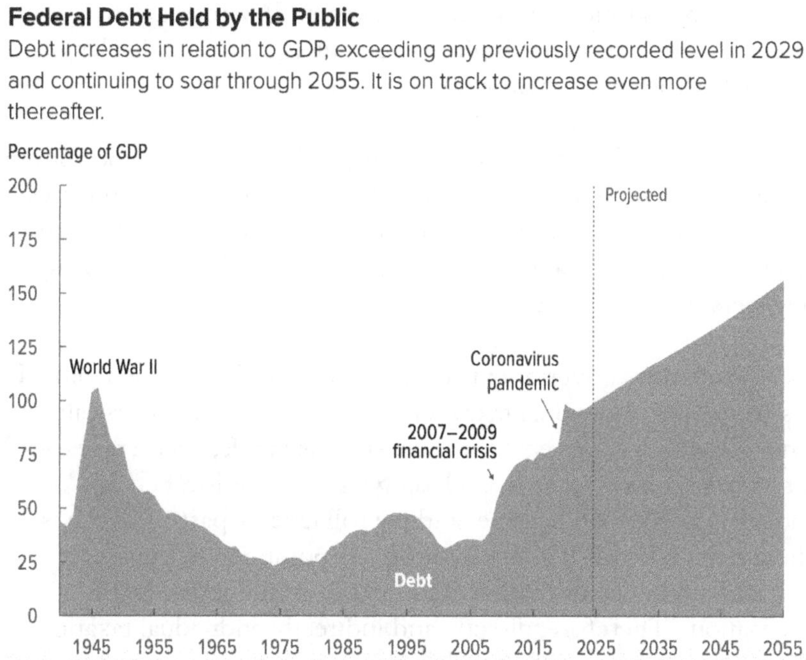

Figure 41: Federal Debt Held by the Public as a Percentage of GDP (CBO)

Note. This figure, based on CBO long-term projections, is known as "debt held by the public" as it credits trust fund balances (Social Security and Medicare) to the gross public debt. The estimated gross public debt for FY 2025 is approximately $38 trillion.

By way of contrast, WW2 was an example of an unexpected exigency requiring deficit spending resulting in a previously unforeseen level of public debt (the alternative, of not defending freedom, of not fighting the war, was obviously off the table). Most would agree that it was America's breathtaking level of munitions production that turned the tide in both the Pacific and European theaters—along with the bravery and selflessness of American and Allied combatants. The deficit generated accordingly was then also in excess of 100% of GDP (remember America was still recovering from the Great Depression) but it was recovered through taxation, and reduction in military spending in the ensuing years. Further, additional "unplanned" expenditures for both the reconstruction of Germany and Japan, as well as the GI Bill (ensuring free college education for US veterans), the Marshall Plan and the Korean War were equally repaid.

Through spending control and a strong post war economy, the Truman administration successfully moved from a massive wartime deficit to budget surpluses in three fiscal years. In a message to Congress in 1948 that in hindsight stands out as a historic display of prudential backbone, Truman wrote ...

"As long as business, employment, and national income continue high, we should maintain tax revenues at levels that will not only meet current expenditures but also leave a surplus for retirement of the public debt. There is no justification now for tax reduction." Clearly, we again need leadership such as this.

Where does government revenue (i.e., taxation) come from? It comes from "us", individual taxpayers and corporate taxpayers (along with miscellaneous "non-tax" revenue, such as tariffs, excise taxes, etc.). As far as federal taxes (that is, excluding any state or local taxes) individuals pay taxes on income, and payroll taxes—part of which is withheld from individual compensation, corporations pay taxes on profits, and payroll taxes that are withheld from the individual's compensation. Therefore, directly and indirectly, individual taxation provides approximately 84% of all federal government revenues, corporations about 9%, with various excise taxes and tariffs making up the balance.

As a country we have operated with a tax revenue shortfall to spending each year since the Reagan era—except during the Clinton presidency. Our government (the Department of Treasury) borrows to finance this annual shortfall, plus the interest payments on total prior debt outstanding, through government debt instruments known as "treasuries", often in the form of 2, 5, 10-year notes and 20 or 30-year bonds. Sadly, the impact of the convergence of the three forces we have referenced, and the message of this study, is that this situation, our annual budget deficit, and our cumulative public debt, is about to get worse.

This obligation on the part of our Congress to look ahead, understand and analyze this risk to our country's solvency and to adopt wise countermeasures is at the heart of this study. Reconciling our annual primary budget deficits each year and solving the question of how we finance our growing public debt are both the fiduciary responsibility of our elected Congress. By any objective measure they have unfortunately been and are failing to meet this responsibility.

Statutory tax rates vs. actual tax receipts

A rarely discussed aspect of taxation in America is the sizeable gap between our official (statutory) tax rates and the amounts actually collected (tax receipts).

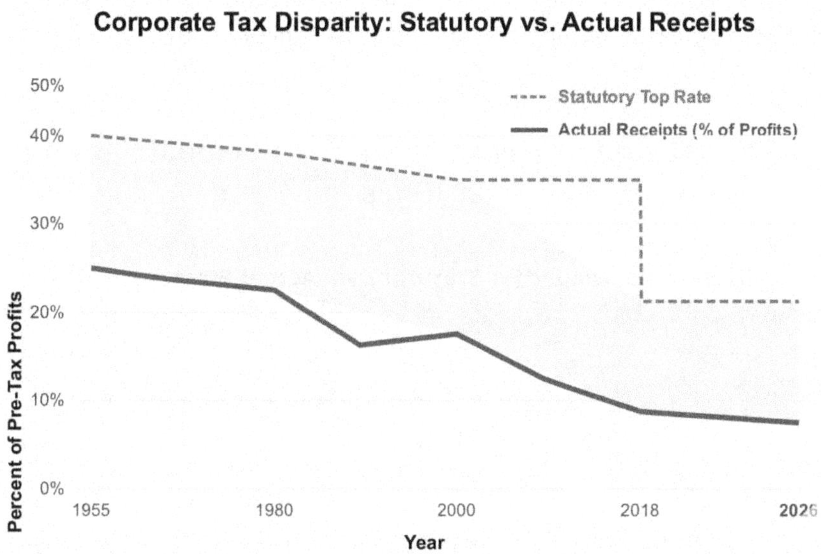

Figure 42: Actual corporate tax receipts vs. statutory rate as percent of Net-Income

Note: Office of Management and Budget (OMB). Specifically, Historical Table 2.1 and Table 2.4; U.S. Treasury Fiscal Data. Monthly Treasury Statements (MTS); Bureau of Economic Analysis (BEA)

There is equally a persistent gap between statutory personal rates (below) vs. actual tax receipts but it is not as vast. Also, as evidenced by tax receipt history, statutory rate changes for the personal had virtually no impact on actual taxes paid by the individual, as changes moreover eliminated loopholes vs. reducing effective tax rates. Conversely, corporate statutory rate changes perpetuated the continuum of granting deduction mechanisms to the corporate sector.

Multiple researchers have pointed out that the 91% top marginal personal tax rate of the 1950s was a fiction; with permissible deductions of that era resulting in top earners paying effective rates closer to 30%. The data suggests that the trend line of effective tax rate not statutory tax rate is what tells the story of tax transformation in the post WW2 era.

"Following the money" we see another vector of evidence that corporate taxation has enjoyed decades of benefit (a 15% net reduction in Federal tax receipts) whereas the personal taxpayer has enjoyed close to none. The reported reason for this is that the stair-step "reductions" in the statutory rate were offset by elimination of tax loopholes that had previously allowed most personal taxpayers to avoid paying the statutory rate. The "bottom line" is that in the last 70 years—on a net receipts basis—there has been virtually no tax relief for the individual taxpayer, contrary to popular perception, and contrary to those enjoyed by the corporate sector.

The Illusion of Decreases in the Personal Statutory Tax Rates

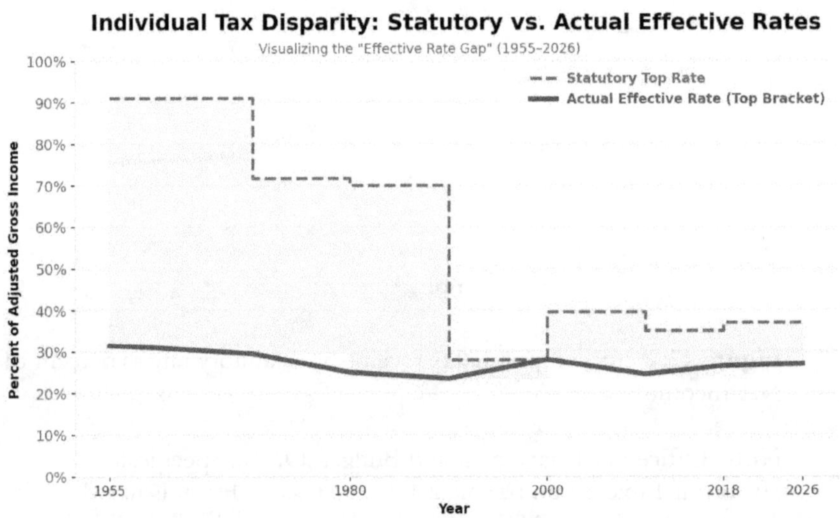

Figure 43: Actual personal tax receipts vs statutory rate 1955 – 2026 percent net income

Note: Office of Management and Budget (OMB). Specifically, Historical Table 2.1 and Table 2.4; U.S. Treasury Fiscal Data. Monthly Treasury Statements (MTS); Bureau of Economic Analysis (BEA)

US Population trajectory impact on the budget and on deficits

In explaining its rather downbeat economic forecasts for the 2024 – 2033 decade, the CBO (Congressional Budget Office) made the following points regarding the continual trend in population decline…

"Demographic trends are key determinants of the long-term budget and economic outlook. In CBO's projections, the U.S. population grows more slowly over the next 30 years than it did over the past 30 years. Without immigration, the population would begin to shrink in 2033, in part because fertility rates remain below the rate that would be required for a generation to replace itself."

"The potential labor force grows by an average of 0.3 percent per year over the next 30 years—much more slowly than the average annual growth of 0.8 percent seen over the past 30 years. Most of that slowdown stems from slower population growth and increases in the average age of the population." (CBO 2025)

Further…" The growth of potential labor force productivity slows over the next 30 years because of two key factors: the slower accumulation of capital (mainly attributable to increased diversion of funds to service the growing public debt, which results in a lower level of private investment) and slower growth of total factor productivity (the average real output per unit of combined labor and capital services) in the nonfarm business sector (as a consequence of said diminution of investment)."

With respect to their (CBO) comment regarding the "lower level of private investment" due to debt service obligations, an important concept in the field of both economics and finance is of "crowding out" of private investment due to increasing sums demanded by increasing public debt service (e.g., cumulative federal deficits and interest due on same). Clinton-era Treasury Secretaries Lloyd Bentsen, Robert Rubin and Larry Summers brought this up repeatedly, and it was a purported catalyst in their desire to eliminate the government deficit in the belief that doing so would catalyze private investment.

In terms of validating (at least by correlation) the theory of "crowding out", the 90's, that is during the Clinton presidency, was the decade with the highest level of productivity in the modern era. Since it is economically axiomatic that investment creates demand, conversely a reduction in funds available for investment leads to diminished demand (a.k.a., growth in GDP), thus the dampened CBO growth forecasts for the next few decades.

The role of productivity growth in budgetary economics

The CBO in its 2025 update writes regarding Labor Productivity forecasts: "Given projected slowdowns in the accumulation of capital and the growth of TFP (Total Factor Productivity—itself often fueled by investment or technological innovation), the growth of potential labor force productivity ...slows in CBO's projections—from an average of 1.4 percent a year over the first decade of the projection period to 1.3 percent over the third decade. The growth of labor productivity (real GDP per hour worked) is projected to maintain a similar pace over the next 30 years, averaging 1.3 percent in each of the next three decades." (Their forecasts thus far do not account for any level of productivity increases we might enjoy from AI.)

By contrast, labor productivity growth was 2.3% in 2024, often attributed to the impact of AI as well as the stimulative policies and infrastructure investments of the Biden era—as by this time the size of the labor force had recovered post-Covid. The 2025 productivity rate has not yet been released by the BLS but consensus estimate is for about 2.6%, which would indicate an uptrend, most likely due to AI, with a tailwind from a flattening size of our labor force. So, the CBO forecast of 1.3% does indeed represent cooling, but it is arguable we can expect productivity to increase in the coming years if productivity benefits of AI kick-in as expected. For now, for this study, we use CBO numbers and forecasts.

Notably, these recent upticks in productivity present a macroeconomic paradox. According to the CBO and historical precedent, our current environment of high deficits and growing debt service is likely "crowding out" private investment and thus detrimental to productivity. Yet, productivity is increasing. What explains this? The answer is likely the growing impact of AI. Productivity gains generated by early AI integration are potentially overriding the drag of national debt service. As Nobel Laureate Economist Paul Krugman has observed, secular trends—such as AI—attract investment, period. This dynamic further underlines the benefit of and need for implementation of an AI taxation framework. Failure to do so exacerbates the risk; doing so seizes an historic opportunity, which arguably should be a low-friction event politically.

We noted in the introduction that growth in size of the labor force and growth in productivity were the bottom-line determinants of growth in GDP. In economics TFP, or total factor productivity, is a technique used in calculating productivity growth that otherwise cannot be attributed to increases in labor, materials or capital investment such as improvements in technology. The impact of inputs such as improvement in technology are at times subjective and difficult to quantify—or may have a lag effect, thus the expression TFP is typically used to "capture" this impact.

"The slower growth of real GDP in this year's projections stems mainly from slower growth of private investment and consumer spending over the next decade and slower growth of real potential GDP over the last decade of the projection period. (Productivity growth for the prior decade, 2013 – 2023, was 1.4%.) The slower growth of real potential GDP reflects a reduction in CBO's projections of population growth. Changes to population projections also reduce the projected growth of the labor force over the last 10 years of the projection period." (CBO)

Productivity rates are a function of GDP divided by the labor force (and size thereof), thus, e.g., a quarter or year with zero GDP growth but a decline in size of *L* (labor force) would show a productivity increase, and vice versa. Therefore, the following chart shows productivity growth 1990 until 2025 alongside change in size of *L* our labor force.

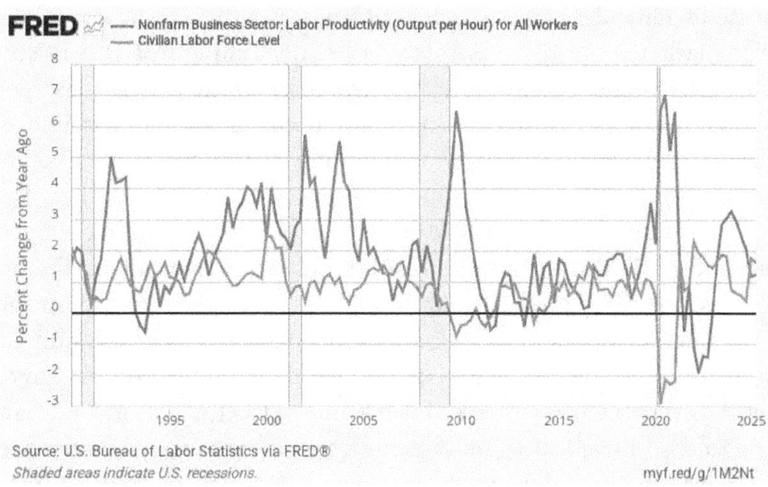

Figure 44: U.S. change in Productivity vs change in Labor Force, Federal Reserve

One can see (above) the occasions in which spikes in productivity are due largely to a sharp event—such as 9/11, the GFC and Covid—as indicated above by gray vertical lines, often resulting in at least a temporary decline in the labor force.

All of which leads us to envisage what we can call an expected output gap vs. prior trend based on the declining size of the labor force and the increased diversion of funds away from investment and into public debt service. Such an occurrence might, if unchecked, begin to resemble a bit of a doom loop, whereby decreases in size of the labor force leads to decreased output leading to decreased investment, leading to decreased output, again leading to decreased investment, further exacerbated by a declining labor force courtesy of negative fertility, not to mention the "diversion" of $1 trillion per year (and growing sequentially) to service our public debt, a.k.a., "crowding out" of potential investment. An unappealing scenario such as this would best be countermanded were it recognized early with necessary actions taken to pre-empt it, which is the goal of this study.

Is the Bond Market a Manifestation of "Unelected" Budgetary Supervision?

An interesting characteristic of our market economy and our democratic process is that in some respects the most powerful voice in our economic policy and decision-making process is that which is wielded by the bond market. The bond market is not elected, it is not mentioned whatsoever in our constitution, it is a manifestation of a dynamic market economy—but its voice is near almighty. It is in some respects the ultimate manifestation of the democratic process, as thousands of voices (those of bond market participants) determine and set pricing based on an intensely active open market process.

Presidents and Finance Ministers around the world have been "brought to heel" if their actions result in adverse reactions by the bond market, such as pricing of 10-year and 30-year treasuries based on the bond market's assessment of risk and hence value. While certainly not a minister of finance, political adviser to President Clinton James Carville, delivered a colorful assessment of the bond market, when in February 1993 he said..."I used to think if there was reincarnation, I wanted to come back as the president or the pope or a .400 baseball hitter. But now I want to come back as the bond market. You can intimidate everybody."

A somewhat worse-case example of its "authority" might be, for example, if the Treasury bond market "judged" that US public debt had become unsustainable, and US Treasury debt auctions were "poorly received", meaning the bond market "required" higher yields than anticipated, this would result in an unpleasant circumstance for America's financial picture. Given American capital markets are the envy of the world and play a foundational role in the size and scope of the American economy and US dollar, fuel investment and therefore growth, no leader in their right mind would put this at risk. Former Treasury Secretary Henry Paulson—Bloomberg's Wall Street Week, April 17, 2026 expressed this exact fear—to paraphrase—he worries that our Congress will not recognize the degree of risk and that it will not exhibit the rigor of response required to meet the moment.

To summarize this topic, we could say …it's a binary world: Congress can choose to fix the deficit itself or perhaps be "told to" one day by the bond market. Or, as Steve Pagliuca (former co-chair of Private Equity company Bain Capital) reminded us on Bloomberg 17 October 2025, with respect to the growth in public debt Congress has presided over …" it's always okay until it isn't okay". Meaning, if displeasure by the bond market with the continuing escalation of the U.S. debt comes to a head, if and when such a day comes, it might come suddenly and without much warning.

Our public debt, like any large problem, would best be solved by addressing it in a serious and comprehensive manner, by planning to evaluate our options and selecting the best one. Waiting until a crisis arrives, such as a failed attempt to issue new debt or refinance existing debt would surely bring with it fewer and less attractive options.

Why are we stuck in Budgetary Purgatory?

Depicted below is the history of deficit spending (red line = federal expenditures and green incoming tax revenue, shaded red area = deficit gap on a rolling annual basis, not cumulative) below chiefly to illustrate that remarkably, we have in our history had only three presidents who have presided over periods of budget recovery: Truman (post WW2), Eisenhower post Korean War, and Clinton (post Reagan era unfunded tax cuts).

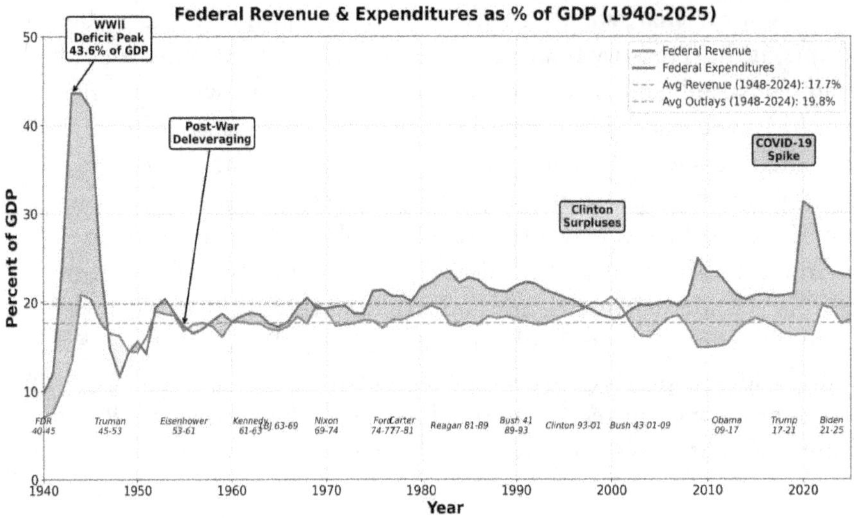

Figure 45: Federal Tax Revenue vs Expenditures as % GDP (OMB/FRED)

Note. Shaded areas represent the primary deficit (red) or surplus (blue) per year. Data compiled by author from OMB Historical Tables.

Surely, we can do better, and surely the consequences we faced by the Great Financial Crisis and Covid—both sources of tremendous deficit in the 21st century, pale in comparison to what our country, our economy and our society endured during the 2nd world war.

As a singular example, the actions of President George H.W. Bush 41 stand as a stark example of fiscal leadership. He recognized the unsustainable trajectory of the Reagan-era deficits, and famously broke his own campaign promise (of "no new taxes") and raised taxes to help facilitate deficit recovery. While he was politically reviled for doing so—an act that partially cost him his re-election bid—his willingness to "take the hit" and absorb the political damage for the sake of what was right for the country arguably helped to lay the foundation for the budget surpluses of the Clinton era.

21. *How to Repay the Public Debt – and Who will Pay?*

The following thought experiment tackles the consequences of our high level of public debt and the "carrying cost" of this burden—specifically the impact of compounding interest service and recurring repayment expense—which are persistently unfunded, perennially digging our deficit hole deeper. We depict a "what if" scenario below with respect to how this might be resolved.

Beginning in the 1980s, we began to run serial deficits, but it was not until the 21st century that these annual deficits seemingly became normalized and cumulatively severe. It is this predicament that we address in this chapter along with the question of, if our Congress were to become serious in their efforts to repay the deficit, what exactly would this entail, who would pay and how long would it take?

U.S. 21st Century Fiscal Policy brought Elevated Deficits

Year	Revenue % GDP	Expenditure % GDP	Deficit % GDP	Key driver
1980	19.0%	21.7%	-2.7%	Pre-Reagan baseline — Cold War defense buildup begins
1990	18.0%	21.9%	-3.9%	Cold War peak spending; S&L crisis adds to deficit
2000	20.6%	18.2%	+2.4%	Post high productivity 90's, Clinton fiscal restraint. Anomaly, not trend
2008	17.6%	20.8%	-3.2%	Post tax cuts, pre-financial crisis, war expenditures vs. decreased taxation
2010	15.1%	24.1%	-9.0%	GFC revenue collapse + emergency spending; worst deficit until Covid

2015	18.2%	20.7%	-2.5%	Post-crisis partial recovery—tax revenue restored to 90's era level
2020	16.3%	31.2%	-14.9%	Covid peak—taxation collapse with dramatic corporate + social stimulus
2024	17.4%	22.8%	-6.0%	Partial but insufficient recovery—deficit begins to appear "structural"
2034 CBO	~18.5%	~24.9%	~-6.4%	CBO baseline projection —gap persists + widens

Table 19: A pattern century-to-date of increased exogenous events coupled with absence of necessary fiscal discipline.

Note: Each year since 2001 has produced a deficit. The structural gap between revenue and expenditure has never closed; CBO projects it will widen to 6.4% of GDP by 2034.
Data source all metrics Congressional Budget Office (CBO), *The Budget and Economic Outlook: 2025 to 2035*

The 21st Century "New Normal": Expenditures Persistently in Excess of Revenue

The 21st century, and the 2000 specifically marked the year of structural crossover to persistent deficits (as depicted both above and below). The transition to persistently lower tax revenue juxtaposed to persistently higher levels of expenditures left no other outcome.

1980 – 2067 Revenue vs. Expenditures: History + Forecast

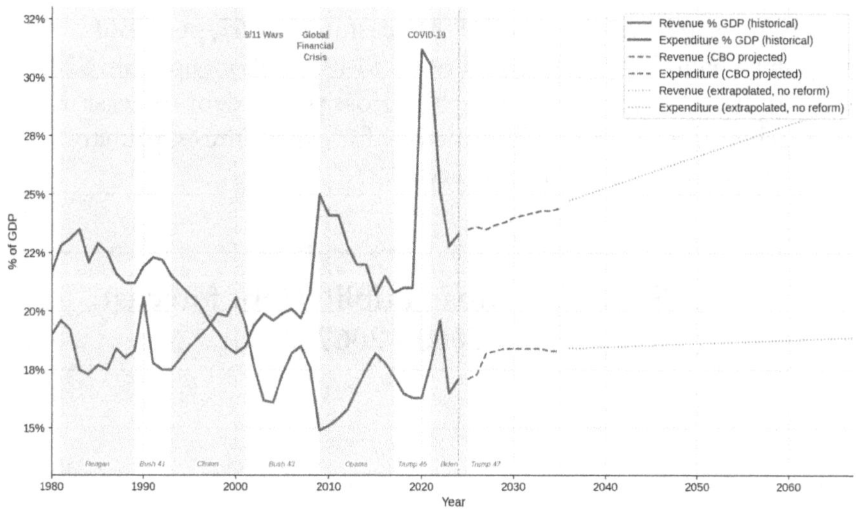

Figure 46: Federal revenue + expenditures as % of GDP, 1980–2067.

Notes: CBO data through 2024 | CBO projections 2025–2035. CBO 2030 forecast expenditures as % of GDP of 24%, revenue % GDP 18.4%, primary deficit 5.5%. CBO Budget and Economic Outlook (January 2025).
Yield forecasts used throughout are CBO estimates, ranging from 3.9% to 3.8% which impacts projected debt service expense as reflected in expenditure trajectory. 2036–2067 per CBO forecasts and author extrapolation.

What will it take to Bend the Public Debt Curve and Restore Fiscal Discipline?

The following calculations use historical data as well as CBO forecasts, with an end target of reducing public debt to 60% of GDP. (We selected 60% as it is near our post WW2 average, whereas a target of 0% might be excessively onerous.) We assume gradual "belt-tightening" of both expenditures and tax rates, in which case it will take until about 2067 to reach our target of reducing gross public debt from 120% of GDP to 60%, such is the magnitude of our debt. Even this means successive generations—the children, grandchildren and great-grandchildren of the baby boomers—will be obligated to pay back this debt.

(Throughout we refer to "gross public debt" as opposed to "debt held by the public" DHBP as it provides a more direct summary of total debt. DHBP refers to gross public debt but deducts prepaid balances in the Social Security and Medicare accounts.)

We begin by depicting GDP forecast until 2067, per CBO metrics, by which date GDP would reach $140.7 trillion, up from $28.3T at the end of 2024. We then overlay the gross public debt forecast until 2067, reaching $469T, using CBO metrics for expenditures, primary deficits and forecast yield on debt service.

U.S. GDP + Gross Public Debt forecast: 2000 - 2067

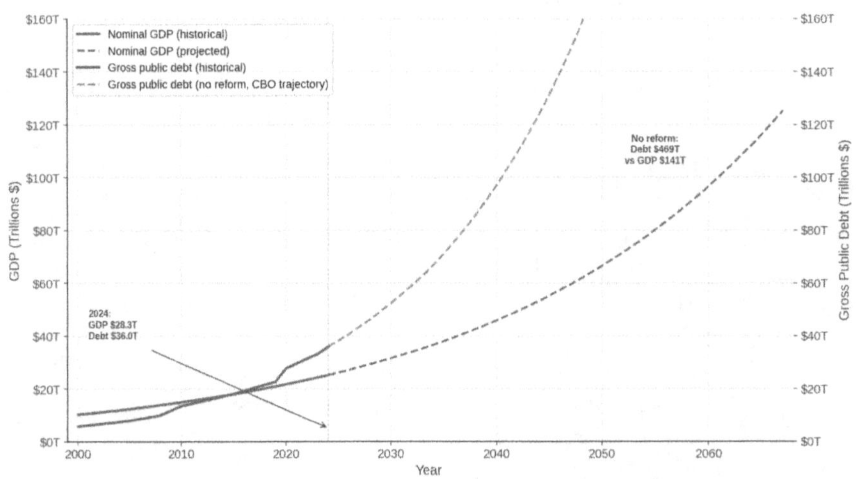

Figure 47: U.S. nominal GDP vs Gross Public Debt, 2000–2067; trend extrapolations

Note: Data per CBO January 2025; Gross public debt per CBO estimates, historical through 2024. Debt reaches $469T by 2067 vs. $141T GDP. Author specification.

The graph below depicts GDP forecast, gross public debt forecast—both per CBO metrics, and overlays our reformed gross public debt estimate, depicted as the curve of debt reform (dot-dash line).

U.S. GDP and Public Debt trends with Proposed Debt Reform

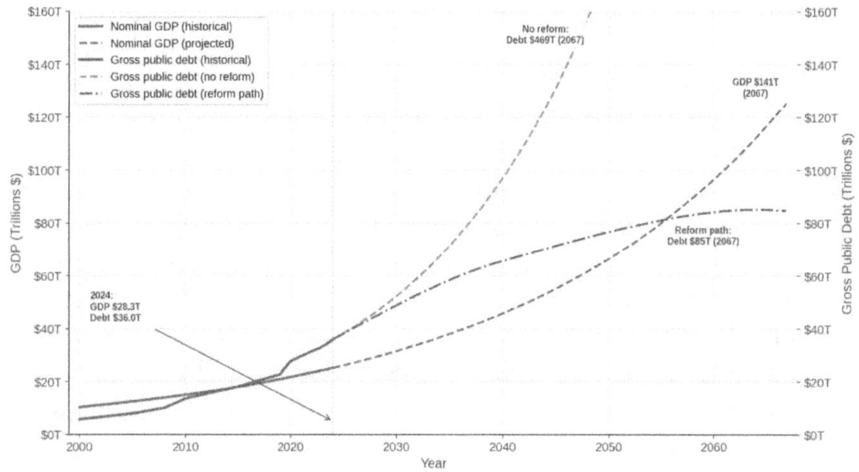

Figure 48: U.S. nominal GDP vs. gross public debt, 2000–2067 + estimated debt reform curve

Note: Nominal GDP (blue line), historical and projected at 3.8%/yr. Gross public debt per CBO estimates, historical through 2024, pre-reform estimates (dashed red line). Debt reaches $469T by 2067 against $141T GDP.
Reform estimate path (dash-dot brown line). Reform estimate curve reduces debt to $85T I n 2067, restoring public debt to 60% of GDP target.
CBO January 2025 forecasts; chart construct author specification.

The Mechanics of How to Restore Public Debt to "only" 60% of GDP

We will not attempt to solve the issue of Federal expenditure reductions in this chapter, which would of course be necessary to restoring debt to 60% of GDP. We will include in the framework below several necessary and unavoidable assumptions.

Taxation revenue obviously must increase—likely through a combination of mechanisms—to achieve deficit stabilization and ultimately partial public debt repayment. Equally, Federal expenditures must be "right-sized" or "reinvented" where possible, but regardless of final ultimate expenditures required they must be funded, including debt service. The act of restoring a primary budget surplus—as will now be necessary—is made much more difficult by virtue of the tremendous "fiscal anchor" our country drags along in the form of our annual debt service of $1 trillion per year—and growing, but failure to account for this budget expense—as has been recent practice—is not an option.

The bottom-line is that for "fiscal recovery" to occur, federal tax revenue must be at a higher rate than federal expenditures for approximately 43 years. Precisely how this occurs—what mixture of revenue increases and expenditure decreases—is up to Congress, but this is the discipline required: we must "spend less than we earn" for 43 years. Doing so does not eliminate our public debt; it merely brings it back to an historic and "manageable" level of 60% that would better position future generations for sustained economic growth. As is well-known by this point in this book, our view is that the additional fourth pillar of revenue offered by taxation of AI would provide a meaningful component of fiscal recovery.

Public Debt Recovery – 43 years of Revenue Greater than Expenditures

Convergence of taxation vs. expenditures first (about 2034), followed by 33 years of revenue approximately 1.5% above expenditures.

Figure 49: Reform path — federal revenue and expenditure as % of GDP required to achieve 60% gross public debt target, 2024–2067.

Notes: revenue intersects expenditures in 2034 at 20.6% of GDP, Reform scenario: primary surplus (revenues – expenditures) growing to 2.5% of GDP by 2042 and maintained through 2067.
Data source: CBO January 2025 baseline; Author extrapolation until 2067.

The Hidden Variable – the Yield Required to Service our Growing Public Debt

Rate of interest, or yield, due on our public debt over a 43-year period is a massive variable, one that greatly affects both annual debt service expense and the compounding effect of unfunded debt service. The current CBO forecast of 4.14% runs through 2033, after which CBO forecasts first 3.9% followed by 3.8%. Thus, one must "hope" that if fiscal discipline is exhibited by Congress, indicating progress in more effectively managing our public debt, that market bond yields will react favorably.

Our erratic yield curve history - distorted by exogenous events

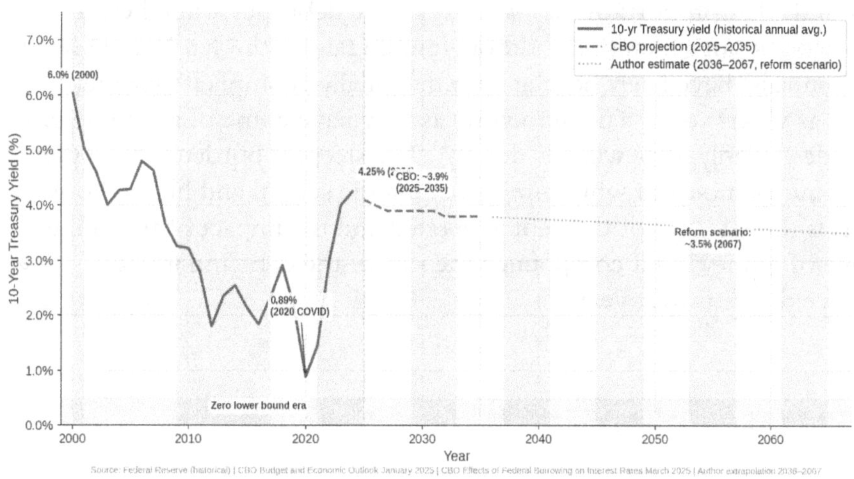

Figure 50: U.S. 10-year Treasury yield, 2000–2067. Historical annual averages through 2024. CBO projection: transitions to ~3.9% average by 2035, declining to 3.8% by end of decade.

Note: Author extrapolation 2036–2067: gradual decline toward ~3.5% under reform scenario, consistent with CBO analysis showing 35bp reduction in yields if debt/GDP were held constant. Zero lower bound era visible 2012–2021.
Source: Federal Reserve; CBO January 2025 and March 2025; Author specification.

Per the above chart, average yield (interest rate paid) on treasury debt instruments was well below the historically normal trend during both the GFC and Covid (at which time interest rates were greatly reduced to stimulate recovery). Yields have since rebounded to a more historically normal level. As treasury debt is gradually rolled over and re-issued it will occur at higher prevailing rates, driving up annual debt service (in fact, this is currently happening, as aggregate debt service payments are sequentially "blending up", increasing cost of debt service).

Theory and history suggest that prevailing yields might decrease slightly if the treasury bond market discounts efforts to reduce the public debt. This occurred during the Clinton administration when the market realized there was a serious effort underway to reduce debt, with a reward of slightly lower go-forward interest rates. In this model they are forecast to stabilize at about 3.8% (above graph).

Repayment burden (of existing public debt) by generation

The following chart (figure 51) summarizes which generations pay and what proportion they will pay of the debt they will inherit from the baby boom generation. Although to be fair, both Gen X and Gen Y (millennials) have lately been at least marginally "complicit" via their roles as voters (or by failing to vote) as they have come of age these past decades. (Sadly, they will pay dearly.) The steepest burden falls to Gen Z, some members of which are still in middle school and high school. This is the "reality" of the debt generated and the impact of the "time value of money" as it compounds the size of the debt and interest service due year over year.

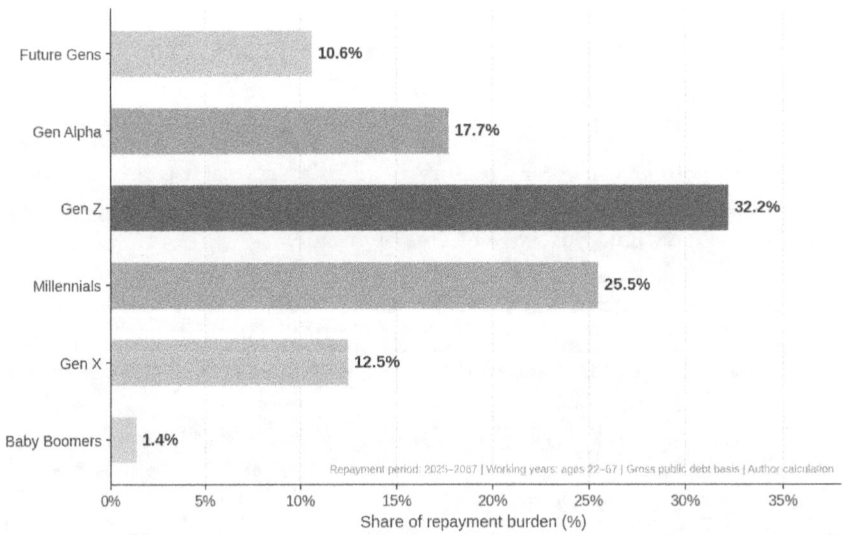

Figure 51: Generational debt repayment burden - share of repayment cost, 2025–2067.

Note: Burden shares derived from each generation's working-year overlap (ages 22–67) within the 43-year repayment period. Gen Z and Millennials bear 57.7% of total burden combined. Baby Boomers bear 1.4%. Total fiscal burden: ~$192T (cumulative interest + surpluses). Gross public debt basis. Yields per CBO forecasts January 2025. Author specification.

The pie chart below (figure 52) dramatically exhibits the "time value of money" as the impact of aggregate gross public debt compounds mercilessly over the extreme length of time needed to pay down this debt. The summary of aggregate payments to retire this debt is $118 trillion in interest plus $36 trillion of principal, a sum total paid of $154 trillion for Congress's $36 T "variable rate loan". ($36T as of the date of CBO estimates used for these estimates; currently $38T.)

Another way to characterize the magnitude of the situation: we will pay $3.28 in interest to reduce each $1 of debt—$4.28 in total when including repayment of principal—much of which will fall on the shoulders of the children and grandchildren of those who caused this debt.

The Price of Requiring 40+ Years to Pay offAccumulated Gross Public Debt

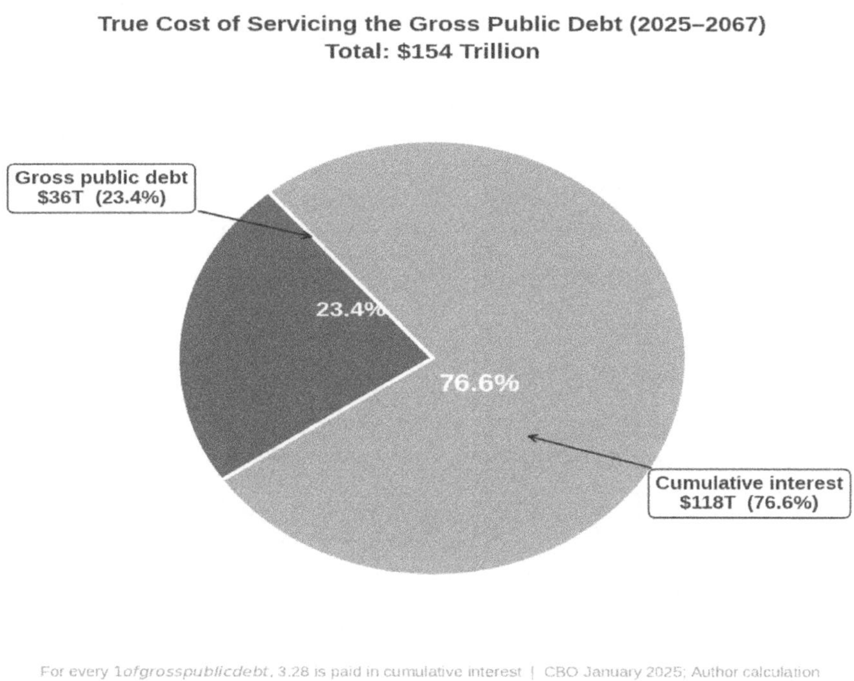

Figure 52: Cumulative cost of servicing gross public debt, 2025–2067. Starting debt: \$36T. Cumulative interest paid 43-year reform period: \$118T. Total fiscal outlay: \$154T.

Note: For every \$1 of gross public debt, \$3.28 is paid in cumulative interest. Data: CBO January 2025; Author calculation.

What is not included in the preceding calculations is the beneficial impact of our proposed AI taxation mechanisms, as detailed in chapter 8. Additionally, Congress faces the exigency of revising our legacy tax revenue system to address the persistent mismatch between share of income vs. share of taxation as allocated. As the Arc of the Production Function makes clear, the historic balance between labor and capital as sources of both income and taxation has fundamentally shifted — and will shift further as AI revolutionizes our economy.

22. The Immediate Gaps in our Labor Force

As reviewed in earlier chapters, the demographic decline in rate of growth of our labor force poses a serious concern both from an economic growth perspective and from a flow of taxpayer revenue perspective. The fact that we also have a growing mismatch between labor force skills available vs. labor force skills needed simply deepens this dilemma. We briefly examine the framework of the aging and skills related gap in our labor force. Regardless of the impact of AI on employment, these trends are in process and are and will affect our economy in their own right.

Per the BLS, non-incarcerated members of the population age 16 or older are considered part of the working age population and eligible for inclusion in the US labor force. There is no upper age limit, with those in the 25 – 54 age range considered "prime working age". Those over 65 are included only if they are employed or actively seeking work.

Labor force participation rate, defined as those actively working or seeking a job, is the percent of the eligible population who comprise the labor force. As of mid 2025 this rate was 62.3% but as the following chart shows, it has been in protracted decline since 2000. The blue line shows labor force size along left axis; green line shows participation percentage along the right. Light gray vertical lines indicate periods of recession. 2020 saw the commencement of Covid.

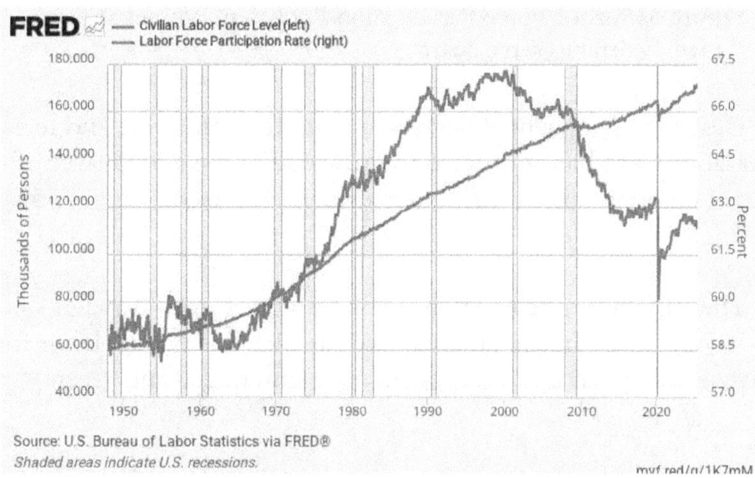

Figure 53: Labor Force with Participation Rate, Federal Reserve

As of 2025, approximately 61.9% of the U.S. population is of working age. This means about 62 out of every 100 people in the U.S. fall within the working-age group. Multiply this working age cohort by labor force participation rate of 62.3% and you have our labor force. Note, average participation rate for foreign-born men is higher than for native-born (app 66.4% vs. 61.6%). The CBO forecasts labor force participation rate to decline to 61.4% over the decade due to our aging population.

The Federal Reserve chart below shows the large disparity in participation rate between foreign-born vs. native-born men.

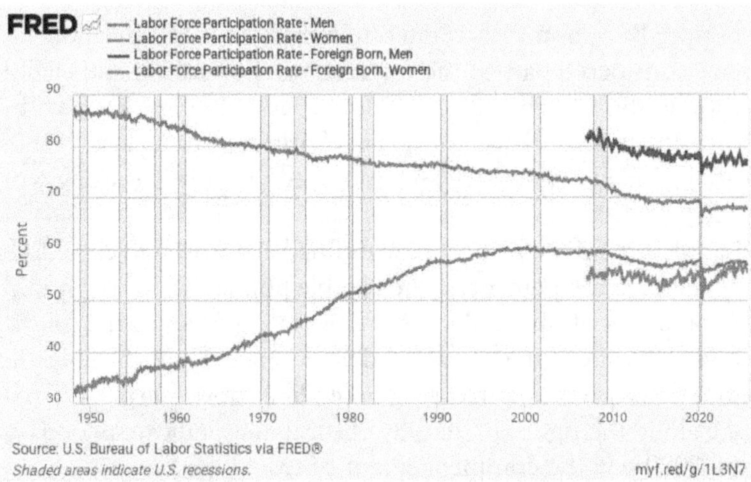

Figure 54: Labor Force Participation Rate Men, Women, Foreign, Native, Federal Reserve chart

Despite the sequential decreases in participation rate and fertility rate, our labor force has continued to grow due to the added layer of immigrants entering our workforce, as evident in the chart (figure 55) below.

The BLS began delineating origin of work force—foreign vs native—about 2009. In the graph above the blue line is total labor force, red is native and green is foreign born. The sum of red and green = blue.

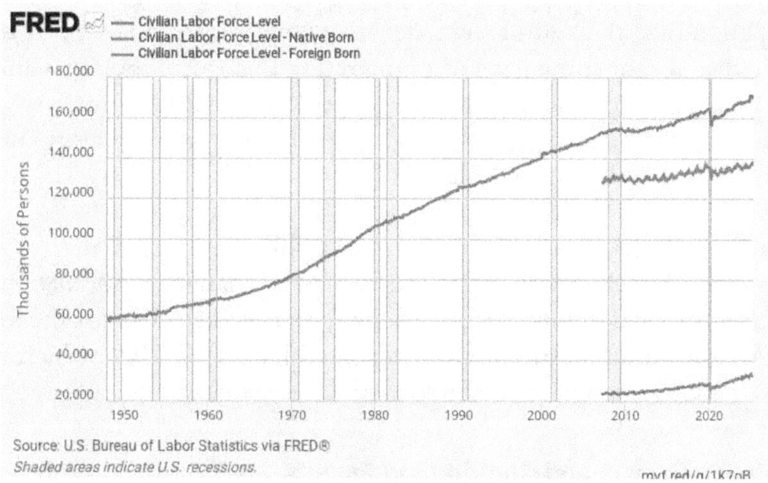

Figure 55: Foreign +Native Born Labor Forces, Federal Reserve

A collective of forces contributes to the decrease in our labor force

The question remains as to why labor force participation rate is in protracted decline, with the inflection point (circa 2000) and subsequent downward trend in participation rate (figure 54), now sufficiently sustained such that it must be accepted as a "new normal". The easy observation is that post 2000, 2010 and 2020 downturns in labor force participation rates followed periods of recession (as depicted by gray vertical lines in the Federal Reserve graph). These participation rate downturns appear to be manifestations of what economists refer to as "scarring" from recession or the "long shadow of recessions" to quote Summers, de Long (2012).

With respect to immigration, the main question we as a country face is not what number we welcome each year but how many will be a match for the needs of our labor force. There is a clear argument (based on BLS data) to be made for more decisively aligning visa issuance to the skill level needs of our labor force, not leaving this to somewhat random selection. There is abundant evidence that there is no shortage of skilled workers who wish to come here, indeed visas for semi-skilled, skilled and highly skilled workers are where the greatest demand vs. supply imbalance exists (per DHS data). Not to mention the prospective pathway of graduating foreign-born STEM students at US universities, constituting an opportunity for the taking should we so desire.

We have reviewed that the trend of negative fertility alone would lead to a decline in the size of our labor force. When one adds the added consequence of an aging population, along with a declining labor force participation rate, then labor force decline comes more apparent. It is unlikely that absent some level of immigration that our population and therefore labor force will continue to grow. Recent CBO estimates conclude that without immigration our population—and therefore our labor force, would begin to decline in 2030.

Due to the dynamic decline in our fertility rate and in net immigration, the CBO (Sep 2025) was forced to change its population assumptions issued in Jan 2025, as follows, and then again—for the same reasons, issued another interim update, dated January 7, 2026, which we depict below.

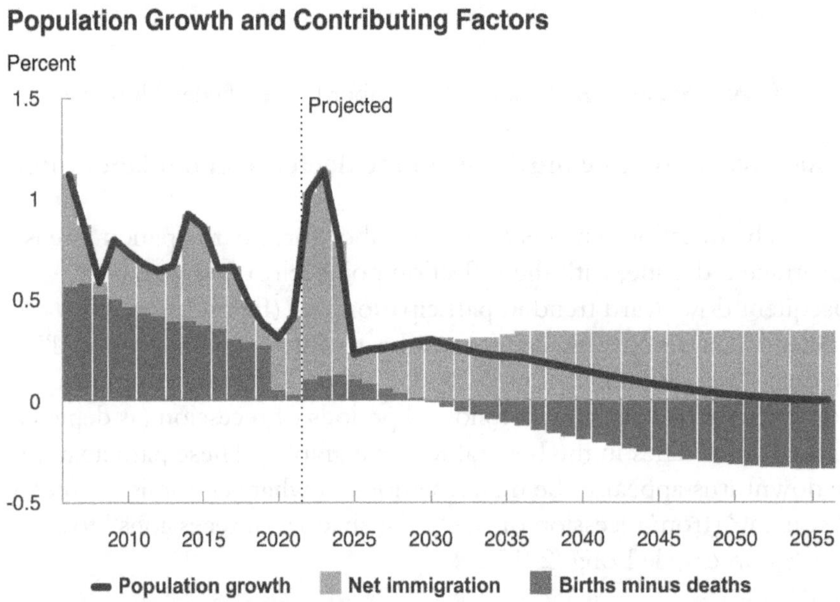

Figure 56: US Population growth forecast (CBO); re-revised January 7, 2026 update

The CBO's September 2025 report, "An Update to the Demographic Outlook, 2025 to 2055," explicitly states that the projected crossover date for deaths exceeding births was then accelerated by two years, and is now—three months later, being revised forward by three.

They specifically indicate these serial changes were driven by two factors:

1. Lower Fertility Rates: The CBO reduced its long-term projections for the U.S. total fertility rate. A lower fertility rate

means fewer native-born Americans entering the population pool.

2. Immigration Changes: The update incorporated new data and the estimated effects of recent administrative actions and legislation (like the 2025 reconciliation act) that were projected to reduce the number of net immigrants over the projection period. An added consequence of fewer immigrants is fewer births in the U.S. in the future.

When on January 7, 2026 the CBO further updated their estimates, reducing fertility rate forecasts (stating we are now at a fertility rate of 1.53), they brought forward the dates of both native born and aggregate population decline.

"The size of the U.S. population and its composition by age and sex have significant implications for the economy and the federal budget. For example, the number of people at the prime working ages of 25 to 54 affects the number of people who are employed, and the size of the population age 65 or older affects the number of Social Security and Medicare beneficiaries."

In this scenario of continued labor force declination there would be direct and indirect consequences. For example, direct consequences would include potential diminished rates of economic output and therefore a reduction in payroll, income and consumption-based tax revenue; indirect consequences would include a diminished rate of investment, due to a lesser rate of economic growth and lesser retained earnings and therefore lesser residual funds available to invest exacerbated by an aging population and rising federal debt service.

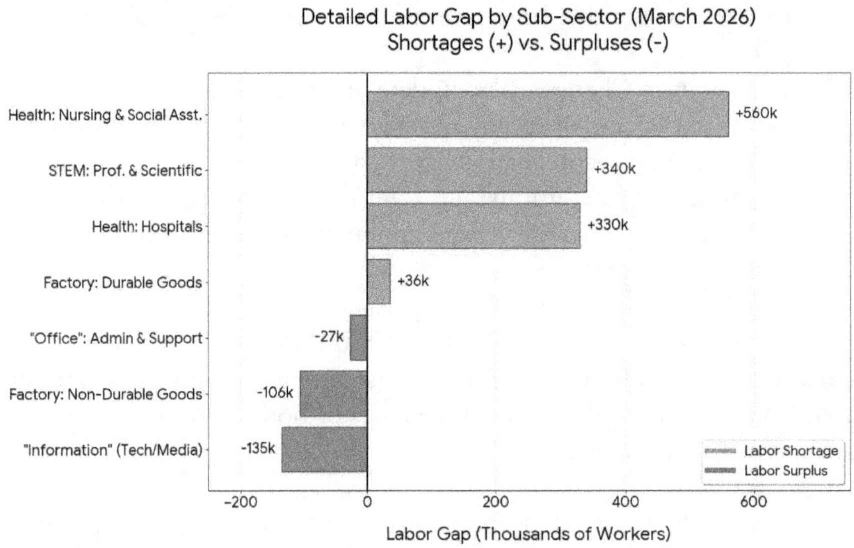

Figure 57: BLS March 2026 Job Openings / Labor Turnover report

Note: U.S. Bureau Labor Statistics Employment Situation JOLTS Reports, March 2026.

In economics, it is axiomatic that investment leads to demand thus diminished investment may become circular in reverse as this reinforces the cycle of diminished output leading to increasingly diminished investment, ad infinitum.

With respect to the CBO population chart (figure 56) there is a direct linkage from a decline in population to a decline in labor force to a decline in tax revenue. This is a crux issue of this study. If it is nigh impossible to alter the trend of a negative fertility rate—not to mention the expected AI-related labor force transformation, there are but three possible alternatives: 1) accept the inevitable reduction in tax revenues and alter government expenditures accordingly, 2) revise our immigration policies—not necessarily sum totals admitted but composition of immigrants admitted via stratified skill type targeting that is modeled to in part offset the loss of tax revenue attributable to a declining labor force, or 3) introduce a new method of taxation that captures the potential loss due to AI-related automation.

The optimal way to approach this would be to elevate the importance of an immigrant's skill level as they correspond to the stratified needs of our labor force as part of the selection process. (This could be described as following the "Singapore model", chapter 23.) A mechanism such as this, adding an economic framework to the immigrant evaluation process would allow us to better address the future shortfall in our labor force by skill level needed and thus better protect individual-based tax revenue.

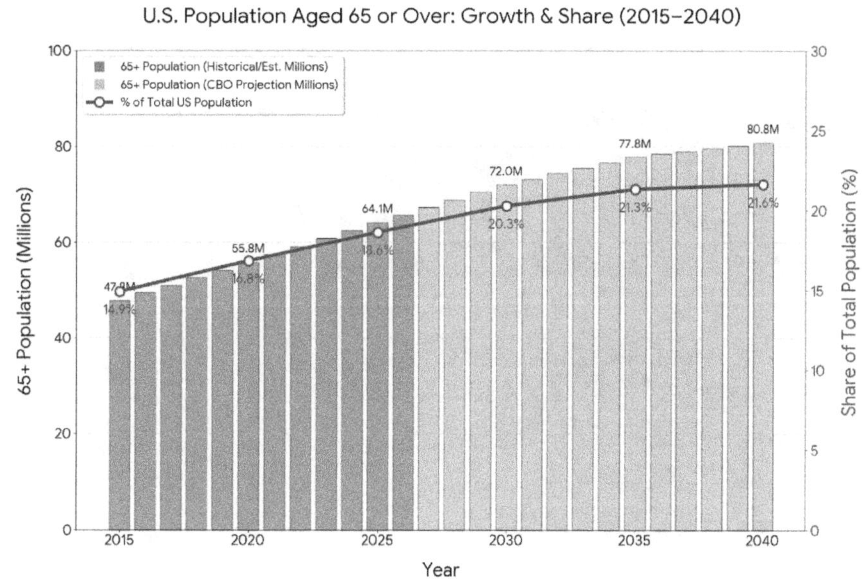

Figure 58: U.S. Population plus age 65 forecast (CBO); the "Gray Tsunami"

Note: CBO Demographic Outlook (2024 & 2026), U.S. Census Bureau (2020 Census), and the Population Reference Bureau (PRB).

The increase in our over 65 population is startling. Meeting the demand for healthcare workers is a clear need to ensure the well-being our aging population.

A shrinking labor force will expose our worker skills vs labor needs mismatch

Throughout the modern era (post WW2) our country has experienced a near steadily increasing labor force, thus the era of a demographically and AI-related labor force cooling puts all of us—economists and politicians, in entirely new territory.

The sub-sectors of greatest need are constantly in the news, from AI related (technical, manufacturing, skilled tradesmen), robotics development, and healthcare, as driven by our demographic transition. Anecdotal reports highlight shortages in two broad areas in particular: STEM related and healthcare (evident in figures 57, 58 & 59). STEM for the reasons stated above, healthcare due to our aging society. The need for low, medium and high skilled foreign-born workers in the healthcare sector is evident in the following chart based on existing share of employment.

Figure 59: Healthcare employment sectors with share of foreign-born workers

Note: Sources - U.S. Census Bureau ACS (2023-2025) September 2025, BLS Occupational Employment & Wage Statistics (OEWS) April 2026, May 2026

We can liken the demographic trend we face to a "gray tsunami". For real-world, seismically driven tsunamis, the warning window is measured in minutes or hours, maximum. Fortuitously, in this case of our demographically driven "gray tsunami", we have had years and decades. Surely, we will be prepared? Regardless, we face this future certainty with one hand tied behind our back, courtesy of a deficit that severely restricts our optionality of response.

Where to next for our labor force?

Connecting these sectors back to current and forecast rates of unemployment—which remain historically low, it is reasonable to estimate that as a country, given current labor force trends, we will struggle to fill these new positions. We can expect that this would hold back our country's economic growth, indirectly weaken our competitive advantage in high growth sectors, and help to create a gap between potential vs actual tax revenue. This would clearly be an undesirable outcome, for the purely economic and competitive reasons, not to mention obvious social implications.

We are agnostic on the number of immigrants admitted legally each year. It is both a premise and an argument of this study that our overall trend level of "legal" immigration (ranging generally between 0.8 to 1.5 million per year, but with a recent average of 1.1 million per year) need not change, but that the composition of these immigrants, that is their suitability for the forecast needs of our labor force, be subject to analysis and targeting to better meet the economic needs of our country. This is for two reasons: 1) protection of future tax revenues to meet our present and future budget obligations, and 2) protection of our competitive stature—as well as simply the needs of our labor force—for important industrial, technological, academic, scientific and medical categories.

At a macro level, the select data reviewed above in conjunction with industry reports and BLS data, consistently corroborate that the areas of highest unfilled need are, and will be, healthcare and STEM-related. We explore STEM at a summary level next.

23. *Why all the fuss about STEM?*

To understand, let's start with a review of the Economic Impact of STEM

The economic case for attracting and retaining foreign STEM graduates is unambiguous — and the cost of failing to do so is measurable. If we ask ourselves, "how can we best assure our continued economic leadership?", apart from growing the most promising citizens, students, future members of our workforce and future leaders, then the short answer would be to "select the best from the rest". This may sound a bit presumptuous, but what if they already want to come here?

We could view the cohort of foreign students who desire to study STEM at America's universities as exactly this group. To generalize, this subset of students often represents the most qualified students from their respective countries, with generally high levels of preparatory (K-12) education, presumably matched by ambition, and therefore with better than average chances for success as students, and if they desire—and if we permit, as members of our future work force.

The numbers on this are clear:

1. In 2024, a total of 1,126,690 foreign students studied at US universities.
2. 56% of which were enrolled in STEM programs, therefore 631,000.
3. Although post-graduation the majority purportedly wished to pursue their long-term careers in the US, only about 20% were able to receive temporary visas allowing this.

The U.S. STEM Talent Pipeline & Immigration Bottleneck (2024)

Pipeline Stage	Count	Context / Bottleneck
1. Total International Students	1,126,690	Total enrolled across all fields of study (IIE Open Doors 2024).

Pipeline Stage	Count	Context / Bottleneck
2. STEM Enrollment	~631,000	56% of all international students pursue STEM fields.
3. STEM OPT Participants	95,384	Students who successfully secured the temporary 24-month STEM OPT extension in 2024 (ICE/SEVP data).
4. Total H-1B Visas Selected	141,205	The total number of H-1B visas granted across *all* fields and professions, strictly constrained by Congressional caps.
5. H-1B Lottery Rejections	617,789	Highly skilled workers (predominantly STEM) turned away in FY2024 due to lack of visa availability (USCIS data).

Table 20: Immigrant STEM students vs employment prospects (BLS, SEVIS)

The primary visa channel for potential STEM workers to immigrate in the US is the H-1B visa. Typically, these applicants are employer sponsored, meaning the applicants have a job offer in hand from an American company who files the registration on their behalf. The employer must attest that said new employee will not displace a native-born worker and that they will pay said employee market rate wages. The employee must demonstrate requisite skill per either university degree and or relevant professional experience.

However, annual H-1B visa entrants are capped at 85,000 plus various exceptions. In total, approximately 18.6% of qualified H-1B (often STEM related) applicants are accepted per U.S. Citizenship and Immigration Services (USCIS) data.

Immigrant STEM employment Applicants vs available Visas

Applicant Channel	2024 Data	Explanation
1. Total H-1B Electronic Registrations – NEW	758,994	Number of eligible registrations submitted for the H-1B cap lottery in FY2024.
2. Approval Rate	18.6%	Percentage of eligible registrations approved after final lottery and USCIS adjudication.
3. New H-1B Petitions Approved (Initial Work)	141,205	New employment petitions approved in FY 2024 (approximate; distinct from continuing employment).
4. H-1B Petitions for Continuing Work Approved	258,000	Petitions approved for continuing employment (renewals, transfers).
5. Annual Shortfall: Qualified H-1B Applicants Denied	617,789	In 2024, 617,789 H-1B applicants, previously qualified by USCIS, were not granted visas.

Table 21: 2024 Immigrant STEM employment applicants vs available visas.

Note: (2024 Data courtesy of USCIS & National Foundation for American Policy (NFAP)

All available (BLS, IRS) data consistently confirms STEM graduates have higher lifetime earnings and therefore contribute a greater level of tax revenue than the average member of our labor force. The following table summarizes projected lifetime earnings and tax revenues for STEM vs. non-STEM cohorts.

Approximate Lifetime Compensation Variance STEM vs non-STEM Workers

Category	Approximate Lifetime Earnings	Estimated Lifetime Income + Payroll Taxes	Notes
1. STEM Graduates	$2.5 million to $3.5 million+	$800,000 to $1.1 million+	Based on progressive tax brackets and payroll taxes (Social Security, Medicare) over 40 years working life.
2. Non-STEM Graduates	$1.19 million to $2.3 million	$380,000 to $700,000	Lower earnings result in proportionally lower taxes paid over lifetime.
3. Difference (The STEM Premium)	$1.3 million to $1.7 million+	$400,000 to $420,000+	STEM grads pay roughly $400k-$420k more in taxes over their working lifetime.

Table 22: STEM vs non-STEM lifetime compensation / taxation estimates

Note: BLS, IRS 2024 data

If we take the number of qualified H-1B applicants denied visas in 2024 (617,789) and (we assume these are largely STEM graduates) multiply these times projected lifetime earnings and tax revenue variance vs non-STEM, we get the following compensation (as a proxy for GDP) and tax revenue lifetime gaps:

Compensation gap = $926.6 billion (617,789 x 1.5 million)

Tax revenue gap = $253.2 billion (617,789 x 410,000)

These are lifetime GDP and tax revenue impact for the *2024* cohort only. As a country we miss out not only on their direct compensation and tax contributions, but also on the presumed "multiplier effect" of their lifetime spending. Of course, this sum and its impact increases dramatically if one adds in the prior and subsequent year cohorts, as this denial of visas to potentially qualified applicants is not a new phenomenon.

With respect to the notion of visa issuance to STEM graduates as a means of extending and enhancing the competitive advantage and stature of US industry and research, in 2007 columnist Thomas Friedman (NY Times) suggested attaching a green card to the diploma of all foreign students graduating from a US university with a master's degree or higher in STEM related curriculum (recent annual average of approximately 170,000 such students—double the number of annual H-1B visa recipients). As a tactic, this would be no less than a pipeline of highly skilled labor into the US labor force. This was and remains a brilliant proposal (assuming appropriate security vetting of each candidate). It coincidentally, represents the notion of "taking the best from the rest", especially those who are already here, are well-educated, and wish to contribute.

A tactic such as Friedman suggests would most probably be immediately additive to our country's per capita GDP (given higher overall income levels of STEM graduates) and additive to our level of taxation per individual worker. Qualitatively, and less immediately measurable, would theoretically be the beneficial impact in scientific and medical fields, disciplines in which the U.S. has exhibited leadership and would be well-served to protect it.

The key intended "take-away" from this topic is that immigration for purpose of employment is one of the smaller categories in terms of overall visas granted but has been demonstrated to be one of the most important drivers of economic vitality as well as fiscal stability. Arguably, student visas, if viewed strategically could be considered a pipeline of future qualified STEM workers, researchers, and scientists for our country. No searching or solicitation needed: many of the world's best and brightest already want to come here.

There is not a path to leadership in the AI-era for our country that does not include excellence and leadership in STEM.

We are not alone in recognizing the potential benefit of foreign-born students and workers with expertise in STEM. DW (Deutsche

Welle) News, a Berlin headquartered English language international news platform reported (August 10, 2025) on the trend of European and Japanese universities targeting Southeast Asian students (often with a STEM orientation) to study and later work in their countries to compensate for their growing shortage of native-born STEM students and skilled workers. Some current examples of this changing competitive set include:

China in October 2025 announced its "K visa" intended to attract young foreign STEM talent to live and work and build their careers in China, in an effort to support its desire to be a technology innovation center.

Canada, while tightening overall immigration caps is creating explicit fast-track mechanisms for high-skilled workers. Canada is offering an accelerated pathway to encourage skilled U.S. H-1B visa holders (tech professionals facing U.S. visa difficulties) to migrate north. They also announced that foreign graduate students applying to public Canadian institutions for master's and PhD programs will be exempt from the new federal study permit.

Australia's skilled migration programs favor IT and specialized roles via their National Innovation Visa.Singapore continues to reinforce its tech hub appeal with passes tailored for high-earners and experts. Their 5-year renewable "One-pass" targets high-achievers with high salaries or outstanding achievements in tech and research. Their "tech pass" targets tech entrepreneurs, leaders, or technical experts to work in Singapore on frontier and disruptive innovations (e.g., AI).

The UK offers special entrée for skilled workers such as potential leaders in digital technology and academia via their Global Tech Pass, as well as encouraging graduate students to stay and work in the UK after studies.

S. Korea just launched several specialized programs and visa reforms to attract and retain top talent in AI, semiconductors, biotechnology, and robotics to prevent "brain drain" and secure technological leadership. This involves long-term residency and financial incentives not available via standard immigration routes.

As a country, it is beyond clear that we have benefitted both academically and economically by the prior flow of STEM students and graduates into our country. The ranks of company founders, company CEOs disproportionately features former foreign-born stem graduates and H-1B visa recipients. The same can be said with respect to our high level of foreign-born Nobel Laureates. It is therefore unequivocally in the best interests of our country that we continue to be a magnet for such talent, and as needed get out of our own way when it comes to deterring this. America's best interests are best served when it exhibits a big, broad, confident vision for its future, with policy to match.

24. U.S. Demography Trends Compared to a Peer Group of Countries

The following section will make use of a comparison of immigration related practices between a peer group of countries – China, Canada, Germany, the UK and Singapore for ease of contrast. (Singapore, while not a "peer" is included because they often seem to have the most "evolved", insightful and targeted policies.) We will find numerous similarities and a few points of difference.

We start with a table depicting best available data on fertility and comparative immigration practices from 2024.

Comparative Fertility & Immigration Metrics 2024

Category	China	USA	Singapore	Germany	UK
Total Fertility Rate	1.04	1.68*	0.98	1.35	1.75
Annual Immigration	420,000	2,220,000	93,000	942,000	940,000
Immigrants % Pop.	0.03%	0.62%	1.5%	1.12%	1.35
Foreign Born % Pop.	0.07%	15.1%	30.5%	19.1%	14.8%

Category	China	USA	Singapore	Germany	UK
Skilled Worker Visa	35,000	160,000	3,000	70,000	125,000
Semi + Low Skilled Visa	75,000	175,000	58,000	130,000	51,000
Student Visas	195,000	988,000	61,000	348,000	450,000
Refugee / Asylee	<5,000	230,000	<1,000	48,000	29,000
Family Reunification	68,000	625,000	17,500	185,000	85,000
Workforce 1st year	37%	51%	60%	47%	52%
Estimated Illegal	650,000	790,000	950	29,000	42,000
Ann. Labor Force Incr.	0.3%	0.4%	1.7%	0.8%	0.5%

Category	China	USA	Singapore	Germany	UK
Data sources OECD, Int Org Migration	Nat Imm. Admin, Bureau Statistics	Census, DHS, USCIS, PEW, Fed Res	Dept Statistics, Ministry Manpower, OECD	Deutsch. Fed Statistics OECD, Eurostat	Home Office, Off Nat Stats

(Estimated illegal immigrants not included in country total immigration)

Table 23: Fertility / Immigration comparison "peer" countries

Note: Date sources - (OECD, IOM, BLS, Census Bureau), * CBO Jan 2026 update = US fertility rate of 1.53

Multiple similarities and contrasts emerge from this comparison. One quick simplification is that the Asian sub-group by far has the lowest fertility rate, and also in many cases have the highest level of specific programs—in place or in test mode—to help countermand this. The Western sub-group, while having higher fertility rates overall, generally have base-line levels of natal care and family care programs in place, so specific fertility-inducing programs as less evident.

Nearly all developed countries face negative fertility issues, thus we endeavor to draw out from our quasi-peer group of countries strategies employed to countermand tis trend along with simple immigration metrics. We will not endeavor to explain why negative fertility is higher in some countries than others (causes of which were partly addressed in chapter 2)—apart from observing some typical correlations, but will mainly focus on what strategies a sampling of countries have undertaken to try to solve the consequences. We will not attempt to characterize them as smart vs. not-as-smart countries but rather observe those who appear to be taking specific steps to countermand this and those that have not yet.

Fertility Rate Evolution by Country - 1960 to present - World Bank

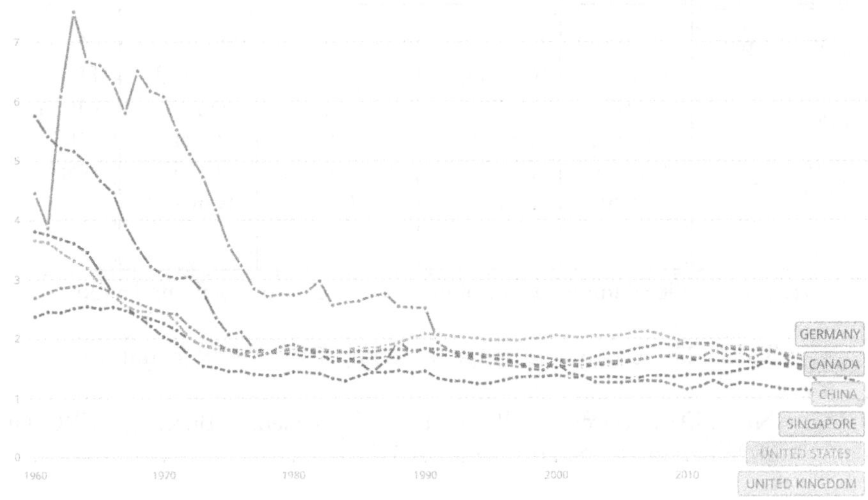

Fertility Rates 2023: Germany 1.4%, Canada 1.3%, China 1.0%, Singapore 1.0%, United States 1.6%, United Kingdom 1.6% (World Bank data)

Figure 60: Fertility rate trends peer group countries (World Bank)

With respect to immigration, for whatever reason, an interesting correlation that emerges is that Western countries appear have higher levels of immigration along with more generous pathways to permanent residency, and conversely many Asian countries have focused on aggressive steps through financial benefits to attempt to countermand their advanced negative fertility trends and protect stability in their societies and their economies accordingly. By any measure, Singapore is an outlier. We devote considerable focus to their policies in order to identify all lessons possible.

Specific Actions taken by China

China, as the data shows, permits very little immigration. As has been broadly reported, they are well into a protracted period of negative fertility, initially mandated via the infamous "one child policy" implemented in 1980 as a reaction to rapid population growth—principally in the countryside, driven by fears that China could not socially and economically support the size of their growing population. Population growth was greatest in the countryside, and accordingly migration to the relatively prosperous urban areas (then 18% of total population) was tightly managed (largely prohibited) in order to not overwhelm services available to urban residents vs. non-urban. This policy was ended, effective 2016, as concern grew regarding the opposite effect, that a shrinking population would not be able to support an aging population along with related fears regarding the consequence of a declining labor force.

China has heretofore hesitated to offer monetary inducements to its citizens to encourage childbirths, except for at the province level where some have been implemented. (For example, Hohhot, capital of Inner Mongolia—a northwestern province, previously announced subsidies of 50,000 yuan ($6,973) to couples who have a second child and 100,000 yuan ($13,947) for a third or more." This has recently changed with the central government announcing a new childbirth incentive program. Reported by *Bloomberg* 29 July, 2025… (to paraphrase)

"China announced it will hand out childcare subsidies in its latest push to boost birthrates after a worrying drop in recent years. The government will spend 3,600 yuan ($502) a year per child under age three."

This followed China's population shrinking for a third straight year in 2024. New births at 9.54 million in 2024 was only half of the 18.8 million registered in 2016 when China lifted its one-child policy (a dramatic drop-off in fertility over an 8-year period).

Last year, China recorded the lowest marriage rate in almost half a century, down 20% from a year before. In the last decade, marriages plummeted from 13.47 million couples in 2013 to 6.11 million in 2024. Chinese are also marrying older, with the average age of first marriage rising from 24.9 in 2010 to 28.7 in 2020. There are cultural factors behind both of these shifts. In China, a male is often expected to have a home, a car and a well-paying job to be considered marriage-eligible, affecting both marriage rate and age. China has regrettably been experiencing higher than expected unemployment rates among the college graduate cohort—since Covid, further exacerbating this.

China's social benefit programs are considered to be at a much lower level than that of other Asian countries experiencing negative fertility (such as S. Korea, Japan, Taiwan and Singapore), with the burden of care falling more principally on the immediate family (i.e., children of retirees).

Where China (or Chinese companies) has been pro-active for more than a decade is in the economic sphere rather than the social. Chinese businesses have been active in outbound foreign direct investment (FDI), that is investment in factories in South Asian countries with relatively abundant low-cost labor, for manufacturing processes predicated upon relatively low-skilled workers. In such a scenario, Chinese companies negotiate a factory development deal--generally at the province level in Cambodia, Viet Nam or Malaysia, typically with guarantees such as constancy of electricity supply, etc., install necessary equipment along with Chinese management and employ local, usually low-skilled, low-cost staff. Tactics such as this, while specifically beneficial at the enterprise level, have the overall effect of addressing the cumulative impact of a diminishing low-cost, domestic labor force.

Alternatively, Chinese companies in more capital-intensive industries have been active in development of manufacturing-based robotics, deployed within factories in China, as a way of both automating manufacturing, lowering cost of production (after capex depreciation) and ensuring quality standardization while at the same time side-stepping labor force shortages within China. Today, China's robotics labor force allegedly surpasses that of all other countries combined, with their robotics "density", i.e., number of robots per 10,000 factory workers behind only S. Korea and Singapore. One could easily view their "push" into robotics as at least a partial reaction to both declining fertility as well as increased cost of labor (supply and demand imbalances of labor naturally create price changes).

Specific Actions taken by the US

The US has had a fairly generous annual allowance as far as number of immigrants permitted—albeit, without skills targeting, but apart from its decades old child tax credits there have been little if any recent policies regarding incenting childbirth. In fact, until quite recently, the topic of negative fertility is barely discussed in public media. In spite of the generally agreed excellence of many US technical universities, the impact of robotics in US factories is still several years away, with indeed most robotic deployment within US factories being produced by joint ventures with European or Japanese producers, domestic offices of same, or by US based Amazon's (and lately, Tesla's) robotics divisions. This is obviously a somewhat painful irony, as was recounted earlier, manufacturing robotics were initially pioneered by American (Stanford University-based) engineers.

Overall, the political and cultural environment in the U.S. is such that there is very little debate at the social, economic or policy level with respect to negative fertility or manufacturing robotics. There has been—of late—considerable attention given to the humanoid robotics category, but this sector is still early-stage, and this masks the fact that as a country we are at present missing out on the economic and labor force benefits available to us through a robotic work force. We believe, transitionally at least, this will be to our disadvantage, but equally can see that as far as implications for our future economy and workforce, robotics penetration in our workforce is gradually beginning to change.

Specific Actions taken by Singapore

(The following dive into Singapore is disproportionately long to offer the historic, political, and economic context that has influenced their highly nuanced set of policies.)

In most senses of the word, Singapore is an outlier. It is an historical outlier, a political outlier, an economic outlier, not to mention a social outlier. Between 1942 and 1965 it had an unparalleled journey as a "state". A former British colony, it was captured by the Japanese in 1942 in one of the more remarkable victories of WW2 (from a western perspective, it was a devastating and embarrassing defeat). At the end of the war, it reverted to its status as a British colony, then became part of the newly created country of Malaysia in 1963, only to essentially be kicked out of Malaysia in 1965 due to irreconcilable differences and began its journey as an independent country at that time. They were at that time, flat-broke and completely alone as a country.

Luckily for Singaporeans, their leader was a legendarily brave, strong-minded and farsighted (none of which are hyperbole) man named Lee Kuan Yew, who through a combination of vision and force of character created one of the more remarkable countries (some say "city-state") in the world today. In the minds of many, Lee Kuan Yew easily makes the list of top ten leaders of the 20th century.

Modeled after the British parliamentary system, largely adhering to democratic practices and *incredibly* completely forbidding and extinguishing corruption, Singapore has become an exceptionally vibrant market economy and society that boasts some of the top metrics in the world as measured by per capita GDP, life expectancy, quality of education and public healthcare. Singapore's National University of Singapore (NUS) now ranks top 10 on a global basis (recently number 8) and ranks top 5 in six specific curriculums. When it comes to government policy, Singapore is often "the reference" for effective governance, even though one could also fairly call it a "curated democracy".

To bring this back to the here and now, and the three forces we focus on in this study, Singapore is in the thick of it, and we will review how they are navigating their way through this turbulence.

1. Negative fertility: Singapore's fertility rate, at approximately 1.0 (vs. a replacement rate of 2.1), is among the lowest in the world. Despite this, their population of 6 million remains stable due to effective policy.

2. Immigration: Singapore has a labor force of 4.01 million, of which approximately 1.6 million are native born and 2.4 million are foreign born. It has developed an extremely "stratified" policy of immigration, with work visas and work permits targeted to address the gap between demand vs. supply in its labor force. In this case, stratified refers to an effective analysis of the needs of its labor force and a system of (skilled and semi-skilled) visas and (basic and unskilled) work permits that is targeted to meet these needs.

3. Adoption of workforce automation: On a density of installed robots per 10,000 manufacturing workers basis, Singapore ranks number 2 in the world, behind only S. Korea, and ahead of China, per 2024 data.

4. Labor force stability: through its stratified and targeted immigration and work permit policies, it maintains labor force stability, and therefore predictable tax revenue.

5. Low statutory rates of taxation (maximum personal rate of 24%, corporate flat tax of 17%, with no special treatment for capital gains) with on a net tax receipts basis (taxable income less allowable deductions) corporate taxes paid as a percent to GDP higher than personal (per 2024 data).

6. All-in their policies result in 2026 IMF reported per capita GDP in nominal USD of $107,758 vs. $94,430 for the U.S.

A key take-away from any study of Singapore is that for nearly all foreseeable impediments, Singapore appears to have indeed foreseen them, planned ahead and generally implemented effective policy to countermand each risk, case by case. They are, 60 years after being "kicked out" of Malaysia, the wealthiest country in Asia with a standard of living that is the envy of most.

Singapore, along with China, Japan and S. Korea has a perilously low fertility rate of about 1%. To their credit, they by far have the most nuanced and targeted immigration and worker visa program of any country. Of Singapore's total population of 6.04 million, only 3.64 million are actual citizens. Added to this are categories of stratified visa and work permit holders, along with dependents allowed for visa holders. There are 400,000 highly skilled and skilled workers under Singapore's E Pass and S Pass system along with 400,000 semi-skilled and unskilled workers with work permits. Dependents of visa holders make up 60,000 residents with foreign students another 50,000. E Pass and S Pass visa holders have a path to permanent residency (PR) per their continuing employment contracts as well as a demonstrated "ability to integrate and contribute to Singapore's society and economy" (per Singapore MOM Ministry of Manpower). Note that the path to permanent residency does not necessarily equate to citizenship.

A little discussed fact, is the size of Singapore's employment tax base—courtesy of its various visa and work permit schemes—in contrast to its actual citizen population. Specifically, Singapore has 6.04 million residents but only 3.64 million citizens. That means roughly 40% of the population — the work permit and visa holders — are contributing payroll and income taxes to the Central Provident Fund (social benefit program), along with consumption taxes while drawing on a comparatively narrow band of social services relative to citizens. Work permit holders in particular have very limited access to Singapore's social safety net — housing subsidies, certain healthcare subsidies, and education benefits are largely reserved for citizens and permanent residents. This little discussed framework may or may not be transferrable to other countries, but it merits thought as it represents a dynamic that benefits all: citizens certainly benefit, and there is a seemingly an endless line of applicants to join Singapore's high wage workforce.

As far as fertility, Singapore previously had a "stop at two" policy to contain population growth which was implemented in 1972 but ended in 1987 (*three decades ahead* of when China ended its one child policy) as fertility trends reversed—they planned ahead and saw the risk coming. Today it offers a variety of financial incentives for third children or more, including parental, educational and health grants. It also has mandatory paternity leave of 4 weeks. Nonetheless, its fertility rate remains stubbornly low, but its work permit and visa programs allow it to maintain—by far, the leading per capita GDP and life expectancy of any Asian country.

Specific Actions taken by Germany

Germany's fertility rate has long been a problem (last reported at 1.4%). Germany's labor force problem has been exacerbated by its 1990 reunification of East with West Germany, which initially resulted in a decline due to a high closure rate of unprofitable East German factories. In 1990 its total workforce post reunification was about 43 million, 2 million of which were foreign born. As of 2024 its total workforce is about 44 million, now with a 9 million (or 20.5%) foreign-born component and therefore a 17% decline in the native-born share. Germany has on multiple occasions revised its immigration policy to facilitate continuity in the skilled worker component of its labor force.

- Issues work permits that can transfer into work visas
- Some stratification targeting for skilled workers
- Experienced professional visas
- Issues work "search permits" allows 1 year to find work
- Free movement within EU, inward and out

Specific Actions taken by the United Kingdom

Immigration in the UK was once driven by "right to freedom of movement" within the EU, which proved to be unpopular enough to fuel the UK's Brexit decision. (The UK joined the European Economic Community, precursor to the EU, in 1973, and nearly five decades later via their Brexit mechanism.) A key driver of the Brexit decision was dissatisfaction with the rate of immigration into the UK. However, this decision seems to have created more problems than it solved, both through its unintended impact on immigration and the fact that Brexit limited the UK's trading partners and led to a predictable economic drag.

Post-Brexit the UK implemented a points-based immigration system, focusing on immigrant skill set, but due to presumed mal-administration or absence of targets for total number of permissible immigrants per year, the annual number of immigrants post-Brexit increased dramatically. By any measure, this consequence of a dramatic increase in immigration caught the average U.K. citizen by surprise, as it had the complete opposite effect of what they thought they were voting for.

The Consequence of an "Unanchored" Immigration Policy: Post-Brexit Era (2020) brought Accelerated UK Immigration

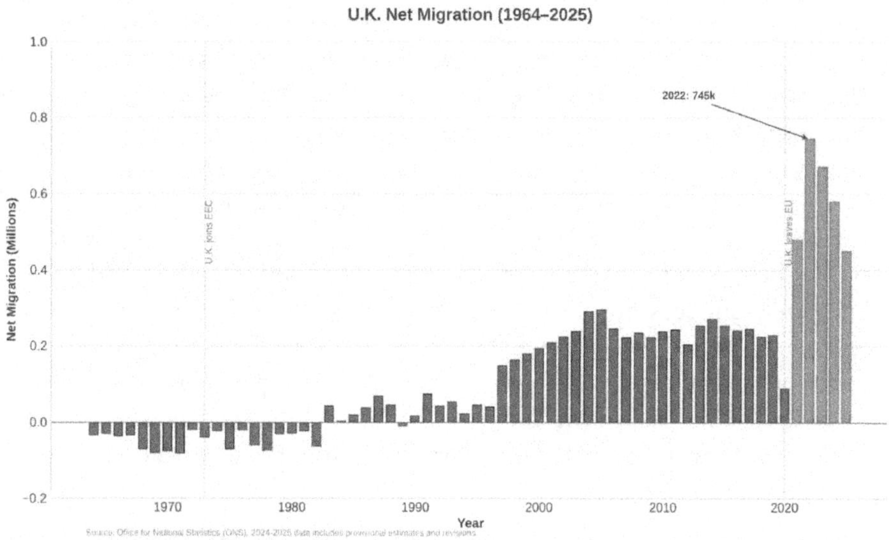

Figure 61: UK Immigration trends 1964 – 2024; UK joins EU 1973 and exited 2020; Deep blue = pre-Brexit, Bright-blue = post-Brexit.

Note: Source - UK Office National Statistics (ONS); ONS (LTIM / IPS Survey 2019); ONS (Admin-based / Home Office 2023); ONS (Provisional Estimates 2025)

Like Canada (below), the UK has not specifically introduced pro-natalist policies to induce childbirth, but also like Canada it has by most standards a widely available set of social and health benefits available to most legal residents and all citizens.

Specific Actions taken by Canada

Over the last decade Canada has increasingly targeted increasing immigration as well as increasing permanent residency for both temporary workers and students. Specifically in 2015 they introduced their Express Entry program facilitating ease of entry via their Federal Skilled Worker Program and Federal Skilled Trades Program. Additionally, Canada grants a high degree of autonomy at the province level to determine their targets and recruit accordingly. Prior to their express entry program, they admitted 260,000 immigrants in 2014 and then 484,000 in 2024.

While Canada has long had an employment focus with respect to immigration, including their "points-based" system adopted in the 1960's, the shift to a more aggressive strategy occurred in the term of Justin Trudeau, largely due to the economic necessity of maintaining the tax revenue foundation for Canada's generous social safety net. The political consensus behind this strategy however began to decline about 2023 when lack of housing and other factors created social pressure regarding the affordability of these past measures.

Canada seems to have not specifically added inducements for couples to have children, but it should be noted that Canada's existing level of health and social care, along with parental tax credits rendered this largely unnecessary relative to countries, such as China, where such services are scarce. Consensus is that Canada is perhaps in a period reflection…immigration policy has been tightened post-Trudeau, but it is not as a "wall" like in the U.S. In fact, many Canadian as well as European countries have been actively welcoming recent academic and research exiles from the U.S.

By way of summary, we can say there are more similarities than differences, allowing for what seems to be differences in geographic blocs, Asian vs. Western practices. One cannot help but observe that as far as sheer number of immigrants, the Western countries have to some extent been overwhelmed the past decades by the number of overall immigrants, illegals into both the E.U. and the U.S., and complications posed by freedom of movement with the E.U.

One highly noteworthy point of divergence among our peer group countries comes from Singapore, which via its stratified work visa and work permit policies has created a structure in which "the many"—voluntarily and freely—help pay for the social benefits of "the few". (The "many" being all working residents; the "few" being Singaporean citizens—which comprise 60% of the total resident population.) We posit that the U.S. Congress can and should apply lessons such as this for the day when they finally update our legacy 1952 Immigration Policy.

25. Conclusion – Observations and Summary of Recommendations

Summary of observations:

1. The demographic impact on our population and our labor force from our decades-long below replacement level birthrate is seemingly irreversible.

2. This will result in a demographically induced declination of our labor force that will be exacerbated by the present and expected future decline in immigration.

3. Their combined consequence of a declining labor force will be a protracted decline in tax revenue, which will particularly hard-hitting given that individual taxpayers currently contribute about 84% of total tax receipts.

4. Our current gross public debt is about $38 trillion (Q2 2026), or about 127% of GDP. Our debt service payments for 2025 were about $1 trillion, which increasingly diverts federal expenditures away from priority areas and into debt service.

5. Study of the production function in juxtaposition to our legacy taxation mechanism illustrates that our public debt dilemma was self-inflicted.

6. It is at this exact moment that the AI revolution has arrived, when we have limited fiscal flexibility as a country to respond to any deleterious consequences.

7. The AI revolution brings with it a significant risk that we will experience considerable economic transformation, potentially resulting in job loss for some, employment transition for others, and periods of uncertainty for many.

8. There is, to give credit to the tremendous possibilities that the AI revolution presents, the likelihood that this era will bring productivity increases, new employment opportunities, and increased output as a country—after a transitory period of unknown duration.

9. It is equally likely that an unwelcome feature of the AI economy may be that we have high rates of GDP growth coupled with lower rates of human employment, due to a combination of substitution of AI for human input and new jobs being filled directly by AI entities. This would result in a high-growth, low-tax revenue paradigm, which of course would fuel fiscal uncertainty.

10. Therefore, the paradox we may face as a country is one of having a dynamic and growing economy yet with a collapsing tax foundation.

11. Last, we must be cognizant that—competitively speaking—there is growing evidence that Chinese AI models are making growing inroads in the U.S. economy.

Summary of recommendations:

1. Implementation of AI taxation (now) via the mechanism we propose in chapter 8, which includes: a) cognitive AI token tax with a progressive, shared allocation; and b) a registration fee and renewal fee system of taxation for instances of physical AI.

2. Legislation that would obligate our Congress to put our fiscal policy on a path to returning gross public debt to a reasonable and historic level, such as 60% of GDP (vs. its current 127% level). This would, presumably, involve addressing the ill-advised disparity in the share of income vs. share of tax burden that has been allowed to develop over the last seven decades, as demonstrated in our study of the Arc of Production Function.

3. That Congress be obligated to restore the discipline intended by the 1974 Congressional Budget and Impoundment Control Act, which expects participation by the President, the Congress, the Congressional Budget and Appropriations Committees, and the CBO to conduct a transparent budgetary review process that reconciles expenditures against sources of revenue. (This implies ending the routine use of the continuing resolution process as a short-cut mechanism for budget approval.)

4. Amendment or replacement of our 1952 Immigration and Nationality Act (INA) such that —irrespective of the number of annually admitted immigrants—a hard link is established between labor force skills needed and applicants approved.

26. *Author's note*

The author has received zero outside funding or support of any type for this study, or in the course of this study.

Rather, he wishes to acknowledge the support and warm welcome from both the administrative and professorial staff of the graduate program of the Faculty of Economics at Chiang Mai University (CMU), Thailand upon his decision to pursue a late career return to university for a Master's in Economics. Additionally, he would like to specifically acknowledge the courtesy extended by the professors associated with CMU's undergraduate Econ program, as in approximately a dozen instances, when he wished to attend supplemental (undergraduate level) classes covering foundational Econ theory and policy, they graciously granted permission.

The author without reservation can recommend both CMU and Thai Universities in general for their academic standards (and their international—English language programs), as well as their manifestations of the uniqueness of Thai culture.

The information provided within are the author's non-expert, best assessments based on specific topical research as well as accrued knowledge courtesy of career and academics. The topics of fertility, immigration and AI are all highly dynamic with relevant outcomes and forecasts experiencing frequent updates and changes, including within government and industry issued forecasts. Accordingly, he has endeavored to represent as up-to-date statistics, trends and outcomes as possible. In his opinion, in the instances in which a representation may be modestly out-of-date, or in which unit calculations of dynamically evolving topics—such as rates of U.S. "token generation"—may experience variance, he does not believe any such variance in measured or projected data materially changes any core conclusions or recommendations within.

The author has of course made use of multiple AI frontier models as valuable research assistants, often to cross-correlate and cross-verify findings and conclusions. However, the ideas, conclusions and written text within belong entirely to him, unless specified otherwise.

George Randolph Dirth
April 2026

About the Author

George Randolph Dirth is a self-described "generalist". A U.C. Berkeley graduate, his professional background has centered around business management—from entry-level to CEO, with a late career return to university to study economics at the master's level, with a focus on policy.

His interests therefore include business, economics, the world in general and geo-political topics. He is an expert at nothing (except perhaps boat speed on a sloop), but with a high degree of interest in a wide variety of current events and topics. As for political orientation, he is a "centrist" (having previously made campaign contributions to members of both major U.S. political parties) believing in the benefits of a robust marketplace of policy ideas.

27. References

Amodei, Dario. Interview by Anderson Cooper. *Anderson Cooper 360*, CNN, May 29, 2025. Television Broadcast.

Anjum, A. "Urbanization as a Driver of Demographic Transition: Insights from Europe and South Asia." *International Journal of Research in Social Sciences* https://rsisinternational.org/journals/ijriss/articles/urbanization-as-a-driver-of-demographic-transition-insights-from-europe-and-south-asia/

Anthropic. (2025). *Claude 3 Opus* [Large language model]. Retrieved August - November 2025, from https://claude.ai

Anthropic. "Disrupting the First Reported AI-Orchestrated Cyber Espionage Campaign." Anthropic Blog, November 13, 2025. https://www.anthropic.com/news/disrupting-AI-espionage.

Barnett, Andrew. "UK Tried to Clamp Down on Migration." *The Wall Street Journal*, May 22, 2025 https://www.wsj.com/world/uk/britain-farage-migration-debacle-245baf3e

Blanchard, O. (2017). *Macroeconomics* (7th ed.). Pearson.

Bruner, Jon, et al. "Evolution of National Nobel Prize Shares in the 20th Century." *arXiv preprint*, September 2010. https://arxiv.org/html/1009.2634.

Brynjolfsson et al, "Canaries in the Coal Mine. Six Facts about Recent Employment Effects of Artificial Intelligence" https://digitaleconomy.stanford.edu/wp-content/uploads/2025/08/Canaries_BrynjolfssonChandarChen.pdf

Challapally, Aditya, Chris Pease, Ramesh Raskar, and Pradyumna Chari. "The GenAI Divide: State of AI in Business 2025." MIT NANDA, July 2025. https://nanda.media.mit.edu/ai_report_2025.pdf.

Chi, L. S., et al. (2025). Measuring global migration flows using online data. *Proceedings of the National Academy of Sciences*, *122*(17). https://www.pnas.org/doi/10.1073/pnas.2409418122

Congressional Budget Office. *The Budget and Economic Outlook: 2024 to 2034*. CBO, February 2024. https://www.cbo.gov/topics/reports-policy-options.

Congressional Budget Office. (2025). *The budget and economic outlook: 2025 to 2035.* https://www.cbo.gov/publication/**60870

Congressional Budget Office. *The Budget and Economic Outlook: 2025 to 2035*. CBO, 2025. https://www.cbo.gov/topics/reports-policy-options.

Congressional Budget Office. *The Long-Term Budget Outlook: 2025 to 2055*. CBO, March 2025. https://www.cbo.gov/topics/reports-policy-options.

Congressional Budget Office. *CBO's Current View of the Economy From 2025 to 2028*. CBO, September 12, 2025. https://www.cbo.gov/publication/61236.

Congressional Budget Office. The January 2025 baseline for federal revenue composition and long-term budget outlooks

Congressional Budget Office. September 11, 2025 report: *U.S. Population Growth Will Slow Even More, CBO Says.* https://www.cbo.gov/publication/62105.

Cutter, Chip. "AI Is Coming for the Consultants. Inside McKinsey, 'This Is Existential'." *The Wall Street Journal*, August 2, 2025. https://www.wsj.com/tech/ai/mckinsey-consulting-firms-ai-strategy-89fbf1be.

Darley, J. (2025, August 4). *The Consultants' Conundrum: Should McKinsey Bet Big on AI?* Technology Magazine. (Quotes Bob Sternfels on the 1:1 agent-to-human ratio and Kate Smaje on the "existential" threat).

Delaney, Kevin J. "Bill Gates: This is why we should tax robots." *World Economic Forum.* Quartz, February 20, 2017. https://www.weforum.org/stories/2017/02/bill-gates-this-is-why-we-should-tax-robots/.

Deloitte Touche Tohmatsu Limited. *Accelerating Smart Factory Adoption in the United States.* 2024. https://www.deloitte.com/us/en/insights.html.

De Long, J. B., & Summers, L. H. (2012). *Fiscal policy in a depressed economy.* Brookings Papers on Economic Activity. https://www.brookings.edu/wp-content/uploads/2016/07/2012b_delong.pdf

Diamandis, Peter H., host. "How Life Changes When We Reach Artificial Superintelligence w/ Dr. Fei-Fei Li & Dr. Eric Schmidt." *Moonshots with Peter Diamandis.* YouTube video, November 7, 2025. https://www.youtube.com/watch?v=Q_9KNz7nnlA.

Dirth, G. R. (2025). *Deportations by US President 2000–2025* [Unpublished data analysis].

Dirth, G. R. (2025). *Summary table of immigration visas granted 2024* [Unpublished data analysis].

Dirth, G. R. (2025). *Major US tech company layoffs in 2025* [Unpublished data analysis].

Dirth, G. R. (2025). *Global robotics density and manufacturer comparison* [Unpublished data analysis].

"Governments Going Broke." *The Economist*, October 18, 2025. https://www.economist.com/finance-and-economics/2025/10/18/governments-going-broke.

Federal Reserve Bank of St. Louis. (2023). *Nonfarm Business Sector: Labor Productivity (Output per Hour) for All Workers and All Employees, Total Nonfarm* [Graph]. Retrieved November 13, 2025, from https://fred.stlouisfed.org/graph/?g=1iX1

Fernald, John G. (*A Quarter-Century of Productivity Slowdown*, 2014) or official historical data from the U.S. Bureau of Labor Statistics (BLS) on Total Factor Productivity (TFP) or Labor Productivity.

Goldin, Claudia. "The Downside of Fertility." NBER Working Paper No. 34268, September 2025. https://doi.org/10.3386/w34268. © 2025 by Claudia Goldin. Presented at the Federal Reserve Bank of

Kansas City Economic Policy Symposium, Jackson Hole, Wyoming, August 2025.

Goldin, C. (2006). *The quiet revolution that transformed women's employment, education, and family* (NBER Working Paper No. 12173). National Bureau of Economic Research.

Goldin, C., & Katz, L. F. (2002). The power of the pill: Oral contraceptives and women's career and marriage decisions. *Journal of Political Economy*, *110*(4), 730–770.

Google. (2025). *Gemini 2.5 Flash* [Large language model]. Retrieved August - November 2025, from https://gemini.google.com

Google DeepMind. "Gemini Robotics 1.5 Brings AI Agents into the Physical World." Google DeepMind Blog, September 25, 2025. https://deepmind.google/blog/gemini-robotics-15-brings-ai-agents-into-the-physical-world/.

Google. *Whimsical Cartoon Robot with Briefcase*. 2025. AI-generated image.

The Guardian. (2025, July 22). OpenAI CEO tells Federal Reserve confab that entire job categories will disappear due to AI. *The Guardian*.
https://www.theguardian.com/technology/2025/jul/22/openai-sam-altman-congress-ai-jobs

Internal Revenue Service. *Tax Rate Schedules and Payroll Tax Rates*. U.S. Department of the Treasury, 2025. https://www.irs.gov/forms-instructions.

International Monetary Fund. "General Government Gross Debt as a Percentage of GDP." FRED, Federal Reserve Bank of St. Louis, retrieved November 13, 2025.

International Monetary Fund. *World Economic Outlook Database*. Accessed November 14, 2025.

International Monetary Fund. *Global Financial Stability Report: Managing the Crypto Transition*. October 2024. https://www.imf.org/en/publications.

International Federation of Robotics. (2024). *World robotics report 2024: Industrial robots.* https://ifr.org/worldrobotics/

Jefferson, Philip N. (2026). "Economic Outlook and Supply-Side (Dis)Inflation Dynamics." Speech delivered at the Brookings Institution, Washington, D.C., February 6.

Jones, Paul Tudor. Interview by Stephanie Ruhle. *Bloomberg Television.* Bloomberg, February 2020. https://www.bloomberg.com/news/videos/

Korinek, A. (2026, January 8). *Public finance in the age of AI: A primer.* Brookings Institution, Center on Regulation and Markets. (Reviewed by William Gale and Matthew Weinzierl). Available at: https://www.brookings.edu/articles/public-finance-age-ai-primer/.

Krugman, Paul. "Secular Stagnation, Coalmines, and Bubbles." *The New York Times* (blog), November 28, 2013. https://krugman.blogs.nytimes.com/2013/11/28/secular-stagnation-coalmines-and-bubbles/

Lin, Belle. "Anthropic Lands Cognizant as Enterprise AI Customer." *The Wall Street Journal*, November 3, 2025. https://news.futunn.com/en/post/64304862/anthropic-lands-cognizant-as-enterprise-ai-customer-wsj.

Mankiw, N. G. (2024). *Principles of macroeconomics* (10th ed.). Cengage Learning.

Mayer, H., Yee, L., Chui, M., & Roberts, R. (2025, January 28). *Superagency in the workplace: Empowering people to unlock AI's full potential at work*. McKinsey Global Institute. https://www.mckinsey.com/capabilities/tech-and-ai/our-insights/superagency-in-the-workplace-empowering-people-to-unlock-ais-full-potential-at-work

McKinsey & Company. "AI-Driven Agentification of Work: Impact on Jobs (2024–2030)." March 2025. https://www.mckinsey.com/

MIT Project NANDA. (2025). *The GenAI Divide: State of AI in Business 2025.*

National Academies of Sciences, Engineering, and Medicine. (2024, September 19). *Strengthening U.S. competitiveness by attracting international*

STEM talent. National Academies Press. https://www.nationalacademies.org/our-work/strengthening-us-competitiveness-by-attracting-international-stem-talent

National Foundation for American Policy (NFAP). (2026, February). *AI and H-1B Visas: Analysis of FY 2025 Filings.* NFAP Policy Brief. Available at: https://nfap.com/wp-content/uploads/2026/02/AI-and-H-1B-Visas.NFAP-Policy-Brief.February-2026-1.pdf.

Ng, Andrew. "Stanford CS230 | Autumn 2025 | Lecture 1: Introduction to Deep Learning." YouTube video. September 23, 2025. https://www.youtube.com/watch?v=_NLHFoVNlbg.

NVIDIA Newsroom. (2025, April 14). *NVIDIA to Manufacture American-Made AI Supercomputers in US for First Time (Foxconn Houston Partnership).* Available at: https://blogs.nvidia.com/blog/nvidia-manufacture-american-made-ai-supercomputers-us/.

Organisation for Economic Co-operation and Development. (2024). *Number of PCT patent applications in AI-related technologies* [Data set]. STI Micro-data Lab: Intellectual Property Database. http://oe.cd/ipstats

Organisation for Economic Co-operation and Development. *International Migration Outlook 2024.* Paris: OECD Publishing, 2024. https://dfr.oregon.gov/pages/index.aspx.

Peter G. Peterson Foundation. "U.S. Debt Ceiling: Frequently Asked Questions." [Report on Debt Risk], October 2024. https://piktochart.com/blog/fact-sheet-examples/.

PoweredByWITI. (2025, March). *AI-driven agentification of work: Impact on jobs (2024–2030)* [LinkedIn Pulse post]. https://www.linkedin.com/pulse/ai-driven-agentification-work-impact-jobs-20242030-poweredbywiti-zbyfc/

Pugh, Emerson W., Lyle R. Johnson, and John H. Palmer. *IBM's 360 and Early 370 Systems.* Cambridge, MA: MIT Press, 1991.

Reich, Robert B. 2023. *Wealth and Poverty.* Undergraduate Lecture Series, University of California, Berkeley. YouTube video, 12-part series. http://www.youtube.com/watch?v=1f2blKai7HA.

Chan, M. (2024, May 15). *TSMC confirms $165 billion U.S. investment in Arizona with 3,000 direct jobs.* Reuters.

https://ell.stackexchange.com/questions/303133/using-the-a-article-with-specific.

Reuters. (2025, September 6). US immigration agents arrest hundreds at Hyundai plant, mostly Koreans. *Reuters.* https://www.reuters.com/world/asia-pacific/us-immigration-agents-arrest-hundreds-hyundai-plant-mostly-koreans-2025-09-06/

"China's Robotics Industry Generated $23 Billion in Revenue in 2022." *Reuters*, January 1, 2023. https://www.reuters.com/business/china-robotics-revenue-hits-23-billion-2022-2023-01-01/

Reuters. "Foxconn to Deploy Humanoid Robots at Houston AI Server Plant." *Reuters*, October 29, 2025. https://quizlet.com/282770084/chapter-9-flash-cards/.

Rubin, Robert E., Jacob Weisberg, and Strobe Talbott. (*In an Uncertain World: Tough Choices from Wall Street to Washington*, 2003) for the personal account, or CBO/OMB rep

Rubin, R. (2025, October 7). *Former Treasury Secretary Robert Rubin Talks Tariffs* [Audio podcast episode]. *Bloomberg Talks.* Bloomberg. \https://www.reddit.com/r/youtube/comments/152qg3e/why_does_youtube_refuse_to_show_you_the_offending/.

Rubin, Robert E. (2026, January 15). *Why Have Business Leaders Gone Silent?* Council on Foreign Relations (CFR). Available at: https://www.cfr.org/experts/robert-e-rubin.

Schumpeter, J. A. (1942). *Capitalism, socialism, and democracy.* Harper & Brothers.

Singapore Ministry of Manpower. *Foreign Workforce Numbers and Policy Details,* https://www.instagram.com/mom_publishing/?hl=en.

Singapore Ministry of Social and Family Development. *Parental and Family Support Schemes.* https://www.msf.gov.sg/.

Solow, Robert M. "Technical Change and the Aggregate Production Function." *The Review of Economics and Statistics* 39, no. 3 (1957): 312–20.

Steinberger, P. (2026, January 30). *OpenClaw: An Open-Source Agentic Framework.* (Initial release Nov 2025 as Clawdbot). Documentation at: https://openclaw.ai/.

Suleyman, Mustafa, in conversation with Zanny Minton Beddoes, "Are We Prepared for the AI Revolution?" Intelligence Squared, London, September 11, 2023.

Summers, Lawrence H., and David M. Cutler. "The Coming Crisis Could Be Worse Than the Last One." *The Washington Post*, January 12, 2018.

United Nations, Department of Economic and Social Affairs, Population Division. *World Population Prospects 2022: Summary of Results.* https://dfr.oregon.gov/pages/index.aspx.

U.S. Bureau of Economic Analysis. (n.d.). *Gross Domestic Product* (GDP). Retrieved November 13, 2025, from FRED, Federal Reserve Bank of St. Louis: https://fred.stlouisfed.org/series/GDP

U.S. Bureau of Economic Analysis. (2025). *Gross Domestic Product, Fourth Quarter and Year 2024* (National Income and Product Accounts). U.S. Department of Commerce. https://www.bea.gov/news/schedule.

U.S. Bureau of Labor Statistics. "Nonfarm Business Sector: Labor Productivity and Civilian Labor Force Level." FRED, Federal Reserve Bank of St. Louis, retrieved November 13, 2025.

U.S. Bureau of Labor Statistics. "Labor Force Participation Rate (LNS11300000)." FRED, Federal Reserve Bank of St. Louis, retrieved November 14, 2025.

U.S. Bureau of Labor Statistics. "Employment Projections, 2023–33." News release, U.S. Department of Labor, September 2024. https://www.bls.gov/schedule/.

U.S. Bureau of Labor Statistics. "Employment Projections, 2023–2033." News release, U.S. Department of Labor, August 29, 2024. https://www.bls.gov/schedule/.

U.S. Bureau of Labor Statistics. "Earnings and Unemployment Rates by Educational Attainment." U.S. Department of Labor, 2025. https://www.bls.gov/data/tables.htm

U.S. Bureau of Labor Statistics. *Job Openings and Labor Turnover Survey (JOLTS).* U.S. Department of Labor. Accessed November 14, 2025. https://www.bls.gov/jlt/.

U.S. Bureau of Labor Statistics. "Employed Persons by Educational Attainment" (*Current Population Survey*). U.S. Department of Labor, 2025. https://www.bls.gov/data/tables.htm.

U.S. Bureau of Labor Statistics. "Employment Projections, 2023–33." News release, U.S. Department of Labor, September 2024. https://www.bls.gov/schedule/.

U.S. Bureau of Labor Statistics. "Earnings by Major Field of Degree." *Annual Report.* U.S. Department of Labor, 2025. https://www.bls.gov/data/tables.htm.

U.S. Census Bureau. *American Community Survey (ACS) [Year of data release]*. Washington, D.C.: U.S. Census Bureau, 2024. https://sheridancollege.libguides.com/acs/Tables-Figures.

U.S. Census Bureau. *National Population Projections: 2023–2033.* Washington, D.C.: U.S. Census Bureau, 2023. https://justicefirstllp.com/online-will-access-safeguarding-your-personal-information/.

U.S. Census Bureau. *International Database (IDB).* Washington, D.C.: U.S. Census Bureau. Retrieved November 14, 2025. https://www.census.gov/programs-surveys/international-programs/about/idb.html.

U.S. Census Bureau. *American Community Survey (ACS) 2023 Data Release.* https://www.census.gov/programs-surveys/acs/data/data-tables.html.

U.S. Citizenship and Immigration Services. *Green Card Categories and Requirements.* U.S. Department of Homeland Security.

U.S. Citizenship and Immigration Services. *Annual Report to Congress on Immigration and Border Security, Fiscal Year 2024*. U.S. Department of Homeland Security, 2025. https://www.uscis.gov/tools/reports-and-studies.

U.S. Citizenship and Immigration Services. "H-1B Cap Season Update, FY 2024." U.S. Department of Homeland Security, 2024. https://www.uscis.gov/newsroom/alerts/h-1b-faq.

U.S. Congress, Joint Committee on Taxation. "Historical Data on Federal Tax Rates and Tax Revenue." . https://taxfoundation.org/blog/understanding-jcts-new-distributional-tables-senates-tax-cuts-jobs-act/.

U.S. Department of Homeland Security, Office of Immigration Statistics. *Annual Flow Report: Legal Permanent Residents*. Washington, D.C.: DHS, 2024. https://dhsprogram.com/data/Guide-to-DHS-Statistics/Organization_of_DHS_Data.htm.

U.S. Department of State Office of the Historian. "Immigration and Nationality Act of 1952 (McCarran-Walter Act)." *Milestones: 1945–1952*. Accessed November 14, 2025. https://history.state.gov/milestones/1945-1952/immigration-act.

U.S. Department of the Treasury. "10-Year Treasury Constant Maturity Rate (GS10)." FRED, Federal Reserve Bank of St. Louis, retrieved November 13, 2025.

U.S. Immigration and Customs Enforcement, Student and Exchange Visitor Program. *SEVIS by the Numbers, 2024 Annual Report*. U.S. Department of Homeland Security, 2025. https://www.ice.gov/sevis/dso-requirements.

U.S. Office of Management and Budget. *Historical Tables, Budget of the U.S. Government, Fiscal Year 2025* (Table 2.3, Summary of Receipts by Source). Executive Office of the President, 2025. https://obamawhitehouse.archives.gov/omb/budget/Historicals.

U.S. Office of Management and Budget. "Federal Surplus or Deficit [-] (FYFSD)." FRED, Federal Reserve Bank of St. Louis, retrieved November 13, 2025. https://fred.stlouisfed.org/series/FYFSD.

U.S. Office of Management and Budget. (*Historical Tables, Budget of the U.S. Government*, Table 1.1) for budget surplus/deficit figures by year.

U.S. Office of Management and Budget. *Historical Tables, Budget of the U.S. Government, Fiscal Year 2025* (Tables 1.1, 1.2, 1.3). Executive Office of the President, 2025. https://obamawhitehouse.archives.gov/omb/budget/Historicals.

Vaswani, A., et al. (2017). "Attention Is All You Need." Advances in Neural Information Processing Systems

The Wall Street Journal. (2025, September 11). U.S. Population Growth Will Slow Even More, CBO Says. *The Wall Street Journal.* https://www.wsj.com/us-news/u-s-population-growth-will-slow-even-more-cbo-says-75f1c14a?mod=hp_listb_pos1

The Wall Street Journal. (2025, July 1). Amazon Is on the Cusp of Using More Robots Than Humans in Its Warehouses. *The Wall Street Journal.* https://www.wsj.com/tech/amazon-warehouse-robots-automation-942b814f

The Wall Street Journal: *"AI Is Coming for the Consultants. Inside McKinsey, 'This Is Existential'"* published on August 4, 2025

Waymo Blog. (2024, May 15). *How Our Cars Learn from Each Other: The Power of Fleet Data.* Available at: https://waymo.com/blog/.

World Bank. "Fertility Rate, Total (births per woman) (SP.DYN.TFRT.IN)." World Bank Data, accessed November 14, 2025. https://datahelpdesk.worldbank.org/knowledgebase/articles/1886686-advanced-data-api-queries.

"No lights, no workers: AI-powered 'dark factories' are reshaping China's manufacturing." *VN Express International,* November 2, 2024. https://e.vnexpress.net/news/tech/tech-news/no-lights-no-workers-ai-powered-dark-factories-are-reshaping-china-s-manufacturing-4921224.html.

"…Robots at Work." YouTube video, published by Bloomberg Live, June 6, 2025. *Amazon's Warehouse Revolution: Robots at Work [Video]. YouTube."* https://www.youtube.com/watch?v=B6pz2R1UHXw.

www.ingramcontent.com/pod-product-compliance
Lightning Source LLC
LaVergne TN
LVHW060030210926
848481LV00013B/3831
9798996295104